T0330356

Politics as a Peculiar Business

NEW THINKING IN POLITICAL ECONOMY

Series Editor: Peter J. Boettke, *George Mason University, USA*

New Thinking in Political Economy aims to encourage scholarship in the intersection of the disciplines of politics, philosophy and economics. It has the ambitious purpose of reinvigorating political economy as a progressive force for understanding social and economic change.

The series is an important forum for the publication of new work analysing the social world from a multidisciplinary perspective. With increased specialization (and professionalization) within universities, interdisciplinary work has become increasingly uncommon. Indeed, during the 20th century, the process of disciplinary specialization reduced the intersection between economics, philosophy and politics and impoverished our understanding of society. Modern economics in particular has become increasingly mathematical and largely ignores the role of institutions and the contribution of moral philosophy and politics.

New Thinking in Political Economy will stimulate new work that combines technical knowledge provided by the 'dismal science' and the wisdom gleaned from the serious study of the 'worldly philosophy'. The series will reinvigorate our understanding of the social world by encouraging a multidisciplinary approach to the challenges confronting society in the new century.

Titles in the series include:

International Aid and Private Schools for the Poor
Smiles, Miracles and Markets
Pauline Dixon

The Rediscovery of Classical Economics
Adaption, Complexity and Growth
David Simpson

Economic Futures of the West
Jan Winiecki

Entrepreneurial Action, Public Policy, and Economic Outcomes
Edited by Robert F. Salvino Jr., Michael T. Tasto and Gregory M. Randolph

Sweden and the Revival of the Capitalist Welfare State
Andreas Bergh

Competition, Coordination and Diversity
From the Firm to Economic Integration
Pascal Salin

Culture and Economic Action
Edited by Laura E. Grube and Virgil Henry Storr

Politics as a Peculiar Business
Insights from a Theory of Entangled Political Economy
Richard E. Wagner

Politics as a Peculiar Business

Insights from a Theory of Entangled Political Economy

Edited by

Richard E. Wagner

Holbert L. Harris Professor of Economics, George Mason University, USA

NEW THINKING IN POLITICAL ECONOMY

Edward Elgar PUBLISHING

Cheltenham, UK • Northampton, MA, USA

Published by
Edward Elgar Publishing Limited
The Lypiatts
15 Lansdown Road
Cheltenham
Glos GL50 2JA
UK

Edward Elgar Publishing, Inc.
William Pratt House
9 Dewey Court
Northampton
Massachusetts 01060
USA

A catalogue record for this book
is available from the British Library

Library of Congress Control Number: 2015952675

This book is available electronically in the **Elgar**online
Economics collection
DOI 10.4337/9781785365485

ISBN 978 1 78536 547 8 (cased)
ISBN 978 1 78536 548 5 (eBook)

Typeset by Servis Filmsetting Ltd, Stockport, Cheshire
Printed and bound in Great Britain by TJ International Ltd, Padstow

Contents

List of figures   vi
Preface   vii

1. Public choice and the Virginia tradition of political economy   1

2. Alternative paths for a theory of political economy   31

3. Systems theory and parts-to-whole relationships   55

4. The logic of economizing action: Universal form and particular
    practice   83

5. Reason, sentiment, and electoral competition   111

6. Parasitical political calculation   136

7. Societal tectonics and the art of the deal   163

8. Moral imagination and constitutional arrangement   186

References   210
Index   229

Figures

2.1 Political economy as additive object-to-object relationship 37
2.2 Political economy as entangled entity-to-entity relationship 43
3.1 Coffee maker as system 57
3.2 Network pattern and system performance 62
3.3 Orthodox portrayal of public–private resource allocation 66
4.1 Prisoner's dilemma applied to neighborhood development 108
5.1 Transactional relationships in political economy 118

Preface

In light of the many books that in recent years have announced their subject as "political economy," a potential reader will reasonably wonder how this book differs from those books. It differs in many ways. Those other books typically treat polities or states as unitary entities that intervene into economies to change their courses in some fashion. In these treatments, states are single-minded entities that operate independently of the rest of society. To the contrary, I treat democratic polities as plural and not singular, which means that the entities that constitute a state are able in large measure to act independently of one another. There is no single mind that directs what is widely described as state activity. Rather, the activities of states arise through competition among many minds, just as do the activities of the enterprises that comprise a society's market economy. Within this alternative scheme of thought, political and economic entities are deeply entangled. Being entangled means that a business typically cannot determine prudent conduct independently of the desires of relevant political entities. It likewise means that political entities can't determine prudent practice independently of the desires of relevant commercial entities. What results from thinking about an entangled system of political economy is recognition that political practice is a *peculiar* form of business practice.

At the conclusion of the American Constitutional Convention in 1787, Benjamin Franklin is reported to have responded, "A republic if you can keep it," to a question from someone who asked him what kind of government the Convention had established. Franklin's challenge clearly has not been met. Over the past century especially, the original limited republic has morphed to a significant extent into a nearly unlimited democracy where there is little principled limit on the reach of the political into society, and with Richard Epstein (2014) setting forth a lucid description of this transformation. I use the logic of an entangled system of political economy to explain how a regime founded on a *constitution of liberty*, where citizens pretty much can do as they choose so long as they respect the equivalent rights of other people, can morph into a *constitution of control*, wherein political imperatives come to dominate large swaths of societal life.

Recognition that politics can reasonably be treated as a peculiar form of business does not reject Michael Oakeshott's (1975) useful distinction between civil association and enterprise association, but only recognizes that examining polities as peculiar forms of enterprises can lead to useful analytical insights about contemporary political economy. Most significantly, both commercial and political entities operate in large measure through making deals and organizing transactions. Negotiation and transaction occupy the foreground of entangled political economy, with orders and force mostly lurking in the background though still having real presence. Entangled political economy takes seriously the claims of spontaneous order theorizing to the effect that large-scale societies must be organized largely through transactions because they are too complex to be organized through systemic planning. In this respect, I embrace and amplify Craig Roberts's (1971) recognition that the Soviet Union was not a genuinely planned economy but rather was a terribly fouled-up market economy. The qualities of the transactions that arise within any system of complex human interaction can differ across societies due to differences in their particular patterns of entanglement.

I should perhaps note that there are analogies between my use of entangled political economy and the use of quantum entanglement by physicists. All the same, I don't regard analogies as substitutes for theory. In no way do I think you can append an economic-sounding vocabulary to analytical frameworks developed to explain physical phenomena and get anything reasonable out of the exercise, at least not without engaging in free-ranging acts of "interpretation." The social world provides different phenomena for explanation than does the natural world, even though humans are also part of the natural world and so are subject to the forces that are at work there. For natural phenomena, there is no option but to theorize from some vantage point outside those phenomena. For social phenomena, however, much useful theorizing can only occur from a vantage point located inside those phenomena. Societal phenomena require a suitable or *sui generis* orientation toward their material, as Ludwig Lachmann (1971) explains in setting forth Max Weber's legacy to social theory.

Business is a source of livelihood for many people. So is politics. Business practice entails competition among enterprises for customer support. Political practice likewise entails competition among political enterprises. Universities have schools of business administration. They also have schools of public administration. Entrepreneurship lies behind the formation of new businesses and the reconfiguration of old ones. It likewise lies behind the articulation of new political programs and the revision of old ones. Businesses must attract investors to provide capital. So must political enterprises, even though some of the investors in political enterprises are forced and not willing investors. Throughout the gamut of political activity, the patterns of practice that economists associate with business are likewise present in democratic polities, though with substantive differences that reflect the *peculiar* commercial qualities of political enterprises. For instance, businesses can be bought and sold, either in whole or in part. Either way, values are established for those enterprises. Political enterprises are not subject directly to sale even though some of their assets can be sold. The absence of value for political enterprises ramifies throughout a system of entangled political economy, and has much to do with the transformation of a limited republic into what is becoming a nearly unlimited democracy.

Political enterprises can influence the success of businesses, just as businesses can influence the success of political enterprises. It is misleading to speak of governmental intervention into markets because those governmental entities are themselves participants within a society's market arrangements. While political enterprises have tools of force available to them that ordinary commercial enterprises lack, it should also be noted that the exercise of power within societies with democratic polities is rarely a matter of a governing few imposing their will on a governed mass. As Friedrich Wieser (1926) and Bertrand de Jouvenel (1948) explain, power within democratic polities must generally be exercised in a manner that obtains acquiescence if not explicit approval from large numbers of people from among the citizenry.

Within democratic polities, political enterprises must attract supporters just as must commercial enterprises, even though some people are forced to support those enterprises. Commercial enterprises engage in advertising. So do political enterprises. Commercial and political enterprises both seek to be successful in their actions and programs. Success and failure, however, are appraised differently between political and commercial enterprises because political profit manifests itself differently than does commercial profit. Political and commercial activities take place within the same society, and involve interactions and relationships among the same people. It is thus meaningful to speak of entangled systems of political economy and their properties. It is not, however, meaningful to speak of independent systems of politics and economics, as conveyed by the conventional language that speaks of political intervention into economy because there is no point outside economy from which that intervention can proceed. All that exists are various forms of participation inside society, and with no entity capable of acting on society as a whole. This is the vision of entangled political economy within which politics is a peculiar form of business.

Chapter 1 describes different conceptions of political economy within the history of economic thought. The entangled vision I present here has its roots in classical political economy, which was largely a political economy of liberty. The emergence of public choice theory around 1960 sought to carry forward the classical orientation using analytical concepts that were in play at that time, and which led to the oft-used signifier Virginia Political Economy (Wagner 2015a). I seek to infuse the classical orientation with some contemporary schemes of thought that were not available to the classical economists or to the founders of Virginia political economy. Chapter 2 contrasts alternative paths toward a theory of political economy, and I describe those paths as additive and entangled. The additive path treats polity and economy as distinct analytical objects, each of which can be usefully analyzed without taking the other into account, and with polity acting on economy to modify economy in some fashion. In contrast, the vision of entangled political economy starts from recognition that society entails extensive commingling among political and economic entities, and with interaction among those entities proceeding through a mix of consent, duress, and force.

Chapter 3 elaborates the idea of systems theory as an analytical framework in which differently constituted enterprises interact within the same society. While economists typically denote an economy as a system, they also typically describe that system as comprising equilibrium among participants. Doing this renders the system mechanical, which leads almost inexorably to a focus on a political economy of control. In contrast, and hearkening back to Ludwig Bertalanffy's (1968) distinction between robotic and creative systems, I treat human population systems as non-equilibrium systems of creative interaction among participants. Chapter 4 explains that the energy that drives societies forward entails the universal form of people acting to replace situations they desire less with situations they desire more. This universal form, however, can generate a wide variety of specific types of action due to differences in the institutional settings within which people interact. The logic of economizing action becomes the point of entry into a theory of society, recognizing that the social configurations that emerge from interaction among individuals also create a form of downward causation whereby those configurations act upon individuals through influencing the notions of normativity that are in play at any particular moment (Wagner 2010a; Lewis 2012).

Chapter 5 accepts the proposition that competition is a social form that always selects for excellence among competitors, regardless of whether that competition pertains to athletics, politics, or business. The particular qualities that are selected will vary across the forms of competition. Political and commercial competition have both points of similarity and points of difference with respect to the qualities for which competition selects, and with the differences contributing to the morphing from a constitution of liberty into a constitution of control. Chapter 6 explores the universal problem of economic calculation that is present whenever any conscious choice must be made. Political enterprises must engage in economic calculation just as do commercial enterprises, only they can't do so directly because political transactions don't generate the prices necessary both to guide and to evaluate action. In consequence, political calculation must bear a parasitical relationship to economic calculation, in that political action simultaneously uses and degrades the market prices that emerge through market interaction. Consequently, a system of entangled political economy takes on a turbulent and not a placid character. For instance, the financial crisis of 2008 illustrates neither market failure nor governmental failure, but rather is an intelligible product of a highly entangled system of political economy.

Chapter 7 recognizes that all action within a system of entangled political economy has a transactional character. The "art of the deal" (Trump 1987) is central to a theory of entangled political economy. Nearly a century ago, Joseph Schumpeter (1934) explained that entrepreneurship is the locus of leadership in a capitalist society. Commercial activity occupied most of the foreground of the human drama, with political activity residing largely in the background. That was a century ago. Now, new social forms have evolved where politically connected figures have moved increasingly from the background of managing the stage into the foreground as participants in what is, after all, a self-generated drama. Chapter 8 makes a modest shift from an explanatory to a normative focus centered on the necessity of people living well together in relatively closed geographical spaces. While the organizing narrative of this book stems from my effort to explain how an entangled political economy can generate its own momentum to transform a constitution of liberty into a constitution of control, this chapter explores whether this morphing is capable of being reversed or is an inescapable product of an entangled system of political economy. We may grant that eternal vigilance is the price of liberty, and yet we must also recognize that many people might regard that price as being too high to be willing to pay it.

I used earlier versions of this book as textual material for a graduate class on public choice I taught the fall 2013 and 2014 semesters. It was during my student days at the University of Virginia in the classrooms of James Buchanan and Gordon Tullock that I first encountered the practice of using work currently in progress rather than previously published work as the focal point of classroom exploration. Invariably, I find that collections of advanced graduate students generate interesting insights, observations, and reactions that lead me to revisit and revise my material. I should like to express my appreciation to those students, even though it would be invidious of me to single out particular ones among them.

I should also like to express my appreciation to the Mercatus Center at George Mason University for sponsoring a workshop on the manuscript on 12–13 February 2015. The comments and observations the participants offered led me to see more clearly what I was seeking to accomplish with this book, while they also helped me to avoid some of the precipices toward which I was verging on occasion. I am particularly grateful to Paul Dragos Aligica for his deft guidance of those two days of discussion, for he displayed a wonderful facility for recognizing when a conversation should move on and when it should linger. Those two days of discussion led to a considerable transformation of the manuscript, due to the advice generously given by Peter Boettke, Roberta Herzberg, Adam Martin, Matthew Mitchell, Claire Morgan, Eileen Norcross, Shruti Rajagopalan, Filippo Sabetti, William Shughart, Randy Simmons, Solomon Stein, Vlad Tarko, Maria Villarreal-Diaz, and Wolf von Laer.

1. Public choice and the Virginia tradition of political economy

In the nineteenth century, what is known as economics today was known as political economy. The replacement of political economy with economics was never universal, as political economy continues to be a recognizable term and with Dimitris Milonakis and Ben Fine (2009) exploring how political economy underwent transformation into economics. As used presently, "political economy" denotes a relationship between polities and economies conceived as separate entities or realms of action. In contrast, this book treats polities and economies as entangled, which means that prudent political action cannot be determined independently of the interests of relevant economic actors, nor can prudent commercial action be determined independently of the interests of relevant political actors. Recognition of the entangled quality of political economy points toward several points of difference with common theories of political economy.

There is something unavoidably arbitrary about locating the origin of any scheme of thought. A thinker's thought always takes place against a background of preceding thought, even if it also entails a projection of a thinker's imagination into new analytical territory. While today's thought might have some original aspects, it will also bear the imprint of preceding thought that can reasonably be described as precursory to the present thought (Lovejoy 1936). Despite this unavoidable arbitrariness, it is often informative for readers to know something about the most significant precursors of a particular scheme of thought, to locate that scheme within the broader *Commons of the Mind* (Baier 1997) in which all thought occurs. As Melvin Reder (1999) explains, economics is a controversial and contested discipline that features several schools of thought with distinct orientations.

Public choice is one style of political economy, and is widely described as the application of economic reasoning to politics.[1] This definition has informative value because it tells the reader that the text will use an economic-sounding vocabulary to discuss material that sounds like politics. Yet this definition is also ambiguous because it says nothing about what type of economic theory will be applied to politics. Different types of economic theory will lead to different types of theories of public choice and political economy, as Martin Staniland (1985) exemplifies in his discussion of various approaches to political economy. For instance, one prominent approach to economics holds that a sound economic theory should be based on the twin presumptions that people maximize given utility functions and that markets are in equilibrium (Reder 1982). Many economists deny one or both of those presumptions, which leads to other styles of economic theory that in turn lead to different treatments of political economy and public choice.

This book treats public choice and political economy from within an analytical framework of systems theory and entangled political economy. It does so by treating politics as a practical activity that is cousin to the commercial and industrial activity that is usually thought to be the domain of economic analysis. The scheme of thought that I advance here falls within the spirit of what has been called Virginia political economy, which originated in the late 1950s at the University of Virginia through the efforts of such scholarly notables as James Buchanan, Ronald Coase, Warren Nutter, Gordon Tullock, and Leland Yeager. Individual theorists rarely if ever assign themselves to a school of thought, for they mostly think of themselves as each forming their own tradition. A school of thought is a construction someone applies to a group of scholars to facilitate the making of points about a particular body of scholarship. Sometimes the points made are negative, with the designation of a school serving to concentrate the negative energy on a particular set of scholars and ideas. Virginia political economy became a recognizable term in this manner.

As David Levy and Sandra Peart (2013) document, around 1961 or 1962 the central administration of the University of Virginia hired a consultant to prepare a report to give the administration leverage to undermine the program that had been under construction in Charlottesville since 1956. That report opened by stating that:

> It is generally recognized that at the top professorial levels this Department is staffed by unquestionably capable men and that it enjoys a considerable repute in the profession. On the other hand, the Committee has received considerable adverse criticism of this Department by reason of its close association with a particular viewpoint; and we have been given to understand that the repute enjoyed is regarded by the vast majority of economists as of a distinctly unfavorable character. It does not need to be emphasized here that the Economics Department has associated itself firmly with an outlook now known as that of the "Virginia school."

In identifying a distinctive Virginia approach to political economy, that report helped to marshal the administrative force required to destroy the program in Charlottesville, though part of that program resurfaced in Blacksburg at Virginia Polytechnic Institute under the rubric public choice.

The tradition of Virginia political economy can be identified, as can any scholarly tradition, in terms of a hard core of ideas from which various lines of thought are fashioned, and which both Boettke and Marciano (2015) and Wagner (2015a) explore from different but complementary angles. Virginia political economy can also be identified with two precursory streams of thought, keeping in mind the unavoidably arbitrary elements involved in any effort to identify precursors, especially when referring to a group of scholars. One stream is the classical tradition of liberal political economy whose origin is typically associated with Adam Smith, though Smith did not originate many of the ideas typically associated with him. The central idea of that tradition of political economy is that societies can generate generally orderly patterns of economic activity even though people are mostly free to direct their lives as they choose. This classical liberal vision of political economy sought to explain how a society grounded in a strong presumption for individual liberty and responsibility for one's self-governance can operate in an orderly manner with but modest political participation in economic activity. To be sure, Virginia political economy arose during the height of the neoclassical period in economic theory, and could easily be misidentified with the neoclassical tradition. But misidentification it would be, for the central theoretical claim of neoclassical economics was the formal identity of liberalism and collectivism as systems of economic order, as Baumol (1965) and Dobb (1969), among others, convey. This formal identity reflected recognition that the first-order conditions for an optimal allocation of resources were the same under capitalism and socialism. This identity of liberalism and collectivism was not a claim that would have been advanced within the classical tradition, nor was it a claim that appeared sensible within the tradition of Virginia political economy, for reasons Milton Friedman (1953a: 277–319) identified in his reviews of separate books by the socialist writers Oskar Lange and Abba Lerner, where Friedman contrasts a focus on the technical identity of necessary conditions with a focus on the different operating properties of alternative institutional arrangements for the governance of human interactions.

The second stream of precursory thought was the Italian tradition in public finance that arose in the 1880s and which had mostly disappeared by the late 1930s, which Buchanan (1960) and Fausto (2003) survey, and with McLure (2007) surveying the Paretian-inspired orientation toward this analytical material. Prior to the appearance of this tradition, as well as after its disappearance, public finance was largely construed by its theorists as an exercise in elaborating maxims for applied statecraft.

Most scholars of public finance have sought to offer advice or maxims for rulers about how to advance the public good in some fashion as this was articulated by the expositors of those theories. Hence, public finance addressed such questions as how large public budgets should be, how progressive taxes should be, and how should tax revenues be distributed among items of possible public expenditure. In contrast, the Italian tradition arose as an effort to incorporate political activity into the explanatory framework of economic theory. Within this tradition, political processes reflected the same logic of economizing action as did market processes, with differences between the processes arising because of differences in the institutional environments that governed interactions among participants. Indeed, in the Foreword to the German translation of Amilcare Puviani's (1903) *Teoria della illusion finanziaria* [Theory of fiscal illusion], Gunter Schmölders (1960) explained that:

> over the last century Italian public finance has had an essentially political science character. The political character of fiscal activity stands always in the foreground . . . . This work is a typical product of Italian public finance, especially a typical product at the end of the nineteenth century. Above all, it is the science of public finance combined with fiscal politics, in many cases giving a good fit with reality [my translation].

Antonio de Viti de Marco is particularly notable with respect to the Italian tradition of public finance, with Manuela Mosca (2011) presenting an informative treatment of De Viti's character and work and with Giuseppe Eusepi and Richard Wagner (2013) locating De Viti as a significant precursor to public choice theory. De Viti's working life pretty much shadowed the life of the classical period of Italian public finance. In 1888, De Viti published *Il carattere teorico dell'economia finanziaria* [The theoretical character of public finance]. This small book was expanded three further times during De Viti's lifetime, culminating finally in the 1934 publication of *Principii di economia finanziaria* [First principles of public finance]. This book was translated into English (De Viti 1936), and is the only book-length statement of the classical Italian orientation toward public finance available in English. In the Preface, De Viti explains that "I treat public finance as a theoretical science, assigning to it the task of *explaining* the phenomena of public finance in their historical setting" (De Viti's italics).

The scholars associated with the Virginia tradition of political economy sought to develop a unified approach to political and economic activity within society by bringing forward and combining insights from the British classical and Italian traditions.[2] By the late 1950s, both of those traditions had pretty much disappeared from scholarly radar screens. The classical tradition of liberal political economy had given way to the neoclassical tradition that was wide open to collectivist economic theories and Progressivist political programs. Public finance, moreover, was dominated by the hortatory imperative to offer Progressivist-inspired accounts of how state power could be deployed to improve society in light of widespread presumptions that market failures would otherwise plague societies.

The schemes of thought associated with any scholarly tradition that is a progressive research program can be likened to a river to which numerous scholars contribute. With multiple schemes of thought and research programs being in play at any moment, it is not unusual to find admixtures among schemes sometimes occurring due to strategic and competitive elements entailed in the generation of scholarship (Collins 1998). As the Virginia tradition developed over the half-century following publication of *The Calculus of Consent* (Buchanan and Tullock 1962), the mainline currents of its thought became mixed with currents from the mainstream of economic thought (invoking Peter Boettke's (2007) distinction between the mainline and mainstream branches of economic theory). This chapter seeks to filter those distinct currents to grasp the essence of public choice within the tradition of Virginia political economy (Wagner 2004, 2013, 2015a,b). To do this, some excursion into the history of economic thought is necessary, and with this excursion followed by consideration of the tangled relationship among politics, economics, and property rights that will inform the rest of the book.

1. PAST ECONOMICS AS ECONOMICS OF THE EXTENDED PRESENT

Economists are notorious for having disdain for old books. Few doctoral programs offer fields in the history of economic analysis and many of them don't even offer courses on the topic. Many reading lists for economics courses feature few items more than five years old, and many of the featured items have yet to be published. The image created by such reading lists is that past scholarship has little to offer present scholars. This image reflects what appears to be the widely held presumption that whatever was once valuable in the past has already been incorporated into present economic theory, so avoiding old books avoids wasting time in exploring blind alleys, which in turn makes economic theory more progressive than it would otherwise be. We can honor the past by recognizing that we are standing on the shoulders of giants, but there is no need to read the contributions of those giants because those of their formulations that are still useful are already incorporated into current theory.

This widely held belief is just that, a belief or an article of faith. It has neither evidence nor theory in its support. Indeed, as theory it entails a thoroughgoing embrace of the theory of perfect competition applied to the generation of economic scholarship, along with the claim that perfect competition pertains to that generation in each and every instant of time. Yet very few economists believe that the theory of perfect competition gives a good description of actual economic processes or arrangements. Furthermore, that belief runs afoul of the micro-theoretic basis of the constitution of economic theories, as Arthur Lovejoy (1936: 3–23) explains in the first of his William James Lectures titled "The Study of the History of Ideas." An economic theory is packaged as a macro-theoretic entity. That entity, however, is constituted as a string of micro-theoretic entities. Consider the use by some theorists to explain involuntary unemployment as a consequence of the need for firms to pay efficiency wages above the competitive level of wages. While this idea is packaged as a macro entity, or what Lovejoy described as a "unit-idea," it is actually constituted through stringing together a number of micro bits of theory. Among those bits are assumptions about business firms, agency theory, compensation schemes, marginal productivity theory and its alternatives, and the meaning of competition, among other bits, all of which can be combined in various ways.

The construction of an economic theory is thus an exercise in combinatorial arithmetic. A deck of cards can provide a simple illustration of the complexity that arises quickly from this type of arithmetic. There are some 635 billion ways that a sequence of 13 cards can be drawn from a deck of 52 cards. Keeping with this illustration, suppose a theory of involuntary unemployment of the efficiency wage variety requires a sequence of 13 micro bits to be strung together from among 52 bits that are available. If so, there are some 635 billion ways a theory of efficiency wages can be articulated. Furthermore, suppose it takes a speedy theorist one day to organize and articulate one such theory. If a thousand scholars are involved in constructing efficiency wage theories, it will take 635 million days to articulate all such theories, or around two million years. It is surely implausible and even unreasonable to claim logical support for thinking that present theory inexorably incorporates the best from the past. To be sure, one could recur to argument about statistical sampling to assert that full enumeration would be wasteful. Even a sample size of one percent, however, would require 20,000 years to allow an inference reasonably to be made by standard statistical procedures. Claims on behalf of the proposition that competition among theorists generates some objective notion of Truth are undecidable, as Chaitin et al. (2012) explain in their exploration of the world of undecidability that arises in pursuing Kurt Gödel's insights about the unavoidably arbitrary character of any closed scheme of thought.

Kenneth Boulding (1971) asked: "After Samuelson, who needs Adam Smith?" Boulding's effective answer was "everyone," and he justified his response by locating Smith within what he called the "extended present." Boulding's poetic prose and my combinatorial arithmetic lead to the same recognition that past scholarly contributions and formulations can often provide valuable insight for current theoretical efforts. There is no guarantee that what is carried forward from past to present will prove to be the most useful of all the possibilities. Someone in 1876 looking back to 1776 might select some things for usefulness and discard others. Yet someone in 1976 looking back to 1776 might make a different selection due to any number of things: the questions to be addressed by current theories might have changed; alternatively, new methods of analysis might have been created that brought tractability to formerly intractable ideas. Adam Smith's use of the diamond–water paradox was kept alive for the better part of a century before being abandoned. Adam Smith's interest in increasing returns was set aside in favor of the tractability of constant returns, only to be revived two centuries later when new schemes of thought made it possible to work with those ideas, as Paul Romer (1986) set forth and with Buchanan and Yoon (1994) collecting a set of essays on increasing returns.

Nicholas Vriend (2002) illustrated nicely Boulding's theme about the extended present when he asked: "Is Hayek an ace?" By "ace," Vriend meant an economist who worked with agent-based computational models. As a literal matter, there is no way Hayek could have been an ace because those techniques weren't around when Hayek (1937, 1945) argued that the central problem of economic theory is to explain how coherent macro patterns can emerge in societies when no micro entity knows but a pittance of the knowledge that would be needed actually to construct that pattern. In doing this, Hayek was, among other things, denying the meaningfulness and usefulness of standard theories of perfect competition as based on postulated conditions of full awareness of relevant knowledge. The analytical challenge for Hayek was to explain how orderly patterns could emerge in the face of limited and divided knowledge. This challenge could never be met by postulating equilibrium and supporting that postulation with econometrics because doing that gave no insight into the actual workings of the social world. Hence, Vriend argued that Hayek most surely would have been an ace had those schemes of thought been available when he was wrestling with his ideas about divided and distributed knowledge. Someone who can now work with agent-based computational models can find illuminating formulations in Hayek, and formulations that are much more open to agent-based techniques than the subsequent equilibrium-centered presumptions that such economists as Grossman and Stiglitz (1976, 1980) work with, though it should also be recognized that agent-based modeling also unavoidably butts against the same problems of unavoidable incompleteness, as Stephen DeCanio (2014) examines in exploring the limits of genuine knowledge about economy and society.

2.   THE MISGUIDED DISTINCTION BETWEEN CLASSICAL AND NEOCLASSICAL ECONOMICS

In textbooks on the history of economics, students learn that the principal dividing line in the history of economics is that which separates the classical from the neoclassical tradition. This separation reflects differences in how economists go about explaining differences in prices. Within the classical tradition, prices were explained as differing because of differences in the cost of producing different products. If it took twice as much time to catch a deer as it did to catch a beaver, the price of a deer would be twice the price of a beaver. This cost-of-production theory of value led the classical economists to ponder such observations as the price of diamonds being vastly higher than the price of water, even though people can live without diamonds but can't live without water. To be sure, not all economists from the eighteenth century pondered this matter. Adam Smith and his British successors did. But Richard Cantillon and the physiocrats in France did not. Even more, the Spanish Jesuits associated with the University of Salamanca centuries earlier (Marjorie Grice-Hutchison 1978) did not do this. Those Jesuits, moreover, had developed a theory of the self-organizing features of economic activity within society well in advance of the contributions of the Scottish Enlightenment to this effect. Indeed, Simon Bilo and Richard Wagner (2015) speculate that it is conceivable had some historical events surrounding the discovery of gold on the American continent turned out differently, we would now attribute the idea of societal self-ordering to the Spanish Enlightenment rather than the Scottish Enlightenment.

Still, the diamond–water paradox plagued the British liberal tradition running from Adam Smith to John Stuart Mill. This paradox was resolved finally by the advent of the marginal revolution late in the nineteenth century, with economic theory thereafter described as neoclassical economics, to recur to the difference in how economists accounted for differences among prices. Prices were now explained with reference to the marginal utilities of different items. Gone were explanations grounded in costs of production. With this shift in the explanation of price, the diamond–water paradox dissolved. Without doubt, having water to drink is more significant for human life than having diamonds to wear. This comparison, however, is irrelevant for explaining prices. What matters for doing that in the neoclassical tradition are the relative values of small increments of different items. Water is plentiful relative to the desire people have for it, so its price is low. Diamonds are scarce relative to the desire people have for them, so people are willing to pay high prices for a few more diamonds while paying very little for a little more water.

It is often observed that winners write history. This observation pertains to the writing of the history of economics. Locating the central dividing line in the history of economics as based on different explanations for prices reflects the central orientation of neoclassical economics as primarily a theory of prices and resource allocations. This neoclassical view of the object of economic theory is conveyed often in textbook references to the primary functions of an economic system as being to determine what is to be produced, how it is to be produced, and how that production is to be distributed.[3] While it is necessarily the case that any system of economic interaction can be described in terms of providing answers to such questions, this does not mean that these questions provide a direct focal point for economic analysis. Theories have both foregrounds and backgrounds, and these can be reversed between different sets of theories.

The neoclassical scheme of thought mostly treated resource allocations as the immediate objects of theoretical examination. Adam Smith, David Ricardo, and John Stuart Mill all operated with cost-of-production theories of value, and so would be lumped together as members of the same tradition within a neoclassical construction of the history of economics. Likewise, William Stanley Jevons, Carl Menger, and Léon Walras all operated with a marginal utility explanation of prices, and so likewise are lumped together within the same scheme of economic theory, though William Jaffé (1976) emphasizes the differences among those three theorists.

Prices and allocations are not, however, the only possible objects on which an economic theory can focus. For neoclassical economics, prices and allocations occupy the theoretical foreground. The background is occupied by various institutional arrangements that are thought necessary for economic activity but which nonetheless are thought to be of secondary analytical interest. Within the spirit of much classical economics, however, it was institutional arrangements that comprised the foreground, with resource allocations relegated to the background, as Nathan Rosenberg (1960) explains in his examination of how it was institutions more than allocations that were central to Adam Smith's conception of economic theory. Economics within the classical motif was principally concerned with the governance of human interactions and their consequences: resource allocations were products of human interaction but were not direct products of human choice.

An alternative scheme for organizing the history of economics would locate the prime differences in the accounts different economists give for the observed orderliness of societies. An alternative genealogy of the history of economics could be advanced based on differences in the objects of economic inquiry. One line of economic theorists would run in terms of economists who thought the prime object of economic analysis was relative prices and resource allocations. This line of classification would place David Ricardo and Léon Walras in the same analytical camp because both were centrally concerned to explain prices and allocations. Sure, Ricardo and Walras took different approaches to explaining relative prices; however, both reflected agreement that the explanation of relative prices and resource allocations was the central object for economic analysis.

This alternative scheme for classification would likewise place Adam Smith and Carl Menger in the same analytical camp despite their taking different approaches to the explanation of price and value. Most significantly in this respect, neither of these economists was centrally concerned with prices and allocations. Among other things, they recognized that resources could not allocate themselves but rather were allocated by people in consequence of their interacting with other people inside some institutional framework that governed and structured those interactions. Economics within the Smith–Menger line of analysis was centered on the institutions of human governance.

Looking ahead, Virginia political economy as it emerged in the late 1950s fell clearly within this Smith–Menger scheme of analysis. That scheme of analysis, however, was often misidentified as a libertarian strain of neoclassical analysis, recalling that the first-order conditions for economic efficiency within the neoclassical scheme are identical for liberal and collectivist economies because allocative efficiency is defined independently of any kind of institutional arrangement that governs interaction among people. This misidentification is a product of adopting the neoclassical writing of the history of economics. It is interesting to note in this respect that Virginia political economy has often been identified as a variant of Chicago-style economics in light of high esteem accorded to Frank Knight by so many Virginia faculty members. And yet James Buchanan, undoubtedly the premier figure in the history of Virginia political economy, expressly rejected his Chicago teachings in noting early on that he wanted to construct an entirely different approach to public finance than what he learned at Chicago, as Marianne Johnson (2014) explains in her examination of James Buchanan's early work on the theory of public finance.

3.   PLAUSIBLE VS. DEMONSTRATIVE REASONING IN POLITICAL ECONOMY

Classical economics was grounded on plausible reasoning; neoclassical economics largely embraced demonstrative reasoning. While the natural home for the public choice motif of Virginia political economy lay in the plausible reasoning of classical economics, it arose in the heyday of demonstrative reasoning, so its formulations often used that scheme of thought, leading in turn to misidentification of its analytical hard core. The classical scheme of liberal economics starts with recognition that economic activity entails regularities that call for scientific articulation. The conceptualization of markets and of a market economy took shape as this inquiry into social theory proceeded. The purpose of such inquiry was to explain how generally orderly patterns of activity emerge within socie-ties even though there was no person or office in society who constructed that regularity. The economic theory of a market economy bore a close relationship to the political philosophy of liberalism. The economic theory explained how socially orderly patterns of activity emerged even though individuals were free to choose how to deploy their talents; the political philosophy explained that socially beneficial properties emerged out of individual interaction within the liberal order of society.

The origins of economics as a subject of scientific inquiry lay in recogni-tion that social life presented regular patterns that called for explanation. It was apparent that the prices and quantities of the products exchanged through market transactions were not determined by some person or bureau. While there were plenty of positions of authority within societies in those days, there was also a good deal of scope for people to transact on terms of their choosing. The economic regularities that people observed occurred on both large and small scales. On a large scale, an influx of gold from the newly discovered American continent was followed by a general rise in prices throughout the gamut of market transactions. On a small scale, it was often noticed that such an event as a public mourning that followed some royal death was accompanied by a rise in the price of black cloth.

The classically liberal theory of a free-market economy emerged as the product of interested scholars trying to give a coherent account of such observations. What was especially significant about these theorists is that they were engaged in plausible reasoning, in contrast to the focus on demonstrative reasoning that came into play late in the nineteenth century (Polya 1954). Plausible reasoning is empirical; demonstrative reasoning is logical. This isn't to say that plausible reasoning is non-logical or illogical, for logic is central to plausible reasoning. Plausible reasoning starts from recognition that the object of inquiry cannot be known in full detail to the inquirer. Similar to the position of the blind men from Hindustan, each of whom felt a piece of an elephant but none of whom felt the full elephant, plausible reasoning seeks to develop plausible analyses based on knowledge that is inescapably limited and incomplete.

The liberal economists recognized that regularities pervaded the economic activities of societies, and sought to give coherent accounts of those regularities. The thrust of these invisible-hand types of explanations was to explain that outcomes that often were socially beneficial emerged out of individual activities that mostly were narrowly focused on local concerns and interests and not on some societal or global object of concern. In this setting, a market economy was the term used to describe social arrangements where transactions occurred within an institutional setting dominated by rights of private property and liberty of contract. People could dispose of or acquire property through transactions and in terms that were agreeable to the affected parties. Such transactions were obviously beneficial to the parties or else they would not have agreed to the transactions. To be sure, there could be cases when transactions occurred under duress, as when someone whose wheel came off a wagon in a remote spot accepted help from a passerby at an exorbitant price because of the coming darkness combined with a strong fear of the beasts that might come out of the forest at night. There could also be cases where the buyer accepted the seller's testimony that a mare was fertile only to find later that she had been spayed.

There was, in other words, no presumption that all transactions were mutually beneficial, but only that mutual benefit was the norm of voluntary exchange. In cases of duress and fraud, moreover, there were legal remedies that disgruntled buyers could pursue. These legal options for remedy were likewise addressed within the framework of plausible reasoning. For neither market transactions nor legal actions was there any claim about global perfection, for this awaited the shift of attention from plausible to demonstrable reasoning that came late in the nineteenth century.

Late in the nineteenth century the neoclassical movement in economic theory started. So too did the growth of socialist movements and welfare states in Europe, followed by the emergence of Progressivism in the United States in the early twentieth century. Progressivism called for the replacement of complex systems of governance based on separated and divided powers with a strong administrative state with the reins of power held by right-minded people. Woodrow Wilson's (1885) call for administrative centralization set the analytical stage for theorists to support monocentric over polycentric arrangements of political offices. It was nearly a century later when Vincent Ostrom (1973) set forth a cogent articulation of the polycentric alternative that informed the original constitutional arrangement. This shift in economic theory and political context was accompanied by a shift from plausible to demonstrative reasoning. Within the spirit of plausible reasoning, liberal economists sought nothing more than to explain how a society of largely self-governing individuals could generate coherent patterns of economic activity that were generally recognized as being beneficial. The plausible nature of such reasoning meant that differences of opinion were always in play within a general presumption in favor of self-ordered liberal governance, as Lionel Robbins (1952) and Warren Samuels (1966) explain in their examinations of the classical orientation toward political economy.

This default setting in favor of self-governance changed as neoclassical economics took shape, not so much due to marginalism *per se* as to the shift to demonstrative reasoning that accompanied the marginal revolution. In conjunction with this path of development, economists came increasingly to articulate claims about market failure. These claims were articulated against a background of a theory of perfect competition, the assumptions of which were rarely to be found in economic life. In the wake of the advance of market failure theories, welfare economics developed into the systematic study of governmental intervention into the market-generated economic organization of societies, classic illustrations of which are James Meade (1952) and Francis Bator (1958). The object of such analytical efforts was to attain demonstrative knowledge about when governmental intervention into market arrangements could represent societal improvement.

While theorists differed in the size of the domain to which market failure arguments pertained, almost invariably they worked with the analytical presumption that political agents would operate with a single-minded dedication to follow the dictates of welfare economics, if only the analysts would speak with the same voice. It is here where modern public choice analysis starts. As with most such beginnings, there is no one instant to date the start. As is almost always the case in these matters, there were precursors and forerunners. In any case, public choice came about when theorists began to treat politicians and public officials as ordinary people. Within the spirit of welfare economics, politicians and public officials were not ordinary people engaged in transactional activity. Transactions were the domain of people in business, who were carriers of the commercial syndrome (Jacobs 1992). Politicians and public officials, however, were carriers of the guardian syndrome and so shunned commerce to carry out their corrective and guardian activities as these were described by theories of welfare economics. Public choice theorists, however, recognized that politicians and public officials had little reason to shun commercial activity and had every reason to get involved with it, possibly creating in the process what Jacobs termed "monstrous moral hybrids."

The so-called marginal revolution in economic theory that started to take shape in the late nineteenth century overcame such logical conundrums as those expressed by the diamond–water paradox, but did so at the expense of narrowing the focus of economic analysis from the governance of systems of social interaction to the analysis of the choices of presumptively maximizing individuals within some given system of social interaction. In conjunction with this narrowing of the object of scientific inquiry came a shift in analytical motif from the earlier concern with plausible reasoning applied to open systems to a treatment of closed systems using demonstrative reasoning. Where the earlier theorists reasoned in terms of social systems that possessed tendencies toward what might be called states of equilibrium, recognizing that such states were mental constructions and not descriptions of reality, the modern or neoclassical theorists reasoned in terms of trying to demonstrate conditions under which systemic equilibrium would occur.

Prior to the advent of marginalism, competition was conceptualized as a normal activity of people who were free to choose their activities. With the advent of marginalism, however, competition came to be treated not as a verb but as an adjective where competition could vary between some notion of perfect competition and various notions of imperfect competition (McNulty 1968). Perfect competition, in turn, was defined in terms of demonstrative reasoning to be a set of conditions under which it must be the case that all items of a product sell for the same price. Absent such conditions, competition would be described as imperfect and hence subject potentially to perfection through appropriate interjections of policy. To be sure, one might wonder why a situation when all participants are price takers would be labeled a state of perfection when it implies that no new products or services are ever created. After all, one cannot be a price taker in creating a new product or service. But to think in this manner is to think in terms of plausible reasoning, and the neoclassical period was infused with the spirit of demonstrative reasoning wherein a good economic theory had to give a precise answer to a well-defined question.

What resulted was recognition that perfect competition was an impossible standard because reality was necessarily imperfect when compared against that standard. With this recognition arose the systematic study of how governments might intervene into market processes to bring about a better state of affairs as this might be judged by market participants. The standard of betterness that economists adopted was that of Pareto efficiency. Within this standard, market imperfection described a situation in which through state action it would be possible to make at least one person better off without making anyone worse off. Such situations were addressed in terms of demonstrative reasoning because of the implausibility of actually trying to do such a thing. From this line of analysis came recognition that there is no principled limit to the reach of state action to improve on the results of market interaction. This doesn't mean that economic analysis counseled a vast increase in the extent of state intervention into economic life. It rather means that there was no principled limit on the reach of political intervention.

The actual reach depended on a calculation of the costs and benefits of intervention. State intervention isn't free. Offices must be created and staffed, and taxes must be imposed. In some cases the potential gains from intervention might exceed the costs. As for who would make such calculations and make such judgments, it was generally left as an article of faith that existing political arrangements would generate the correct answer. Indeed, much of the modern literature on political economy has formalized just this line of analysis, as a later chapter shall examine. For now, however, it can simply be noted that the growth of the Progressivist political program where there is no principled limit on the reach of the political into society fit well with the neoclassical shift to a demonstrative style of reasoning in conjunction with the formalization of that style of reasoning into welfare economics in the middle years of the twentieth century.

4.   ON LIGHTHOUSES, PUBLIC GOODS, AND PLAUSIBLE REASONING

Contemporary economic theory has harbored several controversies about whether particular types of services are better categorized as public or private goods, with television broadcasting (Minasian 1964) and lighthouses (Coase 1974) serving as archetypes of the points at issue. The signals emitted by television stations and lighthouses seem clearly to fit within the purview of Paul Samuelson's (1954, 1955) definition of a public good where a single unit of production can provide unlimited units of consumption, at least within some geographical range covered by the public good. Despite fitting within the rubric of a public good, television signals and lighthouse signals are both capable of being financed by charges paid by users of those services. Yet charging positive prices will exclude some potential users who value the service, even if they value it at less than the price. By the very definition of a public good, excluding anyone who places a positive value on the service violates the first-order conditions for Pareto efficiency. Within the framework of demonstrative reasoning, an observation that vendors can find ways to sell such public goods as television programming and lighthouse signals does not transform those goods into ordinary private goods.

Within the framework of demonstrative reasoning, controversy over whether something is a private or a public good is potentially interminable. There is surely no other possible situation when the classification into private and public is based on some analyst's presumption about individual states of mind regarding their valuations of what are claimed to be public goods. Within the standard Paretian conditions, an efficient level of output is defined as the level of output where the combined willingness of all those who place positive value on the service equals the cost of providing a marginal unit of that service. There is no way to tell whether or not those conditions have been met in any particular case. The willingness of someone to pay for something is revealed only at the moment someone chooses to buy something, or not to buy it. The conceptual categories of orthodox public goods theory are pieces of logic that are part of a scheme of demonstrative reasoning. Such categories can be used as logical exercises, but those exercises cannot be applied directly to reality because they would require the analyst to fill what are nothing but imaginary economic boxes (Wagner 2015b).

To work with such categories requires a scheme of thought grounded in plausible reasoning accompanied by open-ended rather than closed-form modeling. Consider Coase's (1974) treatment of lighthouses in England around the eighteenth century, a treatment that Krause (2015) amplifies by providing relevant illustrations. Those lighthouses were financed by tolls collected from ships that anchored in harbors in the vicinity of those lighthouses. It is easy to understand why proponents of market-based arrangements within society would point to lighthouses as being private and not public goods, given that they think lighthouses are better provided through market-like transactions than through a bureaucratically operated Department of Lighthouses. Such proponents, however, would surely be wrong because the services of those lighthouses are valued by some relevant public. Demonstrative reasoning, however, is incapable of identifying such valuations, for these valuations are revealed only through the actions people take within particular institutional settings.

The public goods quality of lighthouses, and many similar services, resides in the situational logic suitable for plausible reasoning. We can affirm that there is widespread public interest in having ships arrive safely at their destinations rather than crashing on rocks along their paths. That affirmation, moreover, has nothing to do with presuming to know individual marginal valuations for such services. Affirmation rather resides in recognizing that the owners of ships and those who sail on ships value the safe arrival of those ships in harbor. The same goes for the owners of the cargoes carried on those ships, as well as for the merchants who are scheduled to receive the merchandise carried by those ships. This very situation means that profit can be captured through finding ways to create transactions that reduce the danger ships face from crashing on rocks. Just what that might entail is a matter of entrepreneurial and organizational discovery (Kirzner 1973, 1979), of which the possibilities are numerous and open-ended prior to the emergence of particular historical configurations.

For instance, a set of ship owners might form an organization to support a network of lighthouses financed by tolls collected from member ships as they reached port. This scheme pretty much mirrors what Coase (1974) described, though Coase described a situation where a governmental agency collected the tolls. In the absence of government-supported collection, a situation could arise where some ships that arrived at port were not owned by one of the members of the organization. This situation might be sufficiently rare that the members of the organization would ignore it. Alternatively, the ship owners might acquire docking rights at the harbors protected by the lighthouses. In this case, ships would not be allowed to dock without belonging to the organization. To be sure, that organization could well develop a scheme of pricing where dues varied with the number of ships docked during some period. Regardless of how the organization's activities were provided and financed, lighthouse services would reasonably qualify as a good of interest to a relevant public, though that relevant public need not be the set of all people residing within a nation or other political unit.

The analytical boxes labeled "market failure" and "market success" are imaginary boxes that exist only within the framework of demonstrative reasoning (Wagner 2015b). In contrast, plausible reasoning pertains to situations where people perceive situations that render them uneasy and which in turn induces a search for means to reduce that uneasiness. The analytical foreground is thus populated by people seeking to fashion institutional arrangements that allow them to overcome particular sources of uneasiness. Public goods theory in its demonstrative mode presents a caricature of the actual historical possibilities open at any particular moment. Which possible option among a menu of possibilities might be put in play at that moment will be generated through interaction among interested parties within that particular societal setting.

5. INTERPRETING OLD TEXTS AFTER HALF A CENTURY: *THE CALCULUS OF CONSENT*

James Buchanan and Gordon Tullock's (1962) *The Calculus of Consent* is undoubtedly the Ur-text of Virginia political economy, as Wagner (2013) notes. Yet several forms of political economy are in play, and with those forms pointing in different analytical directions. In recognition of this situation, Blankart and Koester (2006) distinguished between public choice and political economics as alternative forms of political economy. Yet the opening line of the Preface to *The Calculus of Consent* reads: "This is a book about the *political* organization of a society of free men" (italics in original). It's clear that there are different ways of bringing economic theory to bear on politics just as there are different ways of constructing economic theories. Any such act of construction will start with some pre-analytical cognitive vision (Schumpeter 1954: 41) which the scholar then seeks to articulate so as to make it intelligible to others. The articulation of that vision will occur through some ordered string of units of thought. How that thought is strung together and how those units are conceptualized will depend on the tools of thought that an author has available to work with. Vriend (2002) explains that agent-based computational modeling offers a solid platform for working with some of Hayek's ideas about knowledge that is fragmented and distributed and nowhere possessed by one person or office. Yet such tools of thought weren't available to Hayek, so he had to resort to literary reasoning that was easily reducible to a statement of equilibrium conditions, the incoherence of which was subsequently set forth by Grossman and Stiglitz (1976, 1980). In doing this, however, Grossman and Stiglitz did not dispute Hayek but ignored him. The ability to articulate a pre-analytical cognitive vision depends on the tools of thought that are available to an author.

The interpretation of *The Calculus of Consent* and its significance for Virginia political economy and public choice is likewise influenced by tools of thought. Ideas about complex systems and agent-based computational modeling were not available to Buchanan and Tullock, though some game-theoretic models were then available. What resulted was an effort at articulation that had a mixed-metaphor quality about it that is subject to misinterpretation, as Wagner (2013) explains. *The Calculus of Consent* was conceived as an effort to explain that the complex constitutional arrangement that was founded in 1789 reflected a coherent economic logic of governance through divided and separated powers. Indeed, Vincent Ostrom's (1987) *Political Theory of a Compound Republic*, first published in 1971, is effectively a flying buttress to *The Calculus of Consent*. Where Buchanan and Tullock took recourse to some of the simple equilibrium models that were then used by economists to illustrate some of their arguments, Ostrom maintained contact with the complex constitutional arrangements that were established in 1789.

The constitutional scheme of separated and divided powers meant that the median voter model was more a fictional construction than a reasonable model of a constitutional arrangement. A median voter model might pertain for a five-member town council that has the sole authority to allocate tax revenues among expenditure items. It would not, however, apply to complex arrangements of separated and divided powers where concurrence among different entities is required before collective action can be undertaken. In these kinds of settings, outcomes are products of interaction and negotiation and not products of choice. The American constitutional system created a complex structure of divided and separated powers that required concurrence among different sets of people. Within a bicameral legislature, for instance, the degree of concurrence that is required varies with the principles by which the two chambers are selected. Within the original constitutional setting, the federal Senate was selected by state legislators while the House was selected directly through election. In consequence of constitutional amendment in 1913, the federal Senate also became selected directly through election. This change surely created more commonality among the electorate than had previously existed (Bueno de Mesquita et al. 2003). In a two-chamber system where both chambers are staffed through at-large elections, selection is likely to operate similarly in both chambers. Quite different properties would result should one chamber be populated by property owners and the other by renters, and with legislation requiring concurrence between both chambers. In this respect, one well cited game-theoretic exposition of fair division occurs where one person slices a cake and the other person takes the first slice. This formulation is similar to requiring concurrence between differently constituted chambers.

In any case, the prime purpose of *The Calculus of Consent* was to explain the complex system of government that the American Constitution established and which had been under strenuous attack by Progressives at least since when Woodrow Wilson (1885) wrote *Congressional Government*, where he extolled the virtues of a strong administrative apparatus in place of continual congressional negotiation and logrolling. *The Calculus of Consent* was conveyed mostly by equilibrium formulations of a relatively simple sort, even though the purpose of the book was to explain how the complex American constitutional system made sense from the perspective of economic logic and even though that sense would vanish if the system were actually reduced to conform to the simplicity of the logic, as Vincent Ostrom (1973, 1987, 1997) recognized with especial cogency.

6.   SIMPLE VOTING RULES AND COMPLEX SYSTEMS OF GOVERNANCE

The central theme of *The Calculus of Consent* has often been reduced to support for a qualified majority voting rule over simple majority voting. *The Calculus of Consent* does present a theory of constitutional choice in terms of a selection of a voting rule for undertaking collective action, and with that choice illustrated in terms of a representative agent who appraises a tradeoff between external costs and decision costs. That individual is imagined as evaluating different rules for supporting collective action by a group, and with Munger and Munger (2015) setting forth a careful analysis of various frameworks for choices by groups. The task the representative agent faces is to select the voting rule that minimizes the full costs of undertaking collective action. As the share of the group that must agree increases, the cost of reaching collective decisions rises but the cost of being victimized by collective action falls. In the limit, the external costs of being victimized by having collective action undertaken of which a representative individual disapproves disappears when unanimity is required. Yet unanimity can entail particularly high decision costs because of the delay in receipt of the benefits of collective action due to increased bargaining costs that accompany increases in the required degree of consensus.

This simple framework of constitutional choice as selection of a voting rule denies any simple identification of democracy with majority rule. Indeed, as an ideal benchmark it embraced unanimity, while also noting that this ideal was unattainable. What resulted was support for some qualified majority rule. The discussion and debate over this constitutional formulation swirled around whether the majority principle was a suitable principle for democratic governance or whether some higher degree of support was a superior principle. The reduction of constitutional choice to selection of a voting rule was analytically tractable as it could be illustrated by summing the two functions of decision costs and external costs, each expressed as the percentage of the group that must agree before it can undertake collective action.

Yet tractability also entails a tradeoff, as Wagner (2010a) explains. Tractability makes it easier to illustrate a point and to explore some implications of a model. Reducing constitutional choice to the action of a representative individual appraising a tradeoff between two functional relationships entailed in a voting rule is a simple framework that is easy to understand and free from ambiguity. Sure, it might be difficult to specify parameters for those functions, but that difficulty points to a lack of knowledge and not to ambiguity about the topic under examination.

Everyone can agree that the topic reduces to specification of two functions even if they aren't sure about how to estimate those functions.

The obverse of securing tractability by using simple models to represent complex phenomena is to obscure what is occluded from view by that model. Instruction about this can be seen by comparing the reduction of constitutional choice to a voting rule with Knut Wicksell's (1896 [1958]) formulation of qualified majority voting along the lines that Wagner (1988) set forth. The English translation of Wicksell was of the second of three essays. Consideration of the full set of essays shows that Wicksell's formulation of the problem of constituting a system of self-governance had significant structural features that were not reducible to a voting rule. In other words, a vote would be taken, but this vote stood at the end of a process that had significant structural features, and it was those structural features that shaped just what it was that would be voted on. In short, Wicksell sought to articulate a set of institutional arrangements that would reflect a roughly *consensual approach* to governance, recognizing that consensus is a plausible and not a demonstrative term. Consensus, however, is not identical with unanimity, for unanimity is a demonstrative term whereas consensus is a plausible term.

One feature common to both Buchanan and Tullock and to Wicksell is the priority of liberalism over democratic or republican government. The anthropological evidence is pretty clear that humanity began in groups, as illustrated by family members being obligated for one another's debts as well as by the absence of last names in the west, as Henry Maine (1864) explained in the context of advancing his claim that the direction of institutional movement in the west had been one of relationships grounded in status giving way to relationships grounded in contract.[4] To be sure, Maine was starting to see signs of a reversal of that direction of movement, and the past century of Progressivist domination has seen an acceleration of the replacement of contract with status. In any case, historically the individual was an extraction from the group. It was not a matter of individuals coming together to form a group. From this point of departure, there is a choice about how to proceed with respect to constitutional formation and analysis. One can start with all property held collectively, as illustrated by family members being responsible for one another's debts and as advocated by Murphy and Nagel (2002). This point of departure, however, is analytically incoherent, at least without sneaking hidden presumptions of private property into the analysis. To posit a collective starting point allows no action to take place unless some prior pattern of structured relationships is also posited, as illustrated by tribal chiefs or councils of elders. While such structured relationships are historically accurate, they also violate the purely collective point of departure. The tribe or family starts with a structured pattern of relationships out of which collective action emerges, and with that action, including action that changes the structure of those relationships, being largely consensual in nature.

The point of departure that starts with individuals and generates groups is likewise mythical. It does, however, fit with certain sentiments held widely in the west, at least until recently when they have come increasingly under challenge. The emphasis in Buchanan and Tullock (1962) reflects this liberal point of departure where the formation of a system of government is a product of people using their prior rights of property. This point of departure, moreover, was asserted in the American Declaration of Independence where it was announced that "governments derive their just powers from the consent of the governed." In their constitutional tradeoff, Buchanan and Tullock (1962) sought to use plausible reasoning to explain how people might accept some modicum of collective imposition because they thought the overall constitutional bargain would nonetheless be a good one. That treatment in terms of plausible reasoning subsequently became misunderstood as economics became dominated by demonstrative reasoning.

Wicksell (1896 [1958]) reasoned similarly, only he placed the voting rule at the culmination of a political structure that he plausibly thought would lead to outcomes that would broadly reflect consensus among the members of Swedish society. In the end, he advocated qualified majority voting within the Swedish parliament, and illustrated what he meant by referring to three-quarters and four-fifths consent to approve fiscal measures. But far more than a voting rule was involved in Wicksell's suggested constitutional framework because a vote would be the last step in a process that he thought would promote government through consensus. Wicksell's constitutional structure featured both executive and parliamentary processes, both constituted so as to work toward consensual outcomes.

With respect to parliament, Wicksell thought that Sweden was a relatively homogeneous nation that could be reduced to a comparatively few types of preference functions. To the extent Wicksell's sociological presumption was accurate, this meant that a system of proportional representation could be developed that would enable a parliament to be selected that would be a miniature representation of Swedish society. If Swedish society were reasonably well represented by, say, seven types of preference functions, it would be plausible to develop a system of proportional representation that had seven parties weighted in parliament similarly to their weights in the society at large. Given this parliamentary arrangement, any proposal for public expenditure would be accompanied by a proposal to finance that expenditure. In light of Wicksell's sociological assumptions, a high degree of support within parliament would plausibly translate into high support within Swedish society. One might dispute whether constructing such a scheme of proportional representation would be an easy task. One might also wonder about how a system of rules of parliamentary procedure might be designed for a system of qualified majority voting when extant parliamentary rules are based on majority voting. However such research questions might be resolved, the point to note is that the Wicksellian scheme is not represented adequately by reducing it to a voting rule because that voting rule is embedded within a structure of parliamentary rules.

It was also embedded within presumptions about the character of the executive part of the government. In Sweden, the executive branch was headed by a monarch, though that scheme could also be adapted to an elected executive. Just as feudal princes derived much revenue from management of their estates, so could the executive in Wicksell's scheme. The executive would operate in a position of residual claimacy by creating programs that parliament would support. To obtain parliamentary support, however, is nothing like obtaining legislative support within a two-party system based on majority rule, where Riker's (1962) size principle comes into play under which successful rule inclines toward minimizing the size of the winning coalition. With multiple parties characterized by heterogeneous preferences and with collective action requiring a high degree of consensus, the consensual properties of collective action would approximate the consensual properties of market action. With market action people don't pay for what they don't choose to buy; with collective action within a consensual framework, the instances of people paying for what they oppose would be rare—and with the extent of rareness varying directly with the degree of inclusivity of the required voting rule.

7. PROPERTY RIGHTS AND SYSTEMS OF GOVERNANCE

The pure theory of a market economy seeks to explain how orderly societal patterns of economic activity arise through interactions among individuals, no one of whom is acting so as to promote particular societal patterns. Such market processes generate societal patterns that have the appearance of being someone's creation even though they are not because they are generated through interaction within a set of institutions that promote such patterns. Those institutions are primarily alienable property rights and freedom of contract. Property can be privately held without being alienable, as illustrated by primogeniture where landed estates could not be subdivided and so had to pass to eldest sons. When alienable property is combined with freedom of contract, a market economy takes shape. Within that form of economic organization, there are strong tendencies for people to deploy their rights of property in ways they value most highly and for people to produce services that other people desire sufficiently to make production worthwhile.

To refer to "tendencies" is to employ plausible reasoning, which is how the classical economists reasoned. Whether the classical scheme of thought is thought to originate with the Spanish Jesuits from Salamanca, the physiocrats from France, or Adam Smith a little later in Great Britain, what arose was a scheme of explanation that was thought to pertain to the preponderance of economic activity which was carried out under private property and freedom of contract. In those days, governments might have accounted for five or ten percent of all economic activity. A theory of market interaction would give a reasonable account of the preponderance of economic activity within society. Collective activity was placed within a type of theoretical black box, as was doubtlessly suitable for the monarchical regimes of the time. Monarchs had their property rights, and with those rights often entailing the ability to impose on subjects. While it would be plausible to describe a monarch as making choices and assimilate a monarch's actions to those of a consumer or a firm, such explanation would be highly idiosyncratic and dependent on autobiographic details pertinent to each monarch. Such explanation stands in stark contrast to the systemic quality of economic reasoning where the analytical emphasis is placed on different systems of relationships and interactions.

In this respect, it is notable that Wicksell sought to embed the Swedish monarch within the market system of Swedish society. It is also notable that Wicksell registered strong objection to how economists treated government in their theories:

> ... with some very few exceptions, the whole theory [of state activity] still rests on the now outdated political philosophy of absolutism. The theory seems to have retained the assumptions of its infancy, in the seventeenth and eighteenth centuries, when absolute power ruled almost all Europe. ... Even the most recent manuals on the science of public finance frequently leave the impression ... of some sort of philosophy of enlightened and benevolent despotism . . . . (Wicksell 1958: 82)

With the advent of democratic regimes, the distinction between private property and public property blurred. In feudal times the prince had his property rights and subjects had theirs within a system of estates and classes. With the disappearance of feudal relations, princely property rights disappeared, to be replaced by the claims of democratic governments.

This replacement creates a challenge for the conceptualization of property rights and the meaning of market economies. Within democratic regimes there are clearly public or political property rights in place. Collective action is impossible without some scheme of political property rights to order relationships among participants within political processes. With feudal regimes, the distinction between rulers and subjects was a fact of birth. With democratic regimes, the distinction is still recognizable but it is an emergent quality of social interaction and not the destiny of birthright. Wagner (2007) argues that both public and private property rights are resident in human nature, even if they manifest themselves differently across institutional regimes. Humans are social creatures, even if not to the extent of the dogs with which we have been associated for so many millennia (Franklin 2009). This sociality provides a bedding ground for public property to grow, though not necessarily in a manner agreeable to everyone. The other side of human nature is a desire for accomplishment and to choose how to live. These two sides of human nature can conflict within an individual as well as conflicting among individuals. Conflict among individuals is easy to grasp, and can be illustrated by conflict among people who appraise differently the communal and individual facets of the structured living together that societies bring in their train.

Conflict within an individual is perhaps more difficult for economists to grasp in light of a long-standing disciplinary convention that everyone necessarily operates with well-ordered utility functions. This convention is a facet of the elevation of demonstrative reasoning that accompanied the ascendancy of the neoclassical style of economic reasoning. Well-ordered utility functions preclude any conflict within an individual, though this preclusion is surely more a feature of a particular scheme of thought than it is a universal feature of human nature. An alternative orientation toward human nature is captured by the ancient concern with the orderliness of the soul, which Isaiah Berlin's (1991) title expresses nicely in its reference to Immanuel Kant's (1784 [1991]) assertion that "out of the crooked timber of humanity no straight thing was ever made." For instance, people surely desire to have a sense of accomplishment and mastery in some sphere of life. This is a rather stoical or ascetic aspect of life. Human nature also contains more hedonistic qualities that can morph into slothfulness and its cousins, perhaps abetted by governmental programs that remove some of the cares and actions that would normally accompany efforts to seek accomplishment. For instance, regulations that restrict competition replace genuine accomplishment with faux accomplishment for the beneficiaries of such regulation.

The pure theory of a market economy is an intellectual construction based on a conceptualization of a system of absolute property rights that is nowhere to be found. One might claim that it pertains to Robinson Crusoe alone on his island, but the very concept of property rights is meaningless in that setting. A property right is not a thing but rather is a relationship between or among people. Property rights have meaning only within societies, so a person's rights of property are limited by the willingness of other people to forbear from interfering with any particular person's chosen activity. Where that forbearance ends, public property begins. Once this is recognized, it must also be recognized that dividing lines between state and market are blurry and subject continually to contestation. This is the vision of entangled political economy, which stands in contrast to the customary notion of additive political economy. It is also the vision of Virginia political economy that was present at its founding around 1960, even if that founding appears somewhat differently when viewed from within the swirling intellectual currents that were then active.

8. TREATING POLITICS AS A PECULIAR TYPE OF BUSINESS PRACTICE

It is easy to see that politics is a particular type of business activity. Pretty much anything that can be said about practical business activity pertains to practical political activity as well. It is through business activity that most people earn their livelihoods; however, a good number of people earn their livelihoods through political activity, as McCormick and Tollison (1981) note in their effort to treat political economy in explanatory rather than in hortatory fashion. Politics is but one of the many career paths that people can pursue. Business is a competitive activity. So is politics. In democracies, elections are perhaps the most visible example of competition, but elections are not the only site of political competition and might not even be the most significant site. Competition is present throughout the political world just as it is present throughout the commercial world. Within the business world, firms compete with one another. A successful firm this year might be gone from the commercial landscape five years later because other firms were more successful in attracting customers. Within firms, moreover, people compete to advance to superior positions within their current firms while also competing to attain superior positions within other firms. It is the same with politics. Politicians compete to attain elected office, and also compete to secure offices they value more highly than their present offices. People who work within governmental agencies likewise compete among themselves for advancement to more desirable positions. Competition is ubiquitous in social life, regardless of whether the activity in question is ordinarily designated as being political or economic.

Entrepreneurship is a creative human activity that bridges present and future. It is through entrepreneurship that old offerings and programs give way to new ones. Entrepreneurship is widely recognized to be significant for commercial practice. Business schools, for instance, often offer courses and some even have programs on entrepreneurship. Political practice likewise exhibits entrepreneurial activity. Whether entrepreneurship is commercial or political, it consists of someone taking a leadership position in trying to insert a new program, product, or service into society. Sometimes those entrepreneurial actions are successful, but often they fail. However particular efforts might fare, they are features of both political and economic practice.

Successful business practice requires the cultivation of supporters of various types. A significant part of that support will come from investors who believe that a particular business might be successful with sufficient capital support. After they have acquired support from investors, businesses will have to attract customers and clients, and will have to keep them despite the ability of those customers and clients to take their business elsewhere. It is the same with political practice. No potential candidate for elected office becomes an actual candidate without acquiring supporters and investors. Linguistic convention refrains from using the term "investor" in connection with the offering of support to candidates and politicians. All the same, the two terms are indistinguishable with respect to the activities to which they point. Someone makes an investment in response to having anticipated that doing so will help to bring about a situation that the investor regards as more desirable than what would otherwise have occurred. Within the commercial world, that greater desirability is customarily expressed in terms of anticipated changes in net worth for the investor. The political world does not generate such a monetary indicator in any direct fashion because political practice is organized within an institutional framework that is incapable of generating prices and transferable claims to ownership rights over cash flows. This institutional difference between political and commercial practice is simply a reflection of the different schemes of ownership that pertain to political and commercial practice. Political practice still generates returns for investors, only it does so in a peculiar manner when compared against commercial practice.

The commercial world is filled with advertising and public relations types of activity in the effort to reach out to customers. So, too, is the political world. Advertising and other public relations activities are prominent within political enterprises just as they are within commercial enterprises. Without doubt, the practice of politics entails a wide variety of activities that are common to both politics and business. Politics, however, is not just one among many instances of the generic practice of business and indistinguishable from the other instances. Politics is rather a *peculiar* instance of business practice, and these peculiar features can ramify throughout the society in which both ordinary and peculiar forms of business activity occur. Among other considerations, there is good reason to think that political enterprises operate in scale-free fashion (Barabási 2002). This scale-free quality means that political entities acquire different operating qualities as their scale of operation expands.

Growing entanglement between the political and the economic can ramify throughout society in the presence of this scale-free quality. The institutions and conventions of private property and free competition operate to give small and large firms pretty much the same properties of being forced systemically to serve consumer desires. The situation can be different with democratic polities, thereby leading large governments to have different properties from small governments. As Jonathan Hughes (1977) explains, governmental involvement in private businesses was present even in Colonial times, but it acquired different qualities as commingling between government and business grew. What Sanford Ikeda (1997) calls the dynamics of intervention undergoes qualitative transformation with increases in the relative number of politically based enterprises in society. To be sure, Patrick and Wagner (2015) explain that intervention is a misleading notion within a framework of entangled political economy. In either case, competition operates differently in limiting the sizes of political and economic enterprises. The peculiar features of the organization of political activity can transform a social system based largely on freedom of enterprise into a cousin of the old systems of feudal relationship where social relations are governed increasingly by principles of status and standing rather than by principles of mutuality and equality.

While successful political practice requires investors, many of those investors are forced investors. A good part of such investment surely occurs under duress, as well as under recognition that such investment can be prudent in light of the ability of political practice to marshal force. Someone might invest in a politician or party because of a simple belief that the politician's program offers a better direction for political organizations within a society than the alternative direction without that investment. Such investments might also be made because it is thought that it will place the investor in the position of acquiring some shield from the undesired taxation or regulation that otherwise might come the investor's way.

Success cannot be gauged the same way in political activity as it is in commercial activity. For commercial activity, success can be gauged by the value of the enterprise. The institutions of private property and freedom of contract operate to generate valuations for all commercial enterprises. In many instances this valuation is generated directly through the operation of stock exchanges. Even for closely held businesses, however, valuation is present because those enterprises can still be sold. Political enterprises are not subject to sale, so no valuation can be attached to such enterprises. A privately held school can be sold, so it can be valued and changes in its value through time can be noted and observed. A publicly held school has no valuation as an enterprise, even though some of its assets can be sold.

Political practice bears an unavoidably parasitic relationship to market practice. Political activity cannot generate valuations for political enterprises and their activities. Yet those enterprises must continually engage in economic calculation because all action requires choices among options, and choice requires valuation. Cost and choice are two images of the same reality (Buchanan 1969). The necessity of making choices requires valuation because the cost of choosing one option is the value associated with the option not chosen. With respect to political activity, market prices can provide useful points of orientation for political enterprises. For instance, it is unlikely that political programs will be created around objects that have little market value to directly affected parties. Political enterprises can gain insight into the substantive construction of their programs by using market prices to gauge where political value might lie, even as those programs also operate to change market prices. After all, the very idea of "reform" would be meaningless if it did not lead to some changes in market prices, even if the actual pattern of such changes is beyond direct control as distinct from influence. In other words, political enterprises require some of the information market exchange generates even though those enterprises are also engaged in changing the terms of trade that are generated through market activity.

Any business has products or services for which it seeks customers. The producer–customer relationship is a universal form that fits numerous particular situations. That universal form holds for political enterprises just as it holds for commercial enterprises. The particular actions that occur inside those universal forms differ to a significant degree, and with those differences being conveyed in large measure by Vilfredo Pareto's (1935) distinction between logical and non-logical action. Logical action pertains to what economists describe as inspection or experience goods (Nelson 1970). These are goods for which consumers can discern relevant qualities simply by inspecting them or sampling them. These are the types of goods that commercial enterprises mostly produce. Within the environment of competition among commercial enterprises, vendors must be able to survive in open competition with other vendors when customers can compare their *ex post* experiences with their *ex ante* imaginations.

It is different for competition among political enterprises. A good deal of the activities of local governments involves inspection and experience goods, as illustrated by municipal playgrounds or golf courses. At higher levels of government, the mix of activity changes with credence goods becoming more common. Credence goods conform to Pareto's notion of non-logical action. For credence goods, it is impossible to test producer claims about the qualitative aspects of the vendor's services, as Emons (1997) examines. In this setting, competition among vendors takes on a significantly ideological character whereby vendors seek to elicit sympathetic responses from potential customers, the results of which can result in people supporting what they would have rejected had they been able to evaluate it directly through inspection or experience (Backhaus 1978). To some degree, political competition revolves around the articulation of images (Boulding 1956) in an environment where those images cannot be subjected directly to some test of their comparative truth values.

NOTES

1. Simmons (2011) is a lucid textbook presentation of public choice ideas; Mueller (2003) is a professional-level treatise; Shughart and Razzolini (2001) is a wide-ranging collection of essays by notable public choice scholars.
2. In Wagner (2015a) I also associate Virginia political economy with the Austrian tradition of economic theory. Austrian ideas were treated with great respect in Charlottesville in the early 1960s, only those ideas were viewed as an aspect of the classical tradition of liberal political economy and not as a distinctive school of economic theory.
3. The neoclassical emphasis on resource allocation finds its political counterpart in Harold Lasswell's (1936) treatment of politics as centrally concerned with who gets what, when they get it, and how they do that.
4. Harold Berman (1983) is a recent treatise that reflects an orientation similar to Maine's.

2. Alternative paths for a theory of political economy

Before Alfred Marshall published the first edition of his *Principles of Economics* in 1890, economics was commonly described as "political economy." Marshall advocated changing from political economy to economics because he thought the shorter term sounded more scientific, and also he was seeking to separate economics from what had been its traditional location inside moral philosophy within the curriculum of British universities. Marshall was successful, and economics became the science that studied the object designated as "economy." This object was described by Marshall as "the study of mankind in the ordinary business of life; it examines that part of individual and social action which is most closely connected with the attainment and the use of the material requisites of wellbeing" (Marshall 1920: 1). The idea of a market economy was an abstract representation of the social organization of such activity. Starting from an institutional framework grounded in principles of private property and freedom of contract, economic theory seeks to explain how complex societal patterns and arrangements can emerge within that framework of simple rules (Epstein 1995).

Within this scheme of thought, politics stands apart from economics. Economics could be extended to considerations of economic policy, but this was separate from economics as a science. There was a science of economics and there was an art of political economy or public policy which is where political activity appeared in intervening into economic life to bring about different outcomes from what otherwise would have been generated within economy. Economics was the study of people dealing with practical problems that arise in earning livelihoods. Politics appeared as an independent source of evaluation and action that was concerned with the social goodness of political intervention into the market-generating institutions of private property and freedom of contract.

What resulted was a scheme of thought where economy and polity denoted independent analytical objects. In those earlier times when governments accounted for 10 percent or less of traditionally measured economic activity and when political regulation of commercial and industrial activity was equally modest, the pure theory of a market economy was perhaps a reasonable approximation to a theory of social economy. While the theory of a market economy didn't explain all activity within society, it explained the preponderance of it. A perfectionist might object to leaving even 10 percent within an analytical black box. Still, a 90 percent or so theory of society was quite a strong analytical performance, for it rendered economic theory as the predominant pathway into a theory of society. Vilfredo Pareto (1935) with his distinction between economic equilibrium and societal equilibrium was perhaps the most notable voice among major economists of the time in rejecting facile acceptance of this approximation-based division of theoretical territory. As an empirical matter consonant with the aggregate accounting of the time, however, separation of economy and polity seemed to be a reasonable analytical scheme, and one that located the bulk of the analytical action inside economic theory.

1.   THEORIZING ABOUT POLITICAL ECONOMY

All theories focus analytical attention in a particular direction or manner. In creating this focus, a theory simultaneously pulls attention away from other possible points of theoretical focus. Furthermore, theories have a combinatorial quality in that they are typically constituted through a set of interlocking elements where those elements work together in helping scholars to develop their analytical propositions within the context of those theories. The term "political economy" denotes the bringing together of economy and polity. There are, however, different ways of accomplishing this bringing together. One way is through a type of addition where the entities maintain their distinctive features. The other is through combination or entanglement wherein an entity with distinctive characteristics and operating properties is created through entanglement. Just as Humpty Dumpty could not be put together again after having fallen off the wall on which he was sitting, neither could an entangled political economy be reconstituted as separate polities and economies.

The neoclassical scheme of economic theory with its emphasis on resource allocation and demonstrative reasoning blends readily with a scheme of additive political economy. This is a scheme of thought that almost begs for some platform from which political power can be inserted into economy to change resource allocations. For this political intervention to be analytically sensible, polity must be construed as acting independently of economy. Economic theory may pertain to and explain the actions of market participants, but it cannot pertain to participants within political processes. Politics must stand apart from economy within the neoclassical scheme of political economy. Politics provides guidance for economic processes, much as the people assembled in Mission Control in Houston provide guidance for spacecraft launched into space.

It is readily apparent that the people working in Mission Control are separate from the spacecraft they are guiding. In somewhat similar fashion, in monarchical times it might be thought that politics was largely separate from market activity. The similarity between Mission Control and the monarchs of old isn't complete, because those monarchs drew various forms of support from market activity. Still, with hereditary monarchs who owned much land which had significant capacity for generating income for the monarch, a monarch would not be confused for an ordinary business person. This situation changes with the advent of democratic forms of government where royalty with independent property gives way to representatives whose support derives from income generated within market processes.

At the time classical political economy took shape, European governments were overwhelmingly monarchical. By the time neoclassical political economy arose, governments were mostly democratic. Yet neoclassical political economy developed within a scheme of thought that reflected monarchical and not democratic governance. Polity stood outside of society's market arrangements, and intervened into those arrangements to pursue whatever it was that the possessor of political power chose to pursue. In the typical formulations of neoclassical political economy, it was some conception of public good that was pursued, or at least some articulation of that good. To support the presumption that political action promotes public good requires clarity about what that promotion requires. Demonstrative reasoning is more suitable than plausible reasoning for providing that clarity. Hence the neoclassical theory of political economy embraced an analytical motif where polity stood apart from economy and intervened into it to pursue objectives that were susceptible to demonstrative reasoning.

While classical political economy took shape during the time when monarchical regimes dominated Europe, the classical motif of plausible reasoning applied to open-ended processes of democratic governance could not intelligibly be pursued by presuming that political action was independent of economic action. There was no longer some monarchical plane of existence that was separate from the citizen plane of existence. The citizen plane is the only plane that exists in a democratic system.[1] To theorize about political economy within a society that possesses a democratically organized polity requires recognition that both the political and the economic actions that are covered by the notion of political economy arise within a common analytical framework. That framework is the scheme of entangled political economy wherein polity and economy are both arenas of practical action that operate in similar but not identical fashion.

While the substantive arrangements of political economy are subject continually to change, the form those arrangements take is pretty much invariant over time. Human nature has a bi-polarity about it that generates the material of both polity and economy (Wagner 2007). The political side of that polarity entails recognition that we are social creatures who live together in close proximity, and with that closeness providing both opportunity for mutual gain and generating antagonism and conflict. The presence of polity is grounded in human nature, and provides a societal space (Storr 2008, 2013) where the substantive content of that living together is worked out through continuing conflict and cooperation. The presence of economy is likewise grounded in human nature, and stems from the need to make a livelihood as well as from desires to be self-directed as against being conscripts in someone's army.

The various forms of activity that occur within business occur within politics as well, though with differences that have significant implications for the qualities of people living together in geographical proximity. To treat polity and economy as entangled is not the common way people talk when they speak of political economy. Such common speech envisions a polity as a kind of lord of the manor who oversees what is denoted as economy. History reveals many substantive instances of lordship. Some of those lords are despotic, others are hereditary, and yet others are elected. However a polity is constituted, it is typically construed as exercising lordship over an economy much as a shepherd manages a flock, or as feudal masters at an earlier time managed their estates. Economy and polity are thus separate spheres of activity, and with polity being the site where economic management occurs. Within the orthodox manner of thinking, the relation between polity and economy is both separate and sequential. Polity is distinct from economy and intervenes into economy. Those interventions, moreover, are thought to repair what someone thinks are defects within an economy.

In the alternative scheme of thought, polity and economy are deeply commingled or entangled. There is some similarity between entangled political economy and quantum entanglement, the latter of which is explained crisply in Susskind and Friedman (2014: 148–234). With quantum entanglement, the state of one particle cannot be described independently of the state of some other particle. With entangled political economy, prudent commercial conduct cannot be determined independently of the desires expressed by political entities; likewise, prudent political action depends on complementary commercial action. Despite some formal similarity, I do not think the humane studies are reasonably reducible to physics.

Recognition of the entangled character of political economy casts a different light upon the governance of human activity, as Patrick and Wagner (2015) explain in their comparison of the distinct though related notions of mixed economies and entangled political economy. In short, conflict and cooperation are two sides of the same proverbial coin (Hirshleifer 2001). They can be separated only in a theorist's imagination. The theory of markets explains patterns of human activity based on prior acceptance of some scheme of property rights that governs the actions that people can undertake. Property rights, however, are just settled quarrels, settled for now anyway. Not too long ago, someone who owned land that had a small swamp on it could drain and fill the swamp, and then build on that land. The ability to do that has now been removed through political action to replace private law with public law. Whether that removal is good or bad, and for whom, is something that people can dispute. Whatever side one might take in such a dispute, that removal from the domain of individual action remains a social fact of entangled political economy. As a fact, it calls for explanation regardless of the evaluation one might have of that fact.

2. ORTHODOX THEORY OF ECONOMIC POLICY: ADDITIVE POLITICAL ECONOMY

By additive political economy, I mean a scheme of thought wherein the analytical object denoted as "political economy" is generated by bringing together two independent entities denoted as polity and economy. Nearly all discussions of economic policy reflect a notion of additive political economy, as illustrated by the long ago articulation of Tinbergen (1952) or the relatively recent articulation of Acocella (1998). Aside from the relationship between the political and the economic being additive, it is also sequential in that the political is treated as acting on previously generated economic outcomes. Within the orthodox theory of policy, market outcomes are presumed to be deficient in providing public goods and controlling the generation of external costs. It is in economy where people write the first draft of the manuscript of social life; however, that manuscript is filled with holes and covering those holes is the task of political action within orthodox political economy. Polity in this scheme of thought is the locus of activity dedicated to improving upon the results of market-generated activity.

The predominant inspiration for public choice theorizing resided in the dual recognition that common claims about market failure often seemed wrong and that, moreover, there is no strong reason to think that political processes would operate in the manner the theory of economic policy envisioned. In contrast to orthodox claims about market failure, there is a public choice literature exemplified by Simmons (2011) and Mitchell and Simmons (1994) that claims that most market failures are really political failures. One difficulty about all such claims, whether of failure or of success, is that clear indicators of success or failure are often absent. A runner's claim to be able to run a mile in less than four minutes can be tested easily. A diver's claim to be able to dive backward from an arm-stand position while making two somersaults and one and a half twists better than anyone in the world can also be tested, though not so clearly or cleanly. The claim of an economist or a politician that a tax on soft drinks would be Pareto efficient is untestable, even if such a proposal were to receive unanimous support within a legislative assembly, because there is no basis for thinking that unanimity within a legislature corresponds to unanimity within the entire society (Buchanan and Tullock 1962).

This additive scheme of thought has several notable features. One is the simple character of each of its objects, polity and economy. An economy, for instance, is characterized by an equilibrium allocation of resources among activities. An economy can, in other words, be reduced to a point-mass entity. Just as a mass of people distributed across some territory can be reduced to a center of gravity, a polity can similarly be reduced to a point-mass entity. How that reduction takes place varies among political forms. With dictatorial forms, that reduction takes place by rendering all political action a matter of maximizing a dictator's objective function. With democratic forms, an election determines which particular objective function will control political action, as portrayed by the median voter model wherein political outcomes are effectively the utility-maximizing choices of the median voter within the polity (Enelow and Hinich 1984, 1990).

Figure 2.1 illustrates the simple logic of this scheme of thought. This figure resembles a billiards table with a cue ball denoted by P set to strike an object ball denoted by E. The position of the object ball corresponds to the outcome of the ordinary market process as presented in standard economics texts. A political actor seeks to change the position of the object ball to either E^L or E^R. Within a democratic system of political economy, it is commonly presumed that an election will select between candidates, and with the winning candidate being able to nudge the object ball to the desired spot on the table. Figure 2.1 captures the core of additive political economy.

The alternative possible locations for the object ball, E^L and E^R, denote different claims about such matters as public goods and externalities. In any case, the conceptual scheme of additive political economy leaves little

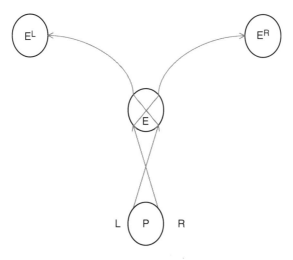

Figure 2.1   Political economy as additive object-to-object relationship

option but to assert that electoral competition will tend to generate allocations in the vicinity of Pareto efficiency. Following Persson and Tabellini
(2000), a government's budget constraint can be written $tY = P + R$, where
t is an average tax rate, Y is aggregate taxable income, P is spending on
public goods, and R is rents for politicians. In competition between two
candidates, the one who promises a larger supply of public goods will tend
to win the election, as these models are typically formulated. By assumption in these models, rents are desired by politicians but not by voters.
A politician who promises larger rents will also have to promise fewer
public goods and higher taxes. Reducing the amount of rents will enhance
electoral prospects within this common framework. While this analytical
framework is common, it is also a bit bizarre. Perhaps most significantly, it
has two candidates competing for the support of what is effectively a single
voter. It's not that there is literally one voter, but it might as well be this
way because all voters are identical in their evaluations of rents and public
goods, as well as in their identification of what constitutes rents and public
goods. There is no room for controversy over such matters as whether
subsidized wind farms in Nevada is a public good that everyone values or
is the creation of a rent for land owners where the farms are located and
which are paid for by taxpayers in general.

   The situation changes once it is recognized that voters are multitudinous
and heterogeneous, as Martin and Wagner (2009) examine. An owner of
desert land on which a wind farm might be installed is surely more likely
than other people to accept claims about such farms being instruments

to reduce global warming through providing cleaner sources of energy, and with the subsidy to such generation being the product of a complex transaction that overcomes free-rider problems. Such claims, moreover, are impossible to dispute, for there are judgments involved that are more like judging diving or figure skating than like running. Epstein (1985) explains that the Fifth Amendment of the American Constitution limits eminent domain by requiring that any taking of property be for a genuine public use and be accompanied by just compensation, which in turn is roughly equivalent to what would have accompanied a market transaction. Judging public use or just compensation, however, is not like judging whether a runner ran a mile in less than four minutes. It is more like judging beauty, where the essence of judgment resides in the eye of the judger. Is building wind farms in Nevada a constitutionally sanctioned public use? Support can be advanced for either type of judgment, and with that judgment probably depending a lot on the position of the judger relative to the cash flows stemming from the wind farm. Wherever judgment is called for (and whether a mile was run in under four minutes does not call for judgment), ambiguity will be present in any instance where that judgment is capable of being rationalized by the judger (Pareto 1935) because any exception to a rule can be rationalized as following the spirit of the rule (Schmitt 1932).

Additive political economy fits the common sense notion that politics and politicians act on market entities and transactions to change market outcomes. In similar fashion, it is commonsensical to aver that the Sun rises in the east and sets in the west. People who are familiar with Copernicus are surely able to understand what is wrong with common sense in this instance. All the same, it surely wouldn't be surprising to find a good share of the population still adhering to this pre-Copernican belief. With respect to direct observation, political entities do appear to be independent from market entities and impose themselves on those entities. All taxes, for instance, are attachments to market transactions. Without market transactions, there would be no tax revenues. All regulations, moreover, change the substantive content of rights of property and contract, and so appear as interventions into economy. As with the relation between Earth and Sun, however, the surface appearance might not withstand deeper examination into the idea of entangled political economy.

Any scheme of thought has both text and subtext. The text is what the scheme plainly says about its object. It is visible from superficial examination, and invites logical manipulation of a what-if type. Text exemplifies explicit knowledge (Polanyi 1958). People can argue about the implications of a text and can ask what-if questions about it. All such questions and exercises, however, stand on a platform that asserts the relevance and primacy of those questions. In this respect, additive political economy stands on a platform that asserts the independence of polity and economy, as well as asserting the primacy of the political over the economic. Political personages are thus reasonably analogized to mechanics whose task is to maintain the economy in good working order. Within this analytical scheme, it is coherent, even necessary to think of political figures as acting to maintain economy in good working order. To be sure, there is plenty of room to dispute which among several possible policy mechanics is the best mechanic, as well as to dispute whether or not the economy really needs repair. While the framework of additive political economy can accommodate much disputation pertaining to policy measures, those disputes are limited and channeled by the subtext of the analytical framework.

By subtext, I refer to the penumbra of thoughts and associations upon which any analytical framework rests, and with other frameworks leading to different thoughts and associations. Subtexts operate at the level of tacit knowledge (Polanyi 1958). Additive political economy brings in its analytical train the presumption that political figures truly know what they are doing in working to modify societal outcomes and configurations. With respect to Figure 2.1, political personages are portrayed as acting directly to reconfigure what are spontaneously generated patterns of economic activity. It further presumes that political action is truly independent of market processes, as against being one set of activities within a market process. In contrast, such reconfiguration is not possible when the situation is examined from within a framework of entangled political economy.

While political personages can still influence societal configurations, they do so as participants inside societal processes and not as outside and impartial social mechanics. The Progressivist vision of political presence and domination throughout society is abetted by the vision of additive political economy because that vision provides rationalization for unlimited political action. In contrast to Knight and Johnson's (2011) assertion that policy provides a unique vantage point for appraising the entirety of society, the vision of entangled political economy recognizes that there is no superior vantage point from which a society can be perceived as a totality. In that ancient fable of the six blind men of Hindustan, each man touched a different part of an elephant (trunk, tusk, and so on) and described what he felt. It took a sighted person to announce that the six men had all touched the same animal.

Entangled political economy, similar to Hayek (1937, 1945), recognizes that there is no sighted person to see the entirety of what the blind men feel individually. Everyone, private citizens and political figures alike, acts on partial and incomplete information, for there is no other option in the presence of the scale and complexity of contemporary societies. A chief and a council of five elders might reasonably know everything of relevance for keeping a tribe of 200 performing as they think it should. For democratic systems of tens or hundreds of millions, however, any such presumption is some combination of arrogance and fatuousness. The subtext of entangled political economy focusses analytical attention on the knowledge-generating properties of different patterns of interaction among persons and entities within society.

3. THE ENTANGLED ALTERNATIVE FOR POLITICAL ECONOMY

Within the orthodox framework of additive political economy, state and market are both reduced to point-mass entities as Figure 2.1 illustrates. Within this conceptualization, there is no option but for polity to act on economy in entity-to-entity fashion. Simple observation, however, puts the lie to any such conceptualization. Political actions are undertaken by particular entities. An Internal Revenue Service might challenge the tax-exempt status of some organizations while ignoring the status of other organizations. A Bureau of Land Management might seek to impose its will on some ranchers while leaving other ranchers alone. To be sure, organizations are not acting entities. Organizations act because executives within each organization direct it to act, though it is linguistically convenient to speak of organizations as acting. In any case, to make analytical contact with these kinds of particularistic details requires a scheme of thought where neither polity nor economy is reduced to an entity with point-mass status because doing that eliminates the possibility of interactions among particular entities as the driving force behind observed societal processes. For a scheme of thought to allow the social world to be generated through a multitude of such activities as interaction between a Bureau of Land Management and various ranchers requires a style of reasoning that theorizes in terms of orders of interacting entities. Within such spontaneous-order schemes of thought (Aydinonat 2008), each entity within the order has some independent freedom of action even as it is also constrained by the actions and desires of other entities. An order is, after all, characterized by both independently acting entities and mutual adjustment among those entities (Hayek 1973).

The distinction between a parade and a pedestrian crowd usefully illustrates this distinction. These are both orderly social configurations. A parade can be reasonably reduced to an entity with point mass. A pedestrian crowd cannot. A parade can be reasonably treated as an organization whose members are united in seeking the same objective. A pedestrian crowd cannot, for it is an order that is constituted through interaction among independent entities that nonetheless operate within the same system of interaction. While most economists would surely recognize that polities and economies are orders and not organizations, they nonetheless work with theoretical frameworks that reduce polities and economies to organizations. For economies, this reduction is achieved by presuming that observations pertain to states of equilibrium. For polities, this reduction is achieved by presuming that political action or policy is directed by a median voter whose identity and preference function are revealed through an election. To theorize about orders with respect to political economy requires a different scheme of thought than one based on market equilibrium and a median voter. To do this requires a scheme of thought suitable for a pedestrian crowd and not a parade.

The political economy of a parade can be reasonably captured by a median voter and equilibrium theory. Through equilibrium theory, a parade can be reduced to a point mass even though it might be one mile in length, 50 feet in width, and contain 5,000 participants. Through this reduction, the parade can be followed by a point on a map as it moves along its route. That route, as well as any changes in direction along the route, will be determined by the parade marshal, who is the equivalent of the median voter in this case. In actual practice, the parade marshal is in place before the members of the parade are selected. Parades are typically organized through the offices of some organizing agent who creates the parade. To be sure, it would be possible to start with a set of musicians and various units suitable for a parade, and have them devise a procedure for selecting a marshal. In any case, the quality of the parade will be governed by such things as the musical and marching abilities of the members and the organizational and instructional skills of the marshal. Similar to the scene depicted by Figure 2.1, a parade marshal who is not content with the look of a parade can change it through an act of policy, as in changing the route of the march, changing the music played, or adding or removing units from the parade. A parade conforms to the standard analytical schema of theories of political economy and public policy.

To avoid this reductionist analytical framework requires some alternative framework that treats both polities and economies as interrelated orders of interacting agents. This would be the political economy of a pedestrian crowd. A pedestrian crowd is not reasonably reducible to point-mass status, at least without distorting significantly what is going on inside the crowd. For instance, someone could freeze the action within a crowd by taking a photograph while hovering in a balloon. A theorist could then declare this observation to constitute equilibrium within the crowd. Having done that, it would be a simple matter to reduce the crowd to a point by computing a center of mass. Doing this, however, would be to convert the crowd into something that it isn't by ignoring some central features of the crowd. The postulate of equilibrium would as a mental operation convert the crowd into a parade, which is nonsensical and which illustrates how our theoretical frameworks can distort our ability to think even though they can also magnify that ability.

A crowd of pedestrians leaving a stadium is clearly an orderly social configuration, even if its movements are not as smooth as that of a parade. The sources of orderliness, however, differ significantly as between the two configurations. The orderliness of the parade is ultimately traceable to the parade marshal, and with qualitative variations in parades being reasonably traceable to variations among parade marshals. A pedestrian crowd is an altogether different social configuration. It is still orderly, only there is no marshal to whom that orderliness can be attributed. To describe a crowd in equilibrium terms, thereby reducing it to an entity with a center of gravity, would be to incur what Mitchel Resnick (1994) describes as the centralized mindset. By this mindset, Resnick means a tendency for people to attribute any observed orderliness to an ordering agent. Resnick applied the inapt use of this mindset to such naturalistic settings as ants looking for food and geese flying. That mindset is also alive and well in social settings, as when markets are described by static notions of equilibrium or when democratic polities are described as reflecting the desires of a median voter.

Figure 2.2 illustrates in three steps how the additive scheme of political economy depicted in Figure 2.1 can be transformed into an entangled system of political economy. Panel A simply duplicates the political and economic entities depicted in Figure 2.1. Panel A provides the analytical point of departure for thinking about entangled political economy. For there to be entanglement rather than distinctiveness or separateness, it is necessary to develop an analytical scheme where there can be interaction between parts of polity and economy without burying that interaction within aggregates. The reason for avoiding averages or aggregates is that these are not acting entities. To the contrary, they are nothing but summaries of the results of previous action, and with the actions that generated those summaries being kept out of sight, as Wagner (2012a) explains regarding the ecological relationship between micro and macro variables within economic theory. Analysis of a system of entangled political economy needs to keep those acting entities in sight.

Shown in Figure 2.2 are two lightning bolts running from Panel A to Panel B. These bolts are meant to illustrate the fragmentation of the unitary entities portrayed in Panel A and also in Figure 2.1. One problem to keep in mind with respect to Figure 2.2 is that it necessarily presents a static portrait of what is really a time-consuming system of continual

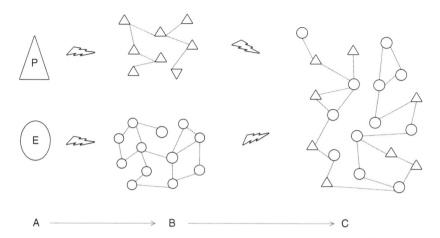

Figure 2.2   Political economy as entangled entity-to-entity relationship

interaction: it uses a snapshot in place of a movie. It is in this distinction where the significant analytical work is done. If this distinction is ignored, the two sets of entities shown in Panel B could each be reduced to point-mass status, as if the members of a parade were caught in a snapshot standing around out of formation. To do that, however, would be to ignore the genuine character of the pedestrian crowd, which entails interaction among the individuals within that crowd who are pursuing their varied intended destinations. Panel B still shows separation between the political and economic entities, so there is no entanglement there. At the same time, however, neither political nor economic entities act in unison. They act independently as such action is channeled by systemic interrelationships among the entities. Panel B shows polities and economies as separate systems of interaction among participants.

Those entities do not, however, comprise separate systems of interaction. They are entangled within the same system, as Panel C shows. There, the lightning bolts between Panels B and C show a pattern of commingling among political and economic entities. Panel C thus portrays a particular configuration among political and economic entities within a system of entangled political economy. Within this system, there is no reduction of polity to a unitary entity that acts on a similarly reduced economy. Political economy still denotes a system of interactions among constituent entities, only the interactions are always between particular entities. To reduce the entities portrayed in Panel C to the singular entities widely denoted as state and market is to misconstrue the nature of political economy and thus to lead astray clear thinking about political economy.

Entangled political economy seeks to render intelligible the changing patterns of political–economic interaction within societies, and to do so within a bottom-up theoretical motif wherein polities are ecologies of political enterprises (Eusepi and Wagner 2011; Smith et al. 2011; Wagner 2014a). The theory of markets is sometimes presented by invoking the image of an invisible hand to indicate that the order of the market emerges through interaction among participants and is not a product of some person's plan; in other words, a market is analogized to a pedestrian crowd and not a parade, as Leonard Read (1958) explains lucidly. Within the analytical schema of entangled political economy as presented in Panels B and C of Figure 2.2, political activity would be characterized in the same invisible hand manner. Roland McKean (1965) sketched such a theme, which Richard Wagner (2007) carried forward. Vincent Ostrom (1962) illustrates this theme in the particular context of water supply. As Ostrom explains, it is nonsensical to ask whether water supply is a political or market activity because myriad entities constituted under a variety of institutional arrangements participate and interact in supplying water. For instance, water might be supplied by a municipal water company, with water carried and stored on equipment produced by private firms and with water quality monitored by a private laboratory acting in light of standards set by a regulatory agency, or, alternatively, a judge.

With respect to entanglement, Jane Jacobs (1992: 92–111) described how social systems operated through interaction among carriers of what she described as two moral syndromes: a commercial syndrome and a guardian syndrome. This distinction does not map fully onto a distinction between political and market entities, though that distinction does have a good deal of correspondence with the distinction between market and political entities. A construction firm is a market entity that largely reflects the commercial syndrome. To be effective, however, that firm will also have to undertake guardian activities. For instance, it will have to engage in various monitoring and auditing activities to guard against theft through employees converting firm assets to their personal possession. While both syndromes are necessary, Jacobs also explains how excessive commingling between carriers of the two syndromes can generate what she describes as "monstrous moral hybrids."

4. CAPITALIZING POLITIES: HOTELS, MALLS, AND CIVIC ASSOCIATIONS

Hotels and malls provide apt illustrations of how public goods can be provided through market-based arrangements. If we compare cities with hotels, particularly relatively large hotels that offer many services and amenities, we will find little difference in the activities they pursue and the problems they face, as Spencer MacCallum (1970) explains and as Fred Foldvary (1994) amplifies. A city, moreover, represents the urban core of a city-state, and with the city-state serving as an option to the nation state, as Hendrik Spruyt (1994) explains. Hotels and malls are really cities within cities, containing both market-based and collective-based activities. Within both cities and hotels, people individually choose places to live, take meals, and buy clothing. They also are protected by security services, ride on publicly provided transport, and have access to such amenities as parks.

There is a striking similarity in form between cities and hotels even if it seems strange to think in this manner. Hotels operate subways that run vertically, and which are made available without direct charge. They provide parks of various types, some with artificial lakes, some with botanical gardens, and others with yet different types of amenities. The same point can be made about malls, for malls too provide both individual places of business and amenities that are made available to the entire public that frequents the mall. A mall is more than the set of individual shops that it contains, for the mall also provides common services and amenities that attract customers and increase the value of the individual shops. In this recognition lies an important lesson for political economy.

Hotels and malls must attract business in an environment of open competition. To do this they must offer good value for the money they ask customers to pay. This is the central principle of good commercial conduct. Hotels and malls involve governmental activity of the same type that is present in the governance of cities. Among other things, they must make decisions about the type and quality of amenities to provide. Higher quality might bring more business but it will also be more costly to supply. An ordinary commercial calculus of cost-and-gain can be brought to bear on the operation of hotels and malls. Hotels and malls contain governments that provide public services just as surely as do cities and imperial powers.

The main difference between cities and hotels resides in their capital accounts, as Moberg and Wagner (2014) explain with particular reference to municipal bankruptcy. A hotel might be owned by a single person or by many people organized into a corporation. Whatever the particular form of ownership, the hotel faces the problem of having to attract investors and customers in an environment where those customers and investors have options. In contrast, cities are organized as cooperatives without alienable ownership. In a democratically organized city, someone acquires an ownership interest by virtue of residency and loses that ownership through leaving the city. It would be easy enough to imagine a thought experiment to illustrate the impact of different forms of capital account. For instance, a city could be transformed from a cooperative where ownership shares are inalienable and based on residency into a corporation with alienable ownership. Alternatively, the residents of a hotel could wake up one morning to find under their doors not bills but ballots because the hotel had been converted into a polity. In thinking about hotels and cities in this manner, it becomes quickly clear that the governance qualities of different institutional arrangements are of far greater significance than assertions about what is or is not a public good.

A hotel has a market value; a city does not. This difference, however, has nothing to do with the distinction between private and public goods. The difference is a product of the institutional framework governing the capital accounts of hotels and cities (Wagner 2011a). For hotels, the capital account is established through willing participation by investors. Those investors, moreover, can sell their ownership in one way or another. The most direct and common form is through the sale of ownership shares on the open market if the hotel is a publicly held corporation. The hotel could, however, be a partnership or a closely held corporation. In this case there would be no active market in ownership, so no explicit market value would exist at any particular moment. Yet an implicit market value would exist all the same because someone could always offer to buy the corporation or a part of it, in which case valuation would be ascertained through the transaction.

By contrast, there is no market value for cities due to the inalienable character of ownership. All cities have capital accounts, necessarily so, but the character of those accounts is a product of various institutional features. There are institutional arrangements that are similar to those that govern hotels. A city entails a tied ownership of real estate and city assets. Someone who buys property in a city is also buying into the ownership of city assets. Since there is no direct ownership of city assets, the value of those assets is reflected in the value of real estate located inside the city. Actions that increase the value of city assets are thus reflected not in an increase in the market value of the city but in an increase in the value of real estate in the city. One limiting institutional arrangement is where owners of real estate have votes weighted in proportion to their property values and where city activities are financed by a flat tax on property value. This institutional arrangement would approach that of the hotel, but would still fall short because people could not specialize in owning cities or owning real estate inside a city. Other institutional arrangements would widen the gap between cities and hotels (Sonstelie and Portney 1978; Boudreaux and Holcombe 1989).

5.   POLITICAL ECONOMY AND CIVIL SOCIETY

The common conceptual dichotomy between public goods and private goods (Samuelson 1954, 1955) misconstrues in a significant way the characteristics of actual societies, which Buchanan (1968) tries to clarify by exploring how public goods can be provided through transactional processes. Within the Samuelsonian dichotomy, political provision is the only option for market provision of any particular activity or service. This dichotomy comes about in reflection of an asocial analytical schema where people are conceptualized as operating in two capacities: as producers, people step into the market to earn income; as consumers, they step into the market to spend what they have earned. Government then enters the picture to provide the various public goods that are not provided within this very austere market setting.

Contemporary economic theory mostly operates within a two-sector framework of markets and states. The theory of markets pertains primarily to profit-seeking enterprises with relationships among those enterprises governed by free and open competition within a regime of private property, and with states somehow correcting market failures and providing public goods. The institutional arrangements of actual societies are far richer than the common public–private dichotomy portrays. What is typically denoted as civil society includes a wide variety of activities that speak to the social organization of economizing activity, as Alexander (2006), Bruni (2012), and the essays collected in Garnett et al. (2015) examine. Nonprofit forms of organization are present in many parts of society. Philanthropic enterprises are often characterized as constituting a third sector as illustrated by the notion of civil society, which covers everything not covered by profit-seeking firms or political enterprises. Market theory and public goods theory both pertain to adult participants in social processes. It is reasonable to wonder about the social processes through which those adults move beyond childhood. Philanthropy is pivotally engaged in the reproduction of societies through time, which is something about which theories of private and public goods are silent.

In his general treatment of social systems, Kenneth Boulding (1970, 1985) distinguished among three sub-systems: exchange, conflict, and integrative. The integrative system in large measure pertains to the societal processes through which infants become adults. It is here where philanthropy has especial significance in influencing the future character of societies. In this respect, Norbert Elias (1939 [1982]) is a fecund analysis of the processes that necessarily must be in play in any society. Numerous such processes are imaginable and can be found in the historical record, with different processes leading to differences in societal qualities and attributes.

When Hillary Clinton (1996) claimed that it took a village to raise a child, she was right. It would be a truly rare family if, indeed, there is any such family that could raise a child on their resources alone. Raising a child requires the resources found only in a village, as no family has the specialized talents that will be involved in raising a child to adulthood.

While Clinton was superficially right in her claim, she was deeply wrong all the same because her idea of a village resembled a Health and Human Services bureaucracy. Raising a child was all about the contributions of bureaucratic agencies. Parents were pretty much lost from view. Civil society contains many resources that parents can call upon in raising children as part of the civilizing process (Elias 1939 [1982], 1939 [1991]). Beyond some biological minimum, wants are not given but rather are continually being formed and changed through social interaction. Society involves people living together in close proximity, and the processes involved in doing so are often quarrelsome and conflictual and not always peaceful and pleasant. For instance, there is continuing conflict at various margins between holding individuals responsible for their actions, as reflected in traditional private law principles and practices, and replacing personal responsibility with therapy, as Philip Reiff (1966) noted and lamented and as Wagner (1992) amplified.

Carolyn Webber and Aaron Wildavsky (1986) organized their exemplary treatment of budgeting throughout the western world around the theme that budgeting is a never-ending struggle among people over how they are to live together in relatively closed spaces. It is this continuing and contested struggle over the never-ending movement to create the societal qualities that we come to experience that offers analytically useful territory for philanthropy and civil society. This analytical territory can surely be better explored by working with lexicographic orderings than with standard utility functions. Lexicographic ordering can be construed as positing a moral imagination that overlooks and evaluates the particular choices and actions that economists typically describe as utility functions. In any case, philanthropy would be deeply implicated in contested processes of societal reproduction.

While friendship exists inside society, so does antagonism and animosity. A desire for approbation is often posited as producing mutual support within societies due to the operation of processes through which esteem is generated (Brennan and Pettit 2004). While this is surely correct, also correct is Arthur Lovejoy's (1961) recognition that approbation is cousin to envy (Shoeck 1969). People have preferences over other people and their activities, but without arriving at identical rankings. Qualities and actions that elicit admiration from some people will elicit envy from others. To speak of community or society is not to speak only of such friendly things as dancing and playing poker. Fighting, after all, is also a social activity, as is the use of politics as an instrument by which some people dominate others. Societies have natural turbulence, and with the intensity of that turbulence varying across time and place. To keep such ideas in play, however, requires thinking about societies not in terms of integral geometries of smoothness but in terms of non-integral geometries of roughness (Potts 2000). To do this, societies cannot be reduced to representative transactions, as exemplified by reducing the formation of constitutional consensus to the agreement among eight friends to play poker.

6. LIBERTY AND DEMOCRACY: A CONSTITUTIONAL TANGLE

Democracy is often portrayed as the political complement to a free economy. Within this mode of thought, liberty and democracy go together. It is in this manner that democracy is often described as a framework for self-governance, thereby distinguishing democracies from systems where most people are governed by other people. An idealistic version of democratic theory holds that individuals govern themselves both in politics and in markets. They do this in the market arena where their actions are governed by the principles of private property and contractual liberty. When those principles are in play, people are free to make of their lives what they choose to the extent their desires and talents allow. Someone who wants to become a business tycoon is free to try. There is no guarantee of success, for success will depend on the ability of other people being willing to support the potential tycoon's efforts. Similarly, someone who could possibly become a tycoon but is adverse to the effort that would be required could live an easy though Spartan life in some rural area where land prices are low. In contrast to feudal systems where people are born into particular patterns of life, in free societies people are able to choose their patterns of life by choosing how to conduct themselves within the confines of society.

Humans are social creatures, and so will take an interest in other people's activities. How much of an interest doubtlessly varies among people, but such an interest will be active in society all the same. The central claim advanced on behalf of liberal democracy is that the democratic form is the natural complement in the political arena of free markets in the economic arena. This claim, however, is possibly true but not necessarily so. The relationship between liberty and democracy is a knotted and tangled one. Vincent Ostrom (1984, 1996) illustrates that government is a type of Faustian bargain. Following the Faust-type legend that has been repeated in many forms over the millennia, government entails doing something bad to achieve what the actor regards as a greater good. In a liberal political setting, government entails the use of an instrument of evil, the imposition of force over people, in the hope or presumption that damage done by the force will fall short of the good that is done.

In modern democratic settings, the use of force is typically advocated on grounds that it allows people to escape prisoner's dilemmas in which they otherwise would be trapped. The logic behind the prisoner's dilemma is coherent even if it might be difficult or even impossible to determine whether it is relevant for any of those settings where it is invoked. The logic of the prisoner's dilemma has been invoked to support both taxation and regulation. With respect to taxation, someone might assert that free concerts in a park in the center of town might provide benefits throughout the town. While some of these might be reflected in higher property values adjacent to the park, other values might not be so readily captured. With admission not being charged for the concert by assumption, free-riding tendencies will exert themselves and lead to under-supply of such concerts, according to the prisoner's dilemma formulation.

As a logical matter, the formulation is not illogical. It is, however, incomplete and also lacks any way of testing its truth value, as Carl Schmitt (1923) explains in his treatment of the tension between liberalism and democracy. Suppose voluntary donations are insufficient to finance the concerts. Someone who supports such concerts could point to this observation as attesting to the veracity of the prisoner's dilemma formulation. Someone without such an inclination, however, could just as readily point to the lack of support as testifying to the lack of interest in those concerts. There is simply no way to distinguish such contrary claims based on direct observation. There is, however, experimental evidence pertaining to experience in free-riding experiments where free riding diminishes in settings where anonymity gives way to interaction among participants (McCaleb and Wagner 1985; Wagner 2012b). This difference reflects the social nature of humans. In this respect a mayor who wanted to see the town sponsor a series of festivals would never install collection boxes in out-of-the-way places where people could make donations in stealthy fashion. To the contrary, such a mayor would enlist various features of human sociality in support of his desire to secure funding for the festivals. Such an effort would surely have several facets. For one thing, the campaign to support the festivals would have a cellular structure, as perhaps illustrated by the mayor enlisting a set of well-distributed supporters who in turn would work to develop further support in their various precincts of interest and engagement. Furthermore, names of supporters could be placed in newspapers and on the town's website. Even more, reserved seating might be offered for various levels of support.

There is no way to say whether such a scheme of activity would generate the same support as might be envisioned in some model of public goods and free riding. The trouble with such models is that the creator of the model posits knowledge of the data necessary to determine the optimizing outcome. The information required in those formulations, however, is simply not available to anyone in the first place. Without doubt, the scheme I have adumbrated would have higher transaction cost associated with it than would the imposition of a tax with the revenues appropriated to support the festivals. But these two settings are not directly comparable. The scheme I have just adumbrated is a genuine set of transactions that an entrepreneur adopts to secure support for an activity. The imposition of a tax involves no direct transactional structure, though an indirect structure will always be present whenever taxes are imposed and revenues appropriated (Hebert and Wagner 2013). It is always cheaper to steal something than it is to create it. The transactional scheme I adumbrated would create the festivals if the sponsors were successful in their entrepreneurial and organizational efforts. Putting together the festivals would be a costly activity. So, too, would be resorting to tax finance. The direct transaction cost is likely to be lower with tax finance for the simple reason that it is cheaper to take something that someone else has already produced than it is to produce it anew. A comparison of these two settings, however, does not illustrate different costs for doing the same thing. It rather illustrates the accomplishment of two quite different things. In one setting, there is a festival put together where people participate to the extent they choose. In the other setting, participation gives way to compulsion through taxation, which in turn brings along the substitution of instruments of force for cooperation in human governance. The Faustian bargain is invariably present in human governance due to autonomy of the political, though the terms of that bargain might be subject to some measure of control as later chapters shall consider.

7. GENERIC DEMOCRACY AND PARTICULAR DEMOCRACIES

Just as there is a vast number of ways that 13 cards can be drawn from a deck of 52 cards, so is there a vast number of ways a democratic government can be formed. At its most generic level, democracy means only that there is at least one political office within a society that is staffed by an election among candidates. Typically, many more offices than that are staffed through election, especially in larger democracies. Indeed, if only one office were staffed through election, the winner of that election might reasonably be designated an elected monarch, probably more reasonably so the longer the term of office. Typically, democracies will have a multitude of elected offices, and with those offices having various constitutionally specified powers and relationships among one another. One common split within the democratic form is between presidential and parliamentary systems. While there have been numerous papers written on empirical differences between sets of parliamentary and presidential systems, that difference illustrates but the proverbial tip of the iceberg with respect to the great number of particular instances of democratic government that can be created from the generic democratic format of having some political offices staffed through election.

Scholars often treat democracy at the generic level, or close to it in any case. At the generic level, Bertrand de Jouvenel (1948) explains that the democratic form of government has been able historically to marshal far greater military force than monarchical regimes, and also to become far more widely involved in regulating activity throughout society than monarchical regimes. The reach of a monarch is pretty much limited by the range of a monarch's interest. The reach of a democratic polity extends pretty much to whatever some plurality of people want it to extend, and with that plurality often being a quite small number. Hans Hermann Hoppe (2001) develops and elaborates a similar theme in comparing democratic and monarchical regimes with respect to their implications for liberty. On a narrower level of analysis, Persson and Tabellini (2000) present findings that presidential forms of democracy tend to spend less than parliamentary forms. In their case, the comparison is made between two generic sub-forms of democracy, but it is still a generic comparison because no reference is made to the myriad particular ways in which a democratic form can be assembled.

A democratic form can be represented as a network of nodes and connections. The nodes would denote the holders of elected office and the connections would denote the relationships among those office holders. With respect to networks, one significant distinction is between monocentric and polycentric networks. The American constitutional system began with a great deal of polycentricity which has become increasingly monocentric over the past century or so. For a polycentric arrangement, there is no apex to which all nodes might be said to look. A monocentric arrangement features such an apex. At the time of the American founding, for instance, the President and Vice President were each elected, and with the Vice President thereby presumably being the second most popular politician at the federal level. Now, the President and Vice President form a team and are elected jointly. Similarly, until 1913 members of the federal Senate were appointed by state legislatures. Now they are elected directly. Before 1913, the federal senate was a type of council of states within Congress. These two instances illustrate different particular ways of arranging democratic offices and the relationships among the holders of those offices.

One of the central principles of constitutional political economy is that the pattern of outcome generated by any political system will depend on the configuration of that system. If the configuration is changed, the systemically generated outcomes will likewise change. In a two-candidate election for President, should the losing candidate become Vice President, it is surely reasonable to think that different political outcomes will result, as compared with the situation where the President has chosen the Vice President. A democratic arrangement can be constructed in almost limitless ways. Among many of those ways it is surely reasonable to think little difference will result. Just as surely, however, some of those ways will matter a great deal.

The original American constitutional arrangement was constructed against a background of seeking to control the effects of faction whereby winning coalitions were able to impose significant costs on the remainder of society. At the time of constitutional founding, it was thought that controlling majority factions was more of a problem than controlling minority factions. Minority factions, it was presumed, could be controlled by requiring majority approval within the relevant parliamentary bodies. In contrast, controlling majority faction was more a matter of dividing and separating powers within a compound republic. For instance, a bicameral legislature can work against majority faction if it is constituted to do so. If the two legislative chambers are selected on the same basis, one chamber will largely mirror the other, so a majority in one chamber will translate into a majority in the other chamber. As the bases by which the chambers are selected come to differ, the operation of majority faction will be weakened to some extent. For instance, one chamber might be elected through districts of equal population while the other chamber is elected in some different manner. The districts might be counties, where some counties are heavily populated while others are sparsely populated. The requirement that legislation require majority approval in both chambers will lead to different outcomes when the same selection principle governs both chambers than when different principles are followed. In particular, measures that receive majority support in both chambers will reflect a greater degree of support among the population if the two chambers were selected according to different principles than if the two chambers were just mirror images of one another.

More recent scholarship in public choice and political economy has shown that minority faction is far more robust than simple arithmetic might make it appear. That arithmetic is typically performed in terms of polities construed as single entities that undertake some universal action that pertains to everyone. Hence, majorities dominate minorities as a simple matter of arithmetic. This vision of polity fits the image presented in Figure 2.1. Within this vision, there is no room for incomplete and distributed knowledge to do any analytical work. For such work to be done, some such vision of polity as that portrayed by Panels B and C of Figure 2.2 must be used, with polities conceived as networks of structured relationships and interactions. Within this alternative framework, it is straightforward to see the robustness of minority faction within democratic polities. In this respect, Robert Rogowski (1974: 87–9) explains that a faction of just five percent of the population can dominate political outcomes 80 percent of the time. Should that faction increase to 7.5 percent of the population, it will be able to get its way 99 percent of the time. Entangled political economy explains that, contrary to the claims advanced in *The Federalist Papers*, majority rule does not prevent minority factions from dominating political outcomes.

NOTE

1. Save for the slave plane of existence at the time of the American constitutional founding.

3. Systems theory and parts-to-whole relationships

This book examines the analytical object denoted as a democratically generated *system* of entangled political economy. With economics being a contested and controversial discipline (Reder 1999), that contestation and controversy extends as well to the compound term "political economy." While this book falls within the general rubric of what has been described as Virginia political economy, it does this by introducing two analytical frameworks not typically associated with Virginia political economy, or associated with any framework of political economy for that matter. One such framework is conveyed by the idea of entangled political economy, which stands in contrast with the ordinary framework of additive political economy. The other framework is systems theory, which this chapter sets forth as it pertains to political economy, and with systems theory standing in contrast to equilibrium theory.

While economists commonly refer to "economic systems," they typically do so in a manner that effectively neuters any contribution systems thinking might make to political economy. This neutering occurs through thinking of economic systems as entailing an equilibrium set of relationships among participants. The presumption of equilibrium effectively allows a society to be treated as if it were a parade. While a parade is a system of relationships among parts, it is a robotic and not a creative system: the members of a parade follow scripts that someone has written for them; in contrast, the members of a creative system develop their own scripts. The parts of the system respond in mechanical fashion, just as the members of a parade respond mechanically to the marshal's instructions. By contrast, within creative systems the parts have minds of their own.

Presumptions of equilibrium have limited usefulness in thinking about creative systems. A crowd of pedestrians leaving a stadium after an event and heading toward various destinations and traveling at different speeds cannot be reduced to a representative agent whose line of march can be plotted on a map. A parade presents the same face to a spectator and to a participant. From each of these perspectives, the orderliness of the parade would be described in terms of such things as the musical and marching abilities of the participants and the amount of time given to rehearsal. By contrast, the pedestrian crowd appears differently to an observer than it appears to a participant. To an observer hovering in a balloon above the scene, the crowd would surely appear frantic and chaotic as it displayed none of the orderliness of a parade. To a participant, however, the crowd would appear orderly, even if the qualities of that order appeared differently from those of the parade. Each participant within the crowd would be able to arrive at his or her desired destination pretty much as planned, even though the talents and capacities exercised in doing so were different from those exercised by members of the parade. For the crowd, orderliness would be explained in terms of such phenomena as adherence to general principles of courtesy, a desire to avoid colliding with other pedestrians, and an ability to judge possible forthcoming collisions by changing one's speed and direction of walk.

A theory suitable for explaining the qualities of parades would not be suitable for explaining the qualities of pedestrian crowds. Equilibrium theory adopts a parade as the avatar for a society. In contrast, a pedestrian crowd is a suitable avatar for a creative system of human interaction. This chapter sets forth the systems-theoretic idea as it feeds into a theory of entangled political economy. Among other things, what is commonly described as "public policy" turns out to be a form of shell game because there is no outside position from which some purported "policy maker" can intervene in a human population system, as DeCanio (2014) explains. All action takes place inside such systems, which generates different insight into the activities described as "public policy." Among other things, the common analytical disjunction between choosing the rules of a game and subsequently playing the game according to those rules dissolves and is replaced by recognition that humans are simultaneously cooperative and quarrelsome creatures, as Pareto (1935) recognized and as Rajagopalan and Wagner (2013) explore.

1.   REGARDING SYSTEMS IN GENERAL

At its most general or abstract level, a system is a set of entities along with some pattern of connection among those entities. Just as the entities that comprise the system have performance properties, so too does the system itself. The output of the system depends on the performance of the elements that comprise the system, as well as on the pattern of connection among the elements. Systems are everywhere. Economists make numerous references to systems, as illustrated by references to financial systems, tax systems, budgetary systems, welfare systems, and social insurance systems. Within society more broadly, people make numerous references

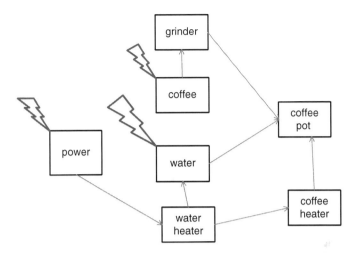

Figure 3.1   Coffee maker as system

to political systems, social systems, cultural systems, and criminal justice systems, among many other systems. From a biological point of reference, people refer to circulatory systems, digestive systems, reproductive systems, and ecological systems, to mention but a few such references. So systems are everywhere, as are references to them. In all such cases, the object described as a system contains a network of parts and connections among those parts, and with the entirety of those parts and connections constituting the system.

Even such a simple device of everyday living as an automatic coffee maker is a system of a robotic type. The coffee maker is constituted through a structured relationship among a set of parts, where the output of the coffee maker is distinct from the outputs of the various parts. The output of the coffee maker depends both on how well the parts work on their own and on how well they fit together. Figure 3.1 presents a simplified sketch of an automatic coffee maker as a system, and does so in a way that corresponds to other diagrams that will be used later in the book—and most certainly not as some engineering schematic to use in actually designing such a system! The three lightning bolts indicate that the system is not self-generating because it requires injections of power, water, and coffee from outside the system.

Those outside injections aside, Figure 3.1 illustrates the point that the performance of the system in generating drinkable coffee depends on how the parts perform and interact. The blade on the grinder can be of varying degrees of sharpness, and these variations will affect the quality of the coffee. Either of the two heating elements might fail, or might just degrade. In either case, the coffee won't taste as hot as it otherwise would. Not shown in Figure 3.1 but a central feature of systems theory nonetheless, is the conduct of the system through time. Figure 3.1 is a static representation independent of the passing of time, and yet a key feature of systems is interaction through time. For instance, the timing mechanism (not shown in Figure 3.1) might be off, with the result that the water is not fully heated before it mixes with the coffee. Alternatively, the water might start pouring over the coffee before the grinder has fully ground the coffee. The system might yield a cup of coffee that lacks excitement, as in being cool or weak. In this very simple robotic system, there is still the problem of determining whether a perceived problem lies in the grinder, one of the power sources, or the timing mechanism that coordinates some of the parts.

Over the years a number of economists have analogized economic policy to the situation faced by a mechanic trying to repair an engine, which is a type of robotic system of interacting parts. This is undoubtedly a comforting image for people who like to think of themselves as having expertise relevant to maintaining the good health of the body politic. The validity of that image, however, is doubtful because creative systems raise problems and issues that don't arise with robotic systems. All systems have the same form in that they can be portrayed as networks of entities and connections. So an engine is a system, as is a forest, and as is an economy or society. As a pure matter of abstract formality, all these systems can be described in graph-theoretic terms as a constellation of nodes and edges, as Figure 3.1 illustrates, and with Potts (2000) organizing his presentation of economic theory within a graph-theoretic framework. As a substantive matter, however, mechanical systems are worlds apart from human population systems, and this makes all the difference in explaining why economists are nothing like automotive mechanics, no matter how strongly some of them might think of themselves in this manner.

Despite the repeated references economists make to economic systems, they mostly do not theorize in terms of systems of interacting and creative agents. Instead, they theorize in terms of equilibrium among the parts, and with the presumption of equilibrium transforming the agents into robots. Through this transformation, equilibrium theory becomes antipodal to systems theory in the presence of creative agents. There is nothing illogical or wrong about the antipodal relationship between equilibrium theory and systems theory. Both have useful domains, but those domains point in different analytical directions, much as the parabolas X^2 and $-X^2$ point in different directions once you move away from their common origin. The equilibrium sketch, as illustrated by Figure 3.1, sets forth a pattern of relationship among the parts that endures whether the system is performing well or badly. For systems that are constructed, as is an automatic coffee maker, an equilibrium sketch is a blueprint for that construction. But not all systems are of this sort. Human population systems, for instance, are not constructed through engineering. Pieces of those systems are constructed, but not the entire system. With respect to Wagner's (2010a, 2010b) formulation of the relation between change and permanence, creative systems theory is Heraclitian while equilibrium theory is Ecclesiastian. Equilibrium theory portrays, similar to the Ecclesiastian recognition that there is nothing new under the Sun, what are thought to be invariant structures independent of time and place. In contrast, systems theory seeks to explain performance through time, as represented by recognition that a person cannot even step twice into the same river. Such performance includes the generation of novelty through continual interaction among creative agents, which amounts to systems effectively acting on themselves, realizing that all such action must be traced to origins in individual agents and their actions.

The systems theory idea applied to human population systems is doubtlessly discomfiting to many people, especially those who envision themselves as social reformers, and in two distinct respects. One respect is that reformers are just as much a part of the system about which they refer in their calls for reform as is everyone else in the system, and with Soros (2013) exploring some possible conceptual avenues along which to incorporate reflexivity into economic theory. The typical posture of those who advance calls for reform is that they stand apart from that system. That posture is an illusion that hides the reality that their calls are but one of the outputs or activities of the system in which they are but one element (Tollison and Wagner 1991). The other though related respect is that systems are often subject only indirectly and not directly to reform, as Donella Meadows (2008: 145–65) explains. As the sociologist Randall Collins put the point:

> The major problem that most prescriptive, action-oriented political philosophies face is precisely the fact that the macro world is a system that we are caught in, but it is not a goal seeking system. Alienation may be a condition of teleological individual human beings making up a social system which is by no means as self-reflexive as themselves. (Collins 1988: 54)

Human population systems are creative systems and not robotic systems, and it is this distinction that leads to recognition that public policy typically resembles a shell game in that it works by deflecting an observer's attention onto the wrong object.

2.   ROBOTIC SYSTEMS AND CREATIVE SYSTEMS

Systems theory has provided fertile ground for thinking about a wide range of complex phenomena where systemic-level qualities are governed by patterns of interaction among the entities that constitute the system. While all systems can be described formally as networks of entities and connections, that structural identity is accompanied by significant diversity. For instance, Bertalanffy (1968: 192–94) contrasts a robot model of a system to an "active personality system" (by which he means what I have described as a creative system). Much of the material of systems theory concerns mechanical relationships among the system's elements. A heating system for a home or office would have such elements as a furnace, a pump, electrical input, and a thermostat. It would also have some pattern of connection among those entities, as illustrated by the vents that carry air to the rooms and by the wiring that connects the thermostat to the pump. The heating system is a mechanical object. The performance of the system depends on how well the elements work together in a non-additive manner. Those elements are mechanical, and so perform as designed until they experience some kind of breakdown, in which case the performance of the system degrades or even stops even though the other elements continue to perform as designed. Such mechanical systems are designed by some designer.

The equilibrium system of additive political economy described by Figure 2.1 is a robotic system. There is a policy maker who acts on an economy denoted as a single entity as constructed through the postulate of equilibrium. Within this scheme of thought, the economy responds mechanically to the policy maker's interventions just as does a billiard ball when struck by a cue ball. While robotic systems are all around us, the focus of this book is on creative systems wherein the components of the system are not just objects to be acted on by some policy maker, but rather exercise their own initiatives and talk back to so-called policy makers, as it were. Indeed, it could well be that robotic systems are limited to the products of human design and not even found in the natural world. With respect to the natural world, for instance, Ilya Prigogine (1997) explores the physical and geological world as a creative system. Andreas Wagner (2014) does the same for the biological world. In any case, for this book the relevant distinction is Bertalanffy's distinction between robotic and active personality systems, and with human population systems being creative and not robotic.

Robotic systems can become highly complex and mired in the undecidability of combinatorial complexity (Chaitin et al. 2012), but human population systems have an additional source of complexity that follows from the creativity of people. While some people may be content to settle into a routine pattern of living unless outside circumstances force them to change, other people will get bored with such routines and will generate change if for no other reason than to avoid boredom. Any system can be described as a set of nodes and connections. The nodes in a robotic system, however, have significantly different qualities from the nodes in a creative system. For the robotic system, the qualities of the nodes are products of design and engineering. With respect to biological nodes, individual organisms will have a repertoire of responses to changes at other nodes which increase systemic complexity. For human population systems, individual nodes are able to imagine and create new patterns of action, thereby injecting novelty into the system (Shackle 1961, 1972).

The central claim of systems theory is that the working properties of a system depend on the pattern of connection among the entities in that system (Potts 2000). For creative systems, it will also depend on the propagation of creative impulses injected into the system at particular nodes. As a formal matter, this claim is independent of the nature of the system. As a substantive matter, however, that claim will play out to strikingly different effect across different types of systems. Such robotic systems as a heating system or a water supply system can be managed so as to keep systemic performance within reasonably close bounds, save for disruptions from outside the system. Someone can adopt the position of managing the system, and feel relatively confident about the systemic effects of various managerial activities. A thermostat is a node in a heating system. If the thermostat's calibration is off, the temperature in the room will not be kept within the desired range. A thermostat is a type of robot. It can be replaced if it is not working well, after which the temperature in the room will be maintained in the desirable range. The system itself will not generate surprises. It is different with biological systems beyond some minimal scale of complexity. A small aquarium for the home is of a much smaller scale of complexity than a coral reef near some island. Introduction of a new fish into the home aquarium will typically be far more predictable than such introduction into a coral reef.

This book is concerned exclusively with human population systems, for it is here where the material of entangled political economy arises. The nodes in a human population system are not robots but are active personality systems. Recognition of this simple fact makes it inapt to speak of controlling such systems, as against speaking of seeking to influence them. To exert influence, however, is different from exerting control. For human population systems there is no systems engineer who can maintain the system in working order because maintenance is a product of interaction among the various active personality systems that constitute the system.

The system maintains itself or it doesn't, depending on patterns of inter-action among the participants. There might be Big Players (Koppl 2002) who exert disproportionate influence over systemic qualities, but this is influence and not control all the same.

3.   PUBLIC POLICY AS SHELL GAME

Entangled political economy emphasizes the structural pattern of relation-ships among the entities that are constituted within different institutional frameworks. Figure 3.2, which is an elaboration of what Wagner (2012a) set forth, illustrates this point. That figure has two levels separated by three lightning bolts. The lower level depicts a network of circles and triangles. This level is denoted as the "action level." This is where all action takes place, and is the only place where action can take place. The upper level is denoted as the "system level." No action takes place on this level, for this level is rather a recordation of various aspects of system performance, both past realizations of performance and future projections. The system level is not an object of action. It is impossible to act directly upon system variables to change system performance, for systemic performance can be

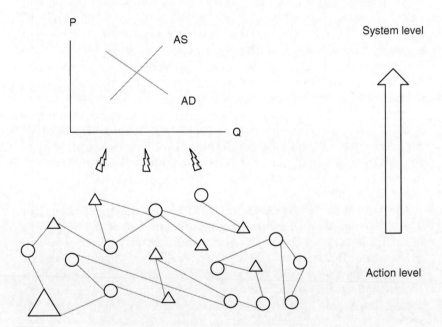

Figure 3.2   Network pattern and system performance

changed only through acting on variables or entities located on the action level. In Figure 3.2, the system level is characterized in terms of aggregate supply and demand, though any set of system-level variables could be used to illustrate the systemic properties that are generated through interaction among the relevant entities at the action level. Regardless of their particular identity, system variables are not direct objects of action but rather are indirect reflections of actions undertaken on the action level.

With respect to the lower part of Figure 3.2, the especially large triangle at the lower left edge can be thought of as representing a central bank as an illustration of Roger Koppl's (2002) identification of central banks as particularly Big Players, meaning not only that they are large but also, and more significantly, that their principles of action differ from ordinary market participants. While monetary and macro theorists commonly speak of a central bank as increasing the supply of money by buying government bonds through open-market operations, those operations occur on the ground level of Figure 3.2. As macro theory is commonly presented, open-market operations would be illustrated by a rightward shift in AD in the upper part of Figure 3.2. But that is only a picture at the end of some expansionary process. With respect to the lower part of Figure 3.2, the central bank would place an order with a brokerage dealer to buy bonds. In turn, that dealer would buy bonds with those market participants who were willing to sell their bonds. The shift in aggregate demand shown in the upper part of Figure 3.2 would derive from the market transactions that are portrayed in the lower part of Figure 3.2. It is in the lower part of the figure where the action takes place, and with the depiction in the upper part being merely a reflection of that action.

With respect to political economy, the circles on the action level denote market-based enterprises while the triangles denote polity-based enterprises. Figure 3.2 portrays 12 circles and eight triangles, which corresponds reasonably closely with private and public shares of GDP in contemporary western democracies. Figure 3.2 is an incomplete graph, which means that each node is connected directly to some but not all of the other nodes in the system. This construction is a graphical representation of Hayek's (1937, 1945) ideas about knowledge being incomplete and dispersed. In contrast, the oft-used assumption of full knowledge would have to be represented as a completely connected graph where any single node is connected directly to all other nodes. The lower level of Figure 3.2 depicts the structural pattern of a system of political economy. Change in that structure can be depicted through changes in the relative numbers of circles and triangles. One could aggregate activity over those circles and triangles to generate a measure of the aggregate sizes of private and public sectors, as Tanzi (2011) exemplifies. Change can also be depicted through changes in patterns of connection. Expansion in the extent of public ordering within a society would appear as an increase in the number of connections between the circles and the triangles in Figure 3.2. As shown in Figure 3.2, a connection is just a connection, and that is about all there is to the matter. With respect to entangled political economy, however, there are different types of connection, as Podemska-Mikluch and Wagner (2013) explain in their distinction between dyadic and triadic relationships in political economy.

Any resort to macro-level explanation in political economy is a form of shell game, in that it diverts people's attention by getting them to look where the action is not. It does this by positing a relationship between or among macro-level variables when no such theoretical relationship exists. A statistical relationship there can well be, but not a theoretical generative relationship.[1] The upper level of Figure 3.2 denotes a kind of projection from the ground level to the system level. This projection takes the form of statistical aggregates compiled through the various national income accounts. It is a collection of statistics. Macro-level theorizing then operates by constructing theoretical-sounding relationships among the statistically constructed objects. Hence, growth in GDP over some period might be related to measure of changes in aggregate years of schooling within a population. Such efforts can readily lead into discussions of what policy measures might change a rate of growth. Those measures, of course, would pertain to the variables captured by the statistical relationship. In the case at hand, this could mean that the discussion would involve whether there were educational policies and programs that might influence the rate of growth.

These kinds of macro-theoretic explanations are examples of shell games in that they misdirect an observer's attention from where the action is truly located, as Marta Podemska-Mikluch (2014) exemplifies in her analysis of the implementation of a Polish program for reimbursing people for medical expenses. This leads to people asking the wrong questions, which in turn can reinforce support for particular political programs. Taking recourse to macro-theoretic styles of argument is to participate in shell games because there is nothing at the macro level that speaks to whatever it is that changes some measure of a rate of growth. In the case at hand, it was presumed that educational spending influenced the rate of growth. But this is just statistics, and these tell us nothing that is truly capable of addressing or answering the question. Spending *per se* can't accomplish anything; whatever might be accomplished will depend on who does the spending, on what they spend, and how they spend. To find answers to the relation between spending and growth requires analytical movement to the ground level, which is the only level where action occurs.

In moving to this ground level, the questions that move into the analytical foreground are not questions regarding how much to spend in the aggregate on education and what will such spending do to the growth rate. These are just statistical questions which in turn are artifacts of a particular scheme of accounting.

This question can be addressed in a conceptually reasonable manner only by moving to the ground level where all questions about structure, interaction, and substance reside. One obvious question of great significance is just what kind of topics will constitute the added educational spending envisioned at the macro level. Another and equally obvious question concerns just who it is that will make such decisions. Will they be made by some official, perhaps aided by an advisory committee, within a governmental department of education? Alternatively, they could be made by parents and students. And if so, there is a further menu of options through which such an approach could proceed. For instance, students could apply for grants to a government agency which in turn could accept or reject the application. Alternatively, the student could make the choice without obtaining any approval, and could even receive payment through the tax system. Continuing in this vein are additional questions regarding the suppliers of whatever particular topics students might study, as part of the increased educational spending. Even if students are allowed to make their own choices of topics, they could be required to secure those services from providers certified by a department of education. Alternatively, that certification might be granted to all public schools but withheld from private schools. As yet another possibility, certification could be limited to schools with unionized teachers.

In all of these ways and the many additional ways that could be readily sketched, the real story of education and growth would play out on the ground level simply because this is the only level where human action takes place. By shifting focus to the macro or systems level, however, many possible actions are hidden. As for which option might actually be pursued in this situation, there is a further story of entangled political economy waiting to be told. Political entities compete among one another just as do market entities, and with political and market entities also engaging in both competitive and collusive activities. Different patterns of entanglement will influence the systemic properties of political–economic interaction, though here I would stress influence and not control. To put the point differently, macro or systemic variables are derivative and not primary variables. A macro-level variable takes its value from the micro-level variables that constitute it. It is as if there were an inverted relationship between puppets and puppeteer, with the actions of the puppets inducing the puppeteer's movements.

4.   PROPERTY RIGHTS AND SYSTEMS OF SOCIAL ECONOMY

At least since Paul Samuelson's (1954, 1955) articulation of a dichotomy between public and private goods, it has been conventional for economists to think in terms of societies facing some tradeoff between public and private output. While not all economists think in this manner, most of them surely do. This scheme of thought leads readily to the conceptualization that Figure 3.3 presents. Shown there is a set of production possibilities denoted by PP which illustrates the various combinations of public and private output a society can attain with the given state of knowledge. In many such formulations, some presumption of a social welfare function is used to choose some optimizing combination as denoted by R. Figure 3.3, however, is not constructed with some social welfare function in mind. Point R is rather placed there in recognition that some set of institutional processes lies behind the generation of such an experienced outcome as that depicted by R. In any scheme of aggregate accounting, there will be some separation between the aggregate of governmental activity, G, provided by political enterprises, and market activity, M, provided by private enterprises, and all of which is generated through non-teleological processes of interaction among people and their entities. Economists, however, have only incompletely characterized those processes. The theory

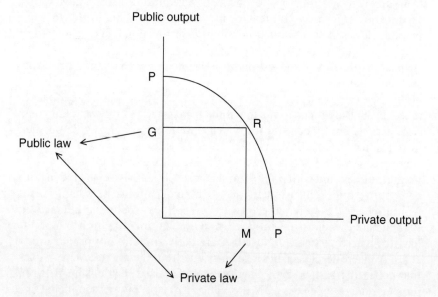

Figure 3.3   Orthodox portrayal of public–private resource allocation

of markets seeks to decompose and explain the structural pattern of M. There is, however, no economic theory that does the same for G, though Buchanan (1967, 1968) and McKean (1965, 1968) made starts, which Wagner (2007, 2012c) moved forward.

The theory of market interaction can give a reasonably coherent explanation of the pattern of market activity that is summarized by M in Figure 3.3, though that theory remains incomplete all the same, especially as the analysis moves outside the confines of equilibrium theory. In any case, there is no comparable theory of political interaction, but only a few pointers toward such a theory. In modern theories of political economy, political outcomes are presumed to be ordered through systemic teleology, either through imposition or through presumption. By imposition, I mean resort to some device that "explains" the outcome as some product of choice, which brings the conceptual paraphernalia of constrained optimization into play. The most common way of doing this is to impose some social welfare function as a fictive device to generate a pattern of collective activity. An equivalent device is to presume a genuine despot who maximizes his or her objective function. By presumption, I mean a scheme of thought that holds that electoral competition selects a particular utility function, that possessed by the median voter with respect to the election in question, to serve as the relevant welfare function. A superficial look might make this scheme of thought less teleological, but it really isn't because it is unreasonable to reduce the entire range of governmental activities to a single person's utility function, even if utility functions are presumed to exist in advance of choice as against themselves being *ex post* rationalizations of or explanations for choice.

A truly explanatory theory of political economy would recognize that G and M in Figure 3.3 are both emergent products of interaction among the members of a society, and in a setting where no person can even see let alone act on the societal entirety. For outcomes to emerge through interaction there must be principles of action that govern the actions of participants in those interactions. For creative agents, moreover, those principles can never be fully specified in advance of action. The pure theory of a market economy seeks to explain how a set of interactions governed by the private law principles of property and contract can yield a coherent pattern of outcomes that, when formulated in equilibrium terms, would be Pareto efficient. This theory can explain M or something like it in Figure 3.3. Subtended to M in Figure 3.3 are the institutional arrangements of private law, namely private property and freedom of contract and association. The pure theory of a market economy explains how societies generate orderly patterns of activity without systemic teleology when individual relationships are governed by the institutional arrangements of private law, though it must also be recognized that those institutional arrangements are not independent of the deployment of political action in society (Schmitt 1932).

An explanatory theory of public activity would have the same features, which is illustrated by subtending the institutional arrangements denoted as public law to G in Figure 3.3. But what are those institutional arrangements? Whatever they are, they must be capable of explaining the observed pattern of public outcomes within the same context of limited and distributed knowledge as the institutional arrangements of private law explain market patterns. Contrary to Samuelson's (1954, 1955) assertion that construction of a theory of fiscal catallaxy was impossible due to failures of preference revelation, Buchanan (1967, 1968) presented some building blocks for constructing an explanatory theory of fiscal catallaxy, and did so by building upon some insights set forth by such Italian scholars as Antonio de Viti de Marco (1936) and Attilio Da Empoli (1941). While Buchanan didn't complete the task he set for himself, he took some significant steps in this direction by putting public institutional arrangements on the same level as private institutional arrangements and pointing toward an analytical schema whereby public outcomes, like private outcomes, were emergent resultants of some institutional framework that could be denoted as public property.

But how can public property be conceptualized in an analytically useful fashion? A collective body can undertake action in the name of the collectivity only in the presence of some framework of rules that governs interaction among the relevant participants, and with Congleton (2011) presenting a comparative history of the generation of such frameworks among western democracies. Even if the collective action summarized by G is traced to a parliamentary assembly, such an assembly of, say, 400 people, is nothing but a mob until that mob acquires some framework of rules that structures interaction among members so as to generate collective outcomes. That framework of rules is what is denoted by institutions of public law that are subtended to G in Figure 3.3. One simple framework, employed by de Viti de Marco (1936) and elaborated in Eusepi and Wagner (2010, 2013), would postulate a universal flat tax on income. A rate of 10 percent would mean that everyone would devote 10 percent of their working time to stocking the fiscal commons. There would be no scope for politics to alter the rate or structure of taxation because the relation between private and public property would be set by the rate of tax. In this manner, market and political processes would operate independently to generate the outcomes denoted by M and G in Figure 3.3. In this framework, polity and economy would operate independently of one another, and would illustrate a form of additive political economy.

Only in a very incomplete sense, however, would this approach account for the size of a public budget. To impose a non-discriminatory flat tax in the fashion of Buchanan and Congleton (1998) would truncate the range of the political in society by removing taxation from political action. Were such a scheme to be in effect, the full weight of parliamentary action would bear on the determination of the uses of tax revenues. This analytical move to truncate the range of the political in society, however, is more a blackboard formalism than it is an effort to account for the social processes and interactions we experience and participate in, as David Primo (2007) explains in his examination of various efforts to bring fiscal processes under institutional control. For one thing, the income on which a flat tax might be based is not a self-defining term. Indeed, Henry Simons's (1938) still-cited and still-controversial treatise on personal income taxation is centered on how income might be defined prior to taxes being imposed. A parliamentary assembly could conceivably agree to operate under a rule whereby the rate of tax would be flat when applied to whatever base the assembly agreed upon. Fiscal politics would still be in play in defining income; moreover, an assembly that cannot work with variable rates would surely work harder in defining what is included in and excluded from the definition of income.

True independence of polity and economy is surely more the stuff of fantasy than of reality, or even of potential reality in light of the autonomy of the political (Schmitt 1932). That independence requires an invariant rate and base along with preclusion of any exemptions or exclusions from the base. Should such an initial situation be defined or attained, experience gives no good reason to think that it would be maintained. Moreover, income is not an object that appears in the natural world, but rather is an object that is constructed through human thought and action. Furthermore, the private law principles of property and contract are often adjudicated through judicial processes populated through public law, which means that there is no necessary reason why those processes execute the terms of private agreements if one party garnered more judicial sympathy than the other party, perhaps as illustrated by ideas about unconscionable contracts.

The institutions that might be denoted as corresponding to private and political property are not decomposable into separate spheres, as illustrated by the double arrow that connects public law and private law in Figure 3.3. They might be partially or incompletely decomposable, but that is the maximal extent of decomposition. Property rights denote a social relationship among people. Private property denotes a relationship of forbearance wherein other people will not contest your actions regarding what you think is your property. If no one contests your desire to cut down a tree on your property and sell the wood to a neighbor, private property pertains to this instance. Should someone contest your desire to fill a marshy area on land to which you hold title and to convert that land into a shopping center, private property is replaced by elements of public property.

This reference to public property, however, is not just another form of private property. With private property there are definite owners who can take action. This is not the case with public property, for relevant action is always collective action; moreover, collectivities can act only inside some framework of rules that generates what are recognized as collective outcomes. Once it is recognized that property rights can for many analytical purposes be usefully conceptualized by the image of a bundle of sticks, it is easy to see that there are myriad margins along which the boundary between private and political property can be contested and potentially change.[2] This is the world of entangled political economy. It is also the world of the anti-commons where the assembly of agreements among individual decision makers can be especially difficult when those decision makers are not residual claimants over the value consequences of their actions (Heller 1998; Buchanan and Yoon 2000). Private property and political property both pertain to the same people inhabiting the same society. If this recognition is applied within a presumption that societies contain some underlying harmony of interests, some definitive equilibrium outcome might be generated despite the fabulous character of both equilibrium outcomes and harmony of interests. Doing this, however, would be to treat politics as an ordinary and not a peculiar business, and would be to step into one of the two main snares Da Empoli (1941) warned against: one snare being to treat politics as disjoint from markets along the lines of Samuelson's later treatments of public goods; the other snare being to treat politics as just one particular manifestation of market activity.

In the world of entangled political economy, however, the governance of human relationships and interactions becomes a pivot of social controversy, as Pareto (1935) recognized with especial cogency in his emphasis on political competition among elites using techniques of wit and power to exercise dominance over ruled masses. Friedrich Wieser (1926), Vilfredo Pareto (1935), and Bertrand de Jouvenel (1948) presented complementary analyses of power in society. In particular, power was not some injection into society from outside of it, as such outside injection is conveyed by numerous references to despotism as a force that stands apart from the ordinary members of society. It is not credible that small numbers of power holders can dominate overwhelmingly large numbers of outsiders without having some modicum of support among those outsiders. For instance, David Skarbeck (2014) explains lucidly that prison guards play but a modest role in maintaining order within prisons. It is the prisoners themselves who bear a great deal of responsibility for maintaining that order, and do so through organizing gangs that promote the maintenance of order within prisons.

Power operates in prisons just as it operates in societies at large. That operation, however, is not a matter of a few outsiders imposing their will on numerous objecting insiders. The situation is rather one where there are margins of commonality across outsiders and insiders, where the relation between prisoners and guards, similar to the relation between citizens and politicians, is entangled and not separable and additive, and with Leeson (2005, 2006, 2008) explaining how socially heterogeneous groups are able to find margins of homogeneity that facilitate trade despite substantial heterogeneity. Daniel Smith (2014) extends Leeson's line of analysis to cooperation among religious groups in medieval Spain despite the presence of religious wars at that time. With respect to the principles governing the determination of G in Figure 3.3, the public law framework can operate neither independently of nor identically with the private law framework. Rather, it operates through what is effectively parasitical attachment to the private law framework, in that political enterprises derive their revenues not directly from customers but indirectly by making tax attachments to market transactions.

5. PROGRESS AND DISSIPATION IN CREATIVE SYSTEMS

Any systems-theoretic explanation can be presented as a graph of nodes and connections, as the lower level of Figure 3.2 illustrates. This figure is also terribly incomplete and requires adumbration to call forth some of the insights that a systems theory can offer, which are hidden both by Figure 3.2 and by the reductionist formulation of equilibrium theory. In particular, I have in mind three analytical items: (1) allowance for the genuine passing of time in the sense of O'Driscoll and Rizzo (1985) and Wagner (2010a, b); (2) recognition that different nodes can operate under different principles of action, and also that those principles can change through time; and (3) consideration of the effects of different ways of fashioning connections between nodes. In view of how these items play out, a creative system can operate in a progressive or dissipative manner.

To distinguish between progressive and dissipative paths of development requires adoption of some standpoint from which to make such judgments. While this book is focused primarily on explanation, beneath that focus lies a normative interest in different ways of organizing the living together that is a fact of all societies. This book embraces the assertion in the American Declaration of Independence that governments derive their just powers from the consent of the governed. This assertion inspires a treatment of politicians as servants of the common interests of the general public and not as lords who oversee what they regard as *their* domain. The image of politicians as lords of the manor, so to speak, was left behind with the American rejection of all things feudal, other than slavery.

When at the close of the Constitutional Convention in 1787, Benjamin Franklin answered "a republic if you can keep it," to a lady who asked what kind of government had been created, Franklin showed that he recognized that a system of political economy could operate in dissipative fashion. There is no doubt that the American system of limited and republican government has experienced dissipation in Franklin's sense, in that what were once positions of servitude have increasingly morphed into positions of mastery, which Wagner (2006a) explores within an analytical framework of emergent order. Within the spirit of the Declaration and the Constitution, public servants had as their accepted obligation the service and advancement of republican liberty (Epstein 2014). While any such obligation will often be honored in the breach, as Jonathan Hughes (1977) explains, the obligation is nonetheless generally acknowledged. This is no longer the case. Political officials, especially at the federal level of government though not only at that level, have taken on some of the status and standing of the feudal estates of old. Without doubt, what some will regard as dissipation others will regard as progress. Any such judgment requires a standard, and in this respect I accept the standard of the American Constitution of a regime grounded on individual liberty along with acceptance of the responsibility to maintain that regime. So when I refer to the ability of systems theory to illuminate processes of dissipation as well as of progress, I have in mind transformation from political figures being stagehands who keep the human drama moving into becoming leading players in that drama.

A. With Respect to Time

Economists often work with spatial images and models. Commercial firms are often described as locating their products within "commercial space." Political candidates are often described as locating their proposed programs in "issue space." Through these kinds of spatial references, success can be ascribed to the firm or candidate who comes closest to the center of gravity of the population to which the firm or candidate is appealing. Within an equilibrium scheme of thought, a snapshot is sufficient to describe and understand the action. Comparative statics is the method that compares two snapshots and seeks to give an account of the change in the observed data. In either case, the observed data is rendered sufficient to infer meaning by virtue of the presumption that what is observed is some equilibrium pattern of relationships.

Someone in this position would have to conclude that horses can fly after seeing snapshots of horses with all four hooves off the ground. No one would actually do this, because the falsity of that claim is obvious. What makes that falsity obvious, however, is experience in watching horses run while time is passing. That experience is not acquired through comparative static reasoning about snapshots. It is acquired through observation over some interval of time where the meaning of what has been observed is intelligible only in consequence of watching a pattern unfold through time. To capture this requires an emergent dynamic scheme of thought. Such a graph as that presented in Figure 3.2 is incapable of doing this. Formulations in terms of differential equations can't do that either because future observations are treated as data at the start, either explicitly or as probability distributions. In any case, it must be kept in mind that the object of analytical interest is a system that undergoes evolution through interactions among the participants within that system. A useful scheme of thought must allow for the internal generation of change due ultimately to conflicts among members of society, sometimes personal conflicts but mostly conflicts regarding the plans of different people and enterprises.

B.   With Respect to Nodes

Keeping in mind that we are dealing with systems that undergo evolution with the passing of time, we recognize that it is the nodes, sometimes conceptualized as persons and sometimes conceptualized as enterprises, that are the carriers of action and the source of novelty. The nodes in a human population system are different from those in a robotic system. Humans have creativity accompanied by volition, some people more than others, probably, but which means in any case that novelty will be continually injected into human population systems. Much of that novelty will take the form of inventions that lead to new businesses and products. Some of these inventions will prove commercially successful while others will be failures. Either way, they will generate changes in the system's structure.

To the extent the nodes are persons, the nodes are carriers of moral sentiments. A market order is the name we apply to a social system when relationships among the members of that society are governed by an institutional framework characterized by the private law principles of private property and freedom of contract (Eucken 1952). As for how that particular institutional framework came about, various answers have been advanced. However such origination might be explained, beneath that institutional framework lies a set of moral beliefs that undergirds it. Private property, for instance, can be summarized by such statements as to leave alone what is not yours. Similarly, freedom of contract can be summarized by such statements as keep the promises you have made or don't interfere with the commitments other people have made.

This kind of morality reflects a social system based on independent people who are able to make their way in the world by rendering services that other people value. People who are unhappy with various features of their life would be counseled first of all to look to themselves in seeking redress for their unhappiness. Perhaps people in this position should work harder or should be polite rather than surly to customers and co-workers. Or perhaps they should change jobs, or change some other aspect of their lives. In any event, the personal sense of independence that would accompany the liberal morality of a market economy is one where people would accept first-order responsibility for their lives and their circumstances. The prime exception to this morality of independence arises in cases where unhappiness can be attributed directly to other people who have violated their rights of property or expectations of contract.

Chapter 5 will explore the extent to which legislation might bring about an alternative moral climate, perhaps due to excessive and misguided kindness of a sort, as a reflection of a form of societal entropy (Georgescu-Roegen 1971) or generalized Samaritan's dilemmas (Buchanan 1975a). Nearly all legislation is accompanied by assertions that there are systemic defects or deficiencies that are behind much of the unhappiness people have about their circumstances. Within a free-market system, someone who would like to live in a nicer house is free to do so by paying the price. That person might not be willing to pay that price, perhaps because it would require working 80 hours a week. If there are a sufficient number of people in this kind of position, as the fact of scarcity almost ensures there will be, a latent demand exists for a political program that would make such housing available on such terms, as illustrated by requirements that mortgages be distributed in stipulated fashion among income categories. Such programs illustrate the operation of politics as a peculiar business.

C. With Respect to Connections

With respect to graph-theoretic illustrations, connections are just lines that connect nodes. Yet there are different kinds of connections, and these do different kinds of work within a system of entangled political economy. Some connections are forged voluntarily, others are forged forcibly. Voluntary connections are the motif of market-based activity. Forcible connections are the province of politics, though not all politically forged connections are extended through force. For market relationships, the magic number is two. It takes two people to make a trade, with both parties being better off after the trade. The magic number for democratic politics, especially on a large scale, is three. There are two people who exchange mutual support and a third person who is forced to offer financial support (Podemska-Mikluch and Wagner 2013). Where market catallactics can be reduced mostly to a set of dyadic relationships, political catallactics typically requires a set of triadic relationships to be characterized accurately.

It is surely a bit ironic that so many people wonder what governments can do to improve the state of trust when a consideration of different ways of fabricating connections gives good reason to think that governments would to a significant degree degrade trust-based relationships, due to the replacement of the voluntarism of dyadic transactions with the compulsion that accompanies politically triadic transactions. The American experience with alcohol prohibition early in the twentieth century provides a good illustration of this point. Within a liberal market economy, there is positive value to rectitude. People mean what they say, and this economizes on the cost of doing business, which in consequence supports trustful states of mind. Someone asks if you would sell him a drink. He's willing to pay your price, so you do. There is nothing funny about this transaction: it is what it appears to be. It's altogether different when Prohibition appears. Someone who asks to buy a drink might be there to entrap you and arrest you. Suspicion replaces trust. With growing suspicion comes change in the way people do business to forestall being victimized through entrapment. Politics is truly a peculiar type of business, and yet a catallactical orientation toward political economy places "the deal" at the center of the analytical stage, similar to John Commons's (1934) placement of the transaction at the center of his analytical stage.

6. MARKETS, POLITICS, AND THE SCALABILITY OF CREATIVE SYSTEMS

Entangled political economy works with network-based representations of relationships and interactions among the relevant entities within a system of political economy. One significant question is whether a network is random and scalable or is non-random and free of scale. If it is random and scalable, the size of a network is pretty much irrelevant because there is no significant change in network qualities as networks become larger. When networks are non-random and scale free, however, significant qualitative changes can accompany expansion in the size of a network. One network might have 40 nodes and 60 connections, another one might have 400 nodes and 600 connections. The second network might look to be just the first network multiplied by ten. But is it? This depends on the pattern of nodes and connections that accompany expansion of the network. The new nodes and connections might locate anywhere at random on the network's graph. Alternatively, they might locate in systematic fashion on parts of the graph. In this latter case, the network is non-scalable or scale free. This distinction matters for a system of entangled political economy because it addresses questions of whether network qualities are invariant to the size of a network. For instance, if economic relationships are scalable while political relationships are not, a system of entangled political economy might feature a form of increasing returns to political power within society.

To illustrate the possible significance of the scale of governance, compare the United States and Switzerland. At the time of its founding, the United States contained 13 states and a population of about 3.5 million. Today's Switzerland contains 26 cantons and a population of nearly 8 million. In comparison, the United States today contains 50 states and a population of around 320 million. Switzerland today has about 285,000 residents per canton, which is similar to the 270,000 residents per state at the time of the American constitutional founding. Now, however, American states average about 6.4 million residents. To achieve a scale of state governance similar to Switzerland today or to the United States when it was founded, something on the order of 1,200 states would be required. No one has proposed any such explosion in the number of states and it is hard to imagine that anyone would support such a thing. Yet this matter of scale raises significant issues regarding the relationship between democracy and liberty, in particular, whether the democratic form might feature a type of increasing returns to power, along with an oligarchic form of democracy which Robert Michels (1962) set forth luminously and which Bertrand de Jouvenel (1961) illustrated pithily. Also highly relevant to recognition of oligarchic features within democratic regimes is Gaetano Mosca's (1947) analysis of democratic despotism based on a distinction between those who rule and those who are ruled.

There is a significant difference between relationships that are scalable and those that are not, and which instead are what are called scale free (Barabási 2002). For the most part, economists work with models that are scalable. This means that the difference between a small and a large firm is a matter of multiplication and little else. A firm with 1,000 employees is just a firm with 100 employees multiplied by 10. If this presumption of scalability could be extended to politics, a state with 10 million people would be equivalent to a city of 100,000 multiplied by 100, or to a town of 10,000 multiplied by 1,000.

There is good reason for economists to think that commercial relationships are reasonably scalable. The market for fresh eggs, for instance, will operate in pretty much the same manner no matter whether that market serves a thousand, a million, or a billion people. With increases in the number of people being served, we would expect to find changes in such things as patterns of wholesaling, retailing, and distribution, as well as increases in the number of market participants. The division of labor does, after all, vary with the extent of the market. All the same, we would not expect changes in scale to affect basic propositions about how free and open competition tends to secure the full exploitation of potential gains from trade among buyers and sellers. It is private property that creates scalability in economic relationships. By becoming larger, a market-based entity might find increasing difficulty in managing its operations, in which case competition from smaller firms will reduce the size of the overly large firm. Open competition tends to generate firms of efficient scale, which means in turn that firms of varying size are able to attract customers and operate as going concerns. At base, commercial relationships must reflect mutual attraction among participants, and this necessity of mutual attraction, which is a quality of private property, tends to render actual market relationships scalable.

Unlike the open competition that market entities typically face, political entities face closed competition. While political entities operate to some extent through mutual attraction, they also employ compulsion which allows scale to expand beyond what free competition would allow. For instance, a town of 10,000 might be governed by a town council of 10 people, each of whom might represent 1,000 people. This would be a relatively personal scale of governance. Members of the council could plausibly know something about many of the people they represent and would often come across them while moving through such daily activities as jogging through a park, shopping in a store, or going to a theater. Beyond this, much council business could be conducted informally, even if the council also operates with regularly scheduled meetings.

It is not plausible to say that a city with 1 million people is just a town of 10,000 multiplied by 100. If the city council still contains 10 members, each member will now represent 100,000 people. It is impossible for someone to know much if anything about 100,000 people. What little that can be known, moreover, will be reducible to census-type forms and aggregated in some fashion. Only a subset of citizens will have direct access to council members, and the pattern of this access will be systematic and not random: power law distributions will dominate random distributions, which means that a relatively few number of people will dominate direct access to political processes. Access to political networks will be the province of people who represent significant interest groups within the city. The same democratic form will reside on the surface, but that superficial view will conceal oligarchic modes of operation.

Alternatively, the city council could be increased to 1,000 members. This would maintain the original scale in which each member represented 1,000 people. In this case, the relationship between population and council size would be scalable; however, the relationship among council members would not be scalable. With a council of 1,000 members, most council members will not even know one another other than as nodding acquaintances. The council will operate with formal rules of procedure, and those rules will include limitations on who can address the council and for how long they can do so. In this setting, possession of the ability to control the agenda and procedures through which political business is conducted will transfer effective control to whatever set of politicians is able to control the agenda. In one particularly absorbing and amusing example of agenda control, Charles Plott and Michael Levine (1978) explain how they were able to develop a decision procedure that led a flying club to buy a plane that the members of the club overwhelmingly thought was inferior to options they had rejected, in consequence of following the procedure that Plott and Levine advocated.

In this respect, Vincent Ostrom (1987, 1997) has explained how democratic oligarchy is a natural tendency of a simple or non-federal republic, the avoidance of which requires some polycentric arrangement of republics (if, indeed, oligarchy can be avoided at all, a proposition that Carl Schmitt (1932) would probably have denied in his treatment of the autonomy of the political). With respect to simple republics that operate with majority rule, public choice principles explain that democracy is more compatible with liberty in smaller rather than larger scales of government. Increases in the scale of governance bring oligarchic characteristics, including domination by entrenched interest groups and an electoral process characterized more by the continuing reelection of incumbents than by competition among political parties. Competition between parties there is, to be sure, but even more notable is the low rate of defeat of incumbents seeking reelection. For large republics, a path that offers compatibility between democracy and liberty is difficult to find and perhaps even more difficult to follow, as Benjamin Franklin appeared to have recognized.

7. FEDERALISM IN SYSTEMS PERSPECTIVE

Federal forms of government feature governments with independent authority, in contrast to a national form where the national government is the ultimate source of governmental authority. The federal form holds out the possibility that the scale-free quality of political governance can be overcome, or at least softened. Much depends in this respect on whether the particular federalism operates according to principles of open competition among governments and also with private entities or whether the federal system operates in cartel-like fashion where the federal government oversees the cartel of governments (Greve 2012; Wagner 2014a, b). A political system based on independent and competitive entities would be the political counterpart of an economic system based on private property. As originally established, American federalism was based largely on open competition. The federal government possessed enclaves of monopoly, not least of which was the so-called supremacy clause, which asserted that federal legislation trumped state legislation in cases of conflict. The federal government also held a postal monopoly, and diplomacy and the prevention of invasion were its province as well. Yet such enclaves were few in number and generally were not topics of controversy. For the most part, the American political system was envisioned as one that carried the principles of free and open competition into the political organization of society.

Each state by itself would be a national or unitary entity, so would be susceptible to rent seeking and rent extraction due to conflict between the majority principle of democracy and the consensual principle of private property, unless there are auxiliary constraints to limit the reach of democratic action. Theories of rent seeking and rent extraction explain how political coalitions can seize gains by restricting the liberties of other members of society to pursue commercial activity.[3] This restriction on liberty is a latent quality of democratic government where majority rule is in conflict with private property and liberty of contract.

States, however, are not independent nations but operate inside a federal system. Each state may be like a small nation in relation to other states, but each state is also a member of a federation, which brings both challenges and opportunities into play that would not confront a single nation. The federal government might have responsibility for maintaining open competition among the states, but there are alternative paths along which this responsibility might play out. One path would have the federal government following its constitutional authority in maintaining open competition (Epstein 2014). The other path would feature the federal government acting as a cartelizing agent, whereby cartels would form mostly under its auspices rather than under state auspices (Greve 2012). For instance, between its creation in 1938 and its elimination in 1984, the Civil Aeronautics Board did not allow a single new airline to carry passengers across state lines, despite the vast growth in air travel that occurred during this period. This is an example of using the federal government to sponsor a form of cartel federalism rather than competitive federalism.

This situation also points to a significant constitutional asymmetry within the American federalist system (Niskanen 1978). Citizens can challenge the constitutionality of state actions in a federal court. This ability fits with the principle that no man should be a judge in his own cause. In this instance, a state should not be able to issue a judgment in a case advanced against it, even if it is different offices of the state that are involved under the separation of powers. Judicial, legislative, and administrative authority may reside in independent offices, but such independence must always be incomplete, because all the offices are staffed through variations on the same electoral process. Hence, the ability of people to challenge state actions in federal courts makes constitutional sense. What does not make similar constitutional sense is the requirement that challenges to the constitutionality of federal actions must be taken to federal and not to state courts. In such cases, the federal government will be a judge in its own cause. Short of a situation in which state courts could render judgment on federal actions to restore constitutional asymmetry, it is not clear whether federalism provides protections for liberty that go beyond what would be part of a national government or whether it simply shifts the locus for the supply of restrictions on liberty and competition to the federal government (Wagner 2014c).

Judicial processes, however, are not the only source of protection against government infringements on liberty and competition. They might not even be the most significant source. Another source, and perhaps the dominant one, is competition among the states (Kenyon and Kincaid, eds. 1991). A national system may entail considerable administrative decentralization and delegation of responsibilities, and yet the extent of competition among subdivisions will be governed by the central government. Within a system of competitive federalism, by contrast, officials of individual states will typically feel more intensely the need to be competitive than would lower-level officials in a national bureaucracy. This does not mean that competition will necessarily trump rent seeking among states within a federal system, for there can still be plenty of gain to politicians from supporting rent-seeking activities. However, genuine federalism does seem better able to accommodate competition than does a national government, due to the need for states to attract residents, which a national government does not face nearly so fully.

Randall Collins (1998) sets forth a model of scholarly competition that has the aim of sketching a framework for the birth and death of schools of thought. Collins's framework of scholarly competition entails scholars competing for what he called attention space. Scholars articulate ideas that they think or hope will prove attractive to other scholars. The number of ideas that are capable of being articulated are vastly in excess of the ability of scholars to follow all those ideas. A scholar's attention space is limited relative to the total stock of ideas to which attention could be paid. Hence, scholars must choose which ideas to follow and which to ignore. This situation of scarcity leads to the formation of schools of thought, where individual scholars tend to pay greatest attention to ideas from those schools with which they most closely associate while also giving some attention to contributions from closely competitive schools.

In some significant ways, political competition resembles scholarly competition. Politicians, like scholars, compete in a setting where attention space is limited. Just as it is impossible for a scholar to read everything all other scholars write, so it is impossible for people to pay attention to everything each politician does or says. Thus, politicians operate in a competitive world, just as do scholars. Politicians typically get their start in local politics, with some advancing to higher levels after success at those lower levels. To be sure, not all politicians follow a path from lower to higher levels, but many of them do. Those who don't typically have reputational bases outside of politics and these bases commend them to influential members of their chosen political party.

It has often been noted that all politics is local politics. This simple observation conveys a deep truth about political competition and the difficulty, if not the impossibility, of maintaining independent action among political entities within a federal system. To a significant degree, electoral success is a matter of becoming familiar in a warm way to voters. An important ingredient in attaining such familiarity is to develop a reputation for addressing issues that your voters care about. Within the original constitutional framework, most of the matters of interest to voters stemmed from local and state levels of government. This isn't to deny the importance of the matters of war and peace that were the province of the federal government. It is only to say that those were not issues that people could do much about. In contrast, the condition of schools, roads, or parks were things of concern to many people and, perhaps more significantly, were issues that ordinary people might conceivably have an impact on.

When faced with this type of setting, what might an ambitious politician do? To gain access to limited attention space, a politician must be able to address issues of interest to the various audiences he or she faces. It seems plausible that an aspirant to federal office, in whichever chamber, could get better access to attention space if the topics that he addressed included matters of local interest. To do this, however, required an expansion in the agenda of topics covered by the federal government beyond what was constitutionally enumerated. Securing grants in aid from federal to state and local governments was one means of achieving this expansion. The

Morrill Act that established land-grant universities, for instance, brought the federal government into education, even though, constitutionally, education was the province of states and of individual citizens.

The position of political parties surely reinforces the emergence and growth of cartel federalism. Political parties did not exist at the time of the constitutional founding, but within a few years they had made their presence felt. In the absence of parties, several candidates might stand for office, and those candidates would likely hold a variety of positions. When political parties appear, there is surely a narrowing of the options over which competition occurs. Indeed, this would be one of the primary consequences of the development of parties, particularly in the two-party system that tends to come about when only one candidate is elected per district.

In thinking of competition, people typically think of the competitors as acting independently of one another. Without parties, competition among candidates would reflect this independence. Political parties, however, act as collusive agents by creating coherence among candidates across different levels of elections. Within this context, a natural progression for politicians is to move from local to state offices and then perhaps to national offices. Electoral competition still takes place, but the diversity of opinion expressed through such elections is narrower than it would be without political parties. In other words, the combination of ambitious politicians and political parties that are vertically integrated across all levels of government creates a cartelizing or centralizing tendency due to the ordinary desire of politicians to advance to higher office.

NOTES

1. In this respect, the essays Joshua Epstein (2006) collects cohere around a research program dedicated to the proposition that explanation in social science must be generative, meaning that some larger social configuration is generated through interaction among simpler elements. Similarly, Bruno Latour (2005) argues that social phenomena cannot be reasonably explained by referring to other social phenomena, but must be explained as emerging from some pre-social condition.
2. In *Boom Towns*, Stephen J.K. Walters (2014) attributes the often poor condition of large cities to the promotion of degradation of both private and public property by city officials and their allies. Private property is degraded through increasing taxes to finance added public spending, and public property is degraded by failure to maintain public property in good working order.
3. Rent seeking originated with Gordon Tullock (1967) and is illustrated across a variety of topics in the essays collected in Rowley et al. (1988). A recent collection on rent seeking is Congleton et al. (2008). Where rent seeking is the political equivalent of bribery, rent extraction is the political equivalent of extortion. Fred McChesney (1997) is a lucid treatise on rent extraction.

4. The logic of economizing action: Universal form and particular practice

Chapter 1 explained that the object of most economic theory shifted during the period of neoclassical ascendancy from society to an optimizing individual within that society, and with the presumption of equilibrium allowing reduction of society to that of a representative individual. Entangled political economy is not some new theoretical orientation. It has a long history. As Maria Paganelli (2014) explains, entangled political economy was the dominant theoretical orientation of the classical period of liberal political economy, for at that time society was the object of economic analysis, and with society not being reducible to a set of exercises in optimization by a representative agent. Entangled political economy is little more than a theoretical effort to render society once again as the object at which economic theory aims. Property rights are social relationships, and in this respect it is good to remember that property and propriety have the same root. Property rights denote relationships among the members of a society, and there are countless specific ways property rights might take shape. Once economics is approached as social theory, entangled political economy comes naturally into the analytical foreground. In this respect, Giandomenico Becchio (2014) explains that Carl Menger incorporated entanglement into his vision of political economy. What one owns depends in large measure on what other people allow, as that allowance is mediated through human nature and the relevant institutional arrangements in place within that society.

Within a framework of private property, the properties and qualities of market interaction emerge through the efforts of participants to seek mutual gain. A car manufacturer, for example, will naturally seek to produce cars with qualities that consumers will buy. This typically means that cars will vary in their qualities, as some customers will be willing to pay for equipment that other customers will not. For instance, only some customers might choose to buy expensive back up cameras, so manufacturers make them available on an optional basis. When public ordering enters the scene, back up cameras might become required equipment. As a formal matter, we still speak of a market for cars. As a substantive matter, however, it is a different market for cars in the presence of public ordering than when that market is governed through private ordering alone. Someone could always argue that most people would prefer to be nudged in this direction of greater safety, as Thaler and Sunstein (2008) do. This claim is untestable, but it illustrates the operation of entangled political economy in any case. For instance, the bulk of consumers may have no desire to be nudged into buying back up cameras. Public ordering might instead operate as a type of manufacturers' cartel that increases their net worth through a political transaction that allows the manufacturers, or at least some of them, to sell items that most consumers otherwise would not buy.

While there are some significant differences in the institutional environments within which commercial and political enterprises operate, those differences do not warrant a sharp distinction between business and politics but warrant only recognition that the practice of politics is a peculiar type of business practice. For instance, how might Greyhound differ from Amtrak? Both enterprises largely carry passengers around the country. Greyhound operates buses and is a private corporation that has market value. Amtrak operates trains and is a public corporation that has no market value. Both corporations compete for customers with other vendors that also offer transportation services. It happens that for Amtrak its customer base includes some significant political figures who are able to secure for it an annual appropriation of over $1 billion. Amtrak secures that appropriation within a competitive budgetary process, and with the outcome of that process suggesting that Amtrak must offer service that significant members of Congress support to the extent that they reduce other appropriations so as to keep Amtrak as a going concern (Eusepi and Wagner 2011). This situation doesn't mean that one should cheer whatever a legislature enacts. It means only that the peculiar business activities of politically sponsored enterprises are as susceptible to economic analysis as are the ordinary business activities of market-based enterprises, keeping in mind that entanglement blurs in some significant respect the distinction between political and market enterprises.

All purposive action follows the form of embracing an end and then choosing among means to attain that end. In this respect, someone who puts together a commercial enterprise within the framework of private property is employing one set of means to achieve a desired end. Someone who puts together a political enterprise within the framework of public property is employing a different constellation of means to achieve a desired end. Both categories of entrepreneurial action are purposive, and with the different courses of action reflecting differences among the members of a society with respect to goals, values, and sentiments. In this respect, it is Sentiment that advances objects for Reason to think about, similar to Daniel Dennett's (1978) formulation of a two-stage model of choice. At the first stage, what Dennett describes as a "consideration generator" and what I describe as sentiment advance particular items for reason to think about. At the second stage, reason does its work. In embracing this relation between sentiment and reason, there is no presumption of universality once it is recognized that humanity constitutes a crooked timber from which it is unreasonable to expect straight things to be built (Berlin 1991). The desire to be effective in action is a universal quality of humanity; however, there is no good reason to think there is homogeneity in the purposes at which action aims, even though ideological articulations can give the illusion of such homogeneity (Pareto 1935).

1. FROM ECONOMIZING ACTION TO SOCIAL THEORY: HOW SO?

Society is the analytical object that a theory of entangled political economy explores, and the analytical point of departure for this exploration is a theory of economizing action. The theory starts with individual action to get to society which is the object of interest. If the object of analytical interest is society or social systems, someone versed in Ockham's razor might wonder why not start directly with society. This route would be shorter. It is also the route economists take with their macro-level theories where they construct direct relationships among macro variables. It is, moreover, a route that can accommodate the making of empirical observations, for any variable can be regressed on any other variable. It is not, however, a route that can accommodate theoretical explanation of social processes and social change. To try to do this is to play a form of shell game. If the object is society, how can change come about? Once society has been reduced to point-mass status, change is impossible other than through society being acted upon by some outside source similar to what Figure 2.1 illustrated, only for a society, unlike an individual within society, there is no such outside source.

The framework of entangled political economy accommodates recognition that societies change only through individual action inside those societies, and with those actions spreading within the society according to the receptivity of other members of that society to those changes. This is the vision conveyed by Figure 3.2, where all change originates at the action level. The object of analytical interest is society, but it is impossible to develop anything other than simple description from a societal point of departure. To develop theoretical explanations, it is necessary to peer into the object denoted as society, which means in turn that society will have to be construed as possessing some form of networked structure. To say this is not to deny meaning to the claim that society as an object acts on individuals through a form of downward causation. It is only to argue for a type of bi-directional interaction (Wagner 2010a; Lewis 2012). Only individuals undertake action, but as social creatures bound up in various practices, conventions, and organizations that have emerged through preceding interactions, societal configurations feed back onto individual action. It is always possible to offer descriptive statements about macro or societal phenomena, as illustrated by statistical associations between interest rates and investment; however, any meaningful analytical statement that pertains to the macro entity denoted as society must make connections with individuals inside the society, for it is those individuals and their connections that drive societal change.

Consider Harold Demsetz's (1967) oft-cited claim that societies shift from common to private property when it is economically efficient to do so. Never mind the claim about economic efficiency, and focus instead on the object called society as making this shift to a more efficient form of ownership. How is it possible that "society" can do this? The answer, of course, is that it can't. As a linguistic convention we speak of a society as making a shift in its property arrangements. Yet we know this is just a manner of speaking. If we truly wanted to explain how this shift comes about, we have to leave the macro or societal level. Immediately, we have an object of theoretical inquiry that is more complex than standard theoretical formulations. Conventional comparative static formulations compare societal states at different moments, t_1 and t_2, and attribute the difference to some difference in relevant data. In the case Demsetz examined, fur-bearing animals were scarcer in t_2 than in t_1, and this could be characterized as a rise in the full price of those animals.

It's possible that this rise in price would lead to the establishment of alienable ownership over animals, but this isn't a necessary or inexorable result of that rise in price. In any event, to deal with movement through time requires some form of emergent dynamics where the object of analytical interest itself changes through time. It is the interval $|t_1 - t_2|$ that is the object of analytical interest. This interval is one where change is taking place within the societal object, and the analytical challenge is to give an account of that change, and with analytical narratives being one means for doing so (Bates et al. 1998). In the case at hand, we might start the analysis of how state t_1 was transformed into state t_2 over some interval by imagining some of the responses people on the ground might have made to the increasing difficulty they found in catching fur-bearing animals. The range of possible responses is perhaps limited only by the imagination of people on the ground.[1] Some responses might be relatively passive, as in some people making overnight trips to catch game where before they were away only several hours. Other responses might be relatively aggressive, as when someone who doesn't feel like taking a long trip ambushes or even kills someone who has already made his catch and is headed home. Whatever kinds of particular responses might arise as this situation unfolds, we would also expect to find concerns about this situation becoming of societal interest. Once again, this interest can be expressed in myriad ways. I use this illustration not to review Demsetz's use of the history in that period, however, but simply to illustrate that a theory whose analytical object is society must nonetheless start with economizing individuals and not society because the only theoretically workable path to the societal level must run through individual action.

The micro–macro distinction within economic theory is a non-informative distinction that reflects the various liabilities that accompanied the ascendancy of neoclassical economics. A far superior distinction is that between praxeology and catallaxy. Praxeology pertains to individual action. Catallaxy pertains to interaction among individuals within society. While economic reasoning begins with praxeology, most phenomena of analytical interest are catallactical. Look at the objects that are commonly treated within micro theory: prices, firms, markets. If micro pertains to individual action, these objects are macro objects. Yet they are treated as micro objects to distinguish them from those aggregate variables that are treated as macro objects. This micro–macro distinction is deeply incoherent because it treats some types of interaction as macro while treating other types as micro, based on nothing more than the size or the extent of the interaction. Hence, the division of firms into distinct industries is to create micro entities, while their aggregation is to create a macro entity. This is nothing but incoherence, for all firms beyond proprietorships involve collective phenomena and are products of interaction or catallaxy. To describe them as products of catallaxy is not, however, to transport them into a different analytical category, as the micro–macro distinction would do, for it is always economizing action that drives catallactical interaction. The only analytically coherent distinction to employ in developing a social-theoretical approach to political economy is the distinction between individual action and societal interaction, or between praxeology and catallaxy.

Social theory in this vein turns on the I–We distinction (Elias 1939 [1991]). The pure theory of a market economy is one idealization of that distinction where all relevant action is carried out by individuals under one of two situations. One situation is a regime of wholly private property as conveyed by standard economic theory. In this case the collective level is truly inert, as it exists only as statistical aggregates. The other situation is in a society bound by tradition. This might fit the feudal scheme with its estates and obligations. While estates and obligations created structure, that structure empirically was treated as fixed and pretty much invariant. We may doubt that any social structure is truly invariant, but once we start traveling down this analytical road we find that structural patterns are generated through interaction in the same manner as market prices are generated through interaction. This brings us into the world of entangled political economy where the I–We relationship is not invariant but rather is subject to change through continuing contestation at one margin of interaction or another. The energy required to drive that contestation is supplied by economizing individuals who are always engaged in seeking preferred states of affairs within their own precincts of interest. To be sure, people can differ in their precincts of interest, and such differences are significant sources of internally generated societal disturbances, as distinct from the placidity of equilibrium theory.

2. ECONOMIZING ACTION: A UNIVERSAL QUALITY OF HUMANITY

All too often economists have portrayed people in such capacities as consumers roaming through a grocery store. People do such things, of course, but this type of activity is only a small portion of the range of purposeful human action that forms the subject matter of economic theory. All purposeful action is open to economic analysis. There is a universal form to which all purposeful action conforms, but it should also be acknowledged that there are myriad differences in the environments in which action occurs, which lead to substantive differences in the content of human action. This distinction between the form of purposive action and its substantive content and context must always be kept somewhere in the mind's background and occasionally brought into the foreground, because otherwise confusion can arise in treating politics as a peculiar type of business.

The first thing to be said about economizing action is that it is action of a practical and not a theoretical sort (Bourdieu 1990, 1998). Such action involves people in doing things that matter to them. All practical activity is capable of being illuminated by economic theory because all of it has the formal quality of people selecting among options to achieve some purpose or objective. All practical action conforms to the form where people make choices among options for attaining the objective of their action. There are different ways an action can be pursued, and people are described as picking what they perceive to be the best option for advancing their purpose. This doesn't mean they will be right or will be happy with the result. It means only that the principle that there is an economizing logic behind all purposive action provides a useful framework for rendering purposeful action intelligible to an outside observer.

Action A is undertaken when action B could have been undertaken because the actor regarded A as offering the more effective path to the desired objective. Many textbook illustrations are of such a simple nature as shopping in a grocery store where a consumer is treated as maximizing a utility function subject to a budget constraint. There is nothing wrong with such simple illustrations so long as it is recognized that these pertain to a small part of the realm of human practice. The praxeological principle is a purely formal principle for ordering thought. It is not a substantive principle whose applicability can be tested in particular situations. Praxeology speaks to the form of practical action and not to its substance. That people pursue their objectives with the intention of being effective rather than ineffective is not something that can be tested. It would be silly to think that people purposively seek to pursue something they desire in a knowingly ineffective manner. Should someone think a person is doing that, that person's objective cannot be what the observer thinks it is or should be. In this respect, Thomas Szasz's (1961) claim that mental illness is mostly a dubious concept is a sound application of the praxeological principle. To be sure, there may be actions open to the person that the person does not know about and would pursue if he or she knew about them. But to raise this possibility is just to say that no one knows everything and that people will often choose courses of action that they might not choose were they omniscient, though they will also dedicate effort to expanding their knowledge relevant for the environments in which they act.

In short, all purposive action obeys the praxeological principle in seeking to economize on the means used in pursuing desired actions. This purely formal principle says nothing about the objectives someone chooses to pursue. We may speak of rational choice as being the formal theory associated with the praxeological principle, but we should also recognize that rationality is associated with deployment of the faculty of reason. The objects that reason thinks about are not themselves outcomes of rational thought *ad infinitum* but are selected by the emotional faculty denoted as sentiment (Damasio 1994; Noteboom 2007). It is sentiment that proposes objects for reason to think about. People do what they do because they choose to do so, and they seek to be effective in what they do. Why they do what they do is in good measure outside praxeology. If there is a widespread belief within a society in the reality of witches, as there was in the Middle Ages, such social practices as trials for witchcraft could be a readily understandable feature of competition among religious orders for support, as Peter Leeson (2012) explains. The different environments within which humans act, moreover, are themselves generated through human interaction and so are emergent products of such interaction. Hence, people act within a particular environment and yet generate new environments in the process, and in a continuing and open-ended manner. This situation doesn't deny the possibility of environmental modification. To the contrary, it asserts the inevitability of such modification; however, such modification is a product of emergent interaction and not of some person's rational choice, even that of a Very Big Player (Koppl 2002), although a Very Big Player typically will surely exert more influence over environmental change than will a Very Small Player.

3. ECONOMIZING ACTION: FROM WHERE COMES SUBSTANCE?

Economizing action is the formal point of entry into a theory of social economy and entangled political economy. It should be kept in mind that praxeology is purely formal. It doesn't speak directly to the substance of action. That substance has both biological and social origins. An isolated Robinson Crusoe illustrates mostly biological sources of action, though with curiosity and imagination also being present. The human organism has natural needs and desires. Some of these reflect absolute needs, the absence of which for long means death. Other of these are relative, or at least more so. People can live outdoors while it is raining or snowing, but they prefer to have shelter from rain and snow. People can tolerate wide variation in temperatures, but they generally prefer temperatures not too far from 70 degrees Fahrenheit or 20 degrees Celsius.

Once Crusoe is recognized to live in society, the substance of action acquires numerous social origins outside of the ordinary gains from specialization that economists typically emphasize. With respect to seeking shelter, for instance, a Crusoe in society will be able to secure better housing than he could on his own, due to the ability of specialization within the division of labor to multiply his effective productivity. This illustrates a biologically based activity where the actor's capacity is multiplied through the division of labor. By activities that have genuine social origin, I mean the types of activity that would never be part of Crusoe's repertoire while living alone. This constellation of activities involves people in interacting with other people and having preferences about their actions and even characters. Life in society involves people living in close proximity to one another. While people can be supportive of one another, they can also be annoying to one another. In these and many other respects, life in society can also be a source of activity that would not be part of Crusoe's biologically based repertoire.

When economics is treated as a science of rational action with society serving merely as background, the activities people pursue are treated as residing wholly within themselves. When economics is treated as a genuine social science, however, other people can also become objects of action in various ways. A Robinson Crusoe might be portrayed as playing a game against nature. When multiple Crusoes inhabit the same space, however, they can also play games with and against each other, which Bernard Suits (1967) conveys to good effect in asking "Is Life a Game We are Playing?" The orientation Suits describes fits with a scheme of thought where social life is a self-organized improvisational drama where the players respond to one another and where novelty is continually injected into the drama through the exercise of creative imaginations. Each person might reflect some teleology, but the drama itself evolves through interactions that occur within a framework of nested games (Tsebelis 1991), in contrast to efforts to inject teleology into the analysis by reducing society to some play of a universal game. Conflict is a significant part of any drama, as nothing but cooperation can easily turn dull. Even with respect to what is generally described as cooperation, it is surely conflict that piques the interest. While people clearly have talent for and interest in being cooperative, they are also nosey and quarrelsome creatures. While a desire for approbation is often noted to work as a generally civilizing sentiment, the rankings that accompany approbation are also a source of envy (Lovejoy 1961). Cooperative activities into which novelty is injected can quickly enter into conflict as some people appreciate the novelty while others don't. While it's true that open competition keeps everyone alert, there is also plenty of evidence that successful competitors also breed a good deal of envy as well as stimulating a good deal of regulation (Schoeck 1969).

No one will appreciate a game where ten people try to pass a ball up and down a court to maximize the aggregate number of baskets they make during 40 minutes. Indeed, we wouldn't even call that a game. To become a game, there must be opposition and conflict. The world surely wouldn't run without opposition, and with cooperation arising out of opposition. What is described as a commercial society entails one characteristic form of game where people compete to provide services that other people will buy. The rules of private property and freedom of contract frame this game just as the rules of basketball frame another game. Human society is an ecology of games, and with there being no prior agreement on the types of games to be played. The games that are played are rather products of the creative imaginations of the participants, where exercise of that imagination entails injecting novelty into the substantive activities that people undertake. On numerous prior occasions where people burned themselves through spilling coffee, the response might have been to apply some salve and let the burn heal. At one moment, however, an imaginative lady retains a lawyer to file a suit, the outcome of which is, among other things, to change the way coffee is dispensed through drive-through windows at fast-food restaurants.

In the sense of Suits (1967), everyone but hermits is playing games, and with myriad different games being played, as Johan Huizinga (1950) explains in depth in his examination of play as a cultural phenomenon. What arises is a self-organized drama where societal characteristics are emergent and not chosen. This emergent quality of societal characteristics can create psychic consternation for people who like to identify themselves as seeking to reform society because emergent qualities are not chosen qualities. In this respect, the sociologist James Coleman (1990: 28) explained:

> Within this conceptual structure the only *action* takes place at the level of individual actors, and the "system level" exists solely as emergent properties characterizing the system of action as a whole. It exists only in the sense that there is behavior of the system. Nevertheless, system-level properties will result, so propositions may be generated at the level of the system. (Coleman's italics)

Within the framework of private property and freedom of contract, the substance of action is directed into types of activity that provide services that other people are willing to pay for from their own wealth. This is the simple economics of mutual gains from trade extended to a societal level, which promotes flourishing among societal participants and leads to societies dominated by commerce. It was in the context of commercial societies that Joseph Schumpeter (1934) explained that entrepreneurship was the locus of leadership within commercial societies. In the time since Schumpeter wrote, political figures have clearly increased their presence in positions of societal leadership. Private property and freedom of contract are necessarily incomplete within societies; moreover, it is doubtful whether such a society can sustain itself against ordinary human sentiments as illustrated by Samaritan's dilemmas writ large (Buchanan 1975a). The pure theory of a market economy maps onto a culture of independent persons each of whom is able to make his or her way in society. Yet modern society has evolved into forms that have significant precincts dominated by dependence. When measured by consumption, few people are truly destitute in the United States. Yet a good number of people avoid destitution not by earning their own way in society but by receiving modern forms of alms.

Within a societal setting of multiple Crusoes, people can be objects of other person's actions. People have 24 hours per day, and work days have shrunk roughly to half of what they were a century ago. What do people do with their added non-working time? Some might spend it watching television, but many people clearly prefer to do things that entail a more active form of engagement. The range of such activities is limited only by one's imagination. Many of these activities would be limited in scope and contained within the principles of property and contract, as illustrated by playing golf or bridge. But other possible activities would expand outside the scope of property and contract, as illustrated by the organization of clubs to contest what other people might do with their property. For instance, a woman whose husband and daughter were killed in an automobile accident on a rainy night involving a clunky old car with defective windshield wipers and brakes, along with a burned out headlamp, might devote a good amount of time to create a public relations campaign to support prohibition on driving cars more than ten years old. Creativity is at work in the games people create and play (Suits 1967), and there is no necessary reason to presume that all of those games would conform to the standard form of commercial game based on acceptance of existing patterns of property rights. In this context there would seem to be good evidence that games of domination and subordination are part of human society and have durability going for them. While economizing action is a universal quality of humanity, the autonomy of the political within society is also a universal quality. Entangled political economy looks to integrate the autonomy of the political with the autonomy of economizing action.

4. ECONOMIZING ACTION AND THE AUTONOMY OF THE POLITICAL

Entangled political economy rests on the twin autonomies of the political and the economic in society, and with interaction between those autonomies being a source of turbulence within society. The autonomy of economizing action is easy enough to understand, for it expresses the idea that people seek to be effective and not ineffective in their intentional actions. The autonomy of economizing action is a metaphysical organizing principle for social theorizing and not a testable proposition derived from a theory. To refer to the autonomy of economizing action is not, however, to treat all such action as genetically or biologically determined, such as seems to be implicit in common references among economists to maximizing given utility functions. Humans are biological creatures for which some categories of action are required to keep the human organism alive.

Yet most of humanity long ago escaped living at the margin of substance, and this escape surely expanded the significance of social interaction in shaping the substance of what economists denote as utility functions, by rendering other people in various ways as objects of action and not just as other acting subjects, despite Martin Buber's (1958) well-known ethical disapproval of people treating other people as objects.

To assert the autonomy of the political seems superficially to clash with the traditional or classical notion of a society of free and independent individuals, perhaps still associated most strongly with John Stuart Mill (1863). This notion of liberalism appears to seek to reduce the political to some combination of economics, law, and ethics. The reduction to economics reflects the autonomy of economizing action. The reduction to law reflects the idea of a rule of law as replacing a rule of men, about which Rajagopalan and Wagner (2013) voice skepticism. The reduction to ethics reflects a presumption that humanity can will itself to be governed along the principles of one of those peaceable kingdom paintings where lions are lying with lambs. This reduction means in turn a denial of Isaiah Berlin's (1991) assertion, following Immanuel Kant's (1784) recognition that the crooked timber of humanity will allow nothing straight ever to be built. In contrast, acceptance of the Kant–Berlin formulation, which is also the formulation of numerous scholars throughout the ages, places the reduction of the political to ethics in the domain of wishful thinking.

These days, the autonomy of the political is most directly associated with Carl Schmitt (1932), whose thinking Renato Cristi (1998) describes as authoritarian liberalism and which Eckhard Bolsinger (2001) describes as political realism.[2] However Schmitt's scheme of thought is described, something similar was voiced by numerous scholars around the same time that Schmitt wrote. Vilfredo Pareto (1915 [1935]) was one such notable scholar whose distinction between logical and non-logical action likewise generated autonomy for the political in society. Similarly, Friedrich Wieser's (1926) exposition of power as rooted in a human nature common to rulers and ruled operates to similar effect despite differences in their theoretical articulations. Furthermore, the untranslated second edition of Carl Menger's *Principles of Economics* is more congruent with the Wieser–Pareto type of formulation than is the first edition, as Giandomenica Becchio (2014) explains in her comparison of the 1871 and 1923 editions of Menger's *Principles*. For the most part, liberal opposition to the autonomy of the political is hortatory in character, as illustrated by Anthony De Jasay (1985, 1997). In contrast, this book embraces the autonomy of the political on explanatory grounds resident within human nature.

The autonomy of the political reflects recognition that power is ever present in society, along with recognition that people differ among themselves in both abilities and interests as these pertain to the relative attractiveness of comparatively introversive and extroversive lines of activity. In this respect, participation in political activity seems likely to hold generally stronger appeal for relatively extroversive types who find public interaction to be a source of energy rather than draining it away. While the autonomy of the political appears in the surface impression that a small number of rulers dominate large masses of citizens, that surface impression hides the sub-surface recognition that power is latent in human nature, and which manifests itself in numerous particular ways historically. That latency and its particular manifestation starts from recognition that humans could potentially be studied within the rubric of ethology as the study of the higher mammals, as against being studied as an independent species. To be sure, we know things about humans by virtue of experience and reflection that we don't know in similar fashion about chimpanzees, wolves, or dogs, among the social mammals that ethologists study (Franklin 2009). While the social mammals engage in cooperation, they are also hierarchical. So, too, are humans. While there may be little difference between a street porter and a philosopher (Levy and Peart, eds. 2008) when operating alone in Crusoe-like fashion, differences arise in societal settings, increasingly so as societal complexity increases as represented by an increasingly stratified division of labor, and with those differences both promoting hierarchy and intensifying the autonomy of the political.

To refer to human sociality is not necessarily to refer to something pleasant. Sociality might be pleasant, but often it is not. Sociality refers simply to orientations and activities that involve a multiple of people, and so are not phenomena recognizable to a Robinson Crusoe. The social mammals mostly exist in cooperative packs. A pack of wolves can bring down a moose even though the aggregate weight of those wolves is less than that of the moose. From time to time, quarrels will arise among the wolves in a pack, and with one of the quarreling wolves emerging as the leader of the pack. The social mammals display cooperation, conflict, and hierarchy as inseparable or entangled qualities, and human societies are no different in this regard.

Sociality can be pleasant, as conveyed formally by the idea of gains from trade and substantively by such images as dancing, going to shows, or playing cards. But sociality can also have an unpleasant side, even if precious few people would prefer to live as isolated hermits, as illustrated formally by the idea of forcible imposition and substantively by such images as being robbed, being prohibited from starting a business, and being imprisoned. Arthur Lovejoy (1961) explains that ranking and respectfulness are qualities of human nature, and with approbation typically treated as a positive virtue. Yet ranking and approbation can also play out negatively, leading to envy, and perhaps with envy inspiring domination. Indeed, approbation is both positive and negative, which is easy to see once it is filtered through recognition of the crooked timber of humanity (Berlin 1991), and which leads directly into recognition of the autonomy of the political. That autonomy is grounded on two reasonable presumptions, one anchored in limited knowledge and the other anchored in human nature.

With respect to limited and divided knowledge (Hayek 1937, 1945), as societal complexity increases, social distance increases among the various instances of street porters and philosophers. The social distance among a farmer, a blacksmith, and a wheelwright is surely relatively small in comparison with the social distance among a refuse collector, an electrician, and a surgeon. With respect to the first trio, it is reasonable to think that each member of that trio could form a genuinely sympathetic understanding of the activities of the others, by which I mean that any one of that trio could observe the actions of the other two and seek to duplicate them. That duplication might be sufficiently awkwardly performed that customers would not want to buy the product, but it would be possible for the one meaningfully to step into the shoes of the other two all the same. In contrast, no genuine sympathy, as distinct from a possibly formal and abstract sympathy, seems plausible among the second trio. The ever increasing division of labor and knowledge would seem to shift the etiology of social sympathy from the realm of substance and experience to the realm of abstraction and conceptualization as a consequence of the limited and divided quality of the entirety of knowledge that is at work within a society.

From this divided quality of knowledge, human nature does the rest of the work in intensifying the autonomy of the political. For Schmitt (1932), the autonomy of the political rested on exceptional circumstances and the friend–enemy distinction. Exceptional circumstances mean that a rule of law cannot be articulated that will cover every possible point of decision that might arise. The presence of exceptions is a point where the autonomy of the political enters into society. The friend–enemy distinction is a feature of the crooked timber of humanity that surely intensifies with increases in societal complexity and the hierarchical ordering in terms of status that comes in the wake of growing complexity. In the wake of their ability to perform one another's activities, it is reasonable to think of the blacksmith and the wheelwright according equal rank on a scale of respect, as that ranking is shaped through actual practice. This situation is surely different as between a refuse collector and a surgeon. The equal ranking between blacksmith and wheelwright would surely give way to an ordering of higher and lower with regard to a scale of respect, at least as this ranking is shaped through experience and practice. To reword one of Pareto's formulations: there is no common metric of respect that can be aggregated across sheep and wolves, even if societal arrangements might be generated that allow both to operate in the same geographical territory.

5. RATIONALITY AND LOGICAL VS. NON-LOGICAL ACTION

Vilfredo Pareto (1935: 75–230) distinguished between logical and non-logical action, and Pareto's distinction has great significance for entangled political economy. The first thing that should be said about this distinction is that it has nothing to do with any distinction between rationality and irrationality. Pareto thought all action was rational, and in this respect his orientation was similar to Thomas Szasz's (1961) claim that mental illness was a piece of mythology in that it applied a medical terminology to what was really a moral issue. Someone who doesn't feel like going to work could be called lazy or labeled a malingerer. Alternatively, that person could be described as suffering from some form of stress disorder. The latter option allows the person to feel better about himself while also perhaps qualifying for some form of welfare relief and also payment for the medical diagnostician. For Pareto, all action was rational, but there were different environments in which action occurred. The substance of rational action varied across environments even though the form of rationality was invariant to environment, which is similar to Gerd Gigerenzer's (2007) treatment of rationality as entailing a relationship between an actor and an environment.

From the point of view of an acting subject, all action is rational, unless the subject has reason to tell you otherwise. Pareto accepted this quality of action from the subject's point of view. Pareto's distinction, however, is formulated from the objective point of view. This is the point of view of an observer who is classifying actions into categories. In this respect, Pareto argued that actions mostly fell into one of two categories and, furthermore, it was generally apparent into which category an action fell. All action has the same formal structure: a person acts in response to a desire to achieve some objective. In some cases there is a direct connection between action and objective that can be rendered sensible to an external observer and which can be tested through experience. In other cases there is no such connection that an external observer could see, and those actions would be non-logical. One quality of the crooked timber of humanity, however, is the desire and the ability to give a logical-sounding account of all actions. These accounts Pareto described as derivations, though they are better known today as rationalizations to denote the use of rational-like language to justify an action.

For the most part, logical action is the domain of markets while non-logical action is the domain of politics and religion, though this mapping from action to domain is not exact. Someone wants to buy a comfortable armchair. After examining a few, the buyer makes a choice. The buyer takes the action of buying an armchair with the objective of having a comfortable place to sit. There is a short link between the action and the objective at which the action aims. Moreover, the chairs carry prices, and these prices facilitate the appraisal of tradeoffs between differences in qualities among the chairs and differences in prices. Within this kind of environment for action, it is plausible to claim that action exhibits the quality of a logical appraisal of options that can also be tested through what Pareto called the logico-experimental method. The speaker will always assert that he or she has made a logical or rational choice. Pareto's logico-experimental approach asks whether an external observer would reach the same judgment of a logical appraisal among options where that appraisal can be tested by experience or experiment. In market settings this is generally the case, but often it is not in political settings. To use an illustration Andrew Bongiorno (1930) used in his exposition of Pareto's sociology, rowing across a sea to go somewhere would illustrate logical action, for it can be demonstrated that rowing moves the boat forward in the water. In contrast, making a sacrifice to Poseidon to calm a storm-tossed sea would be a non-logical action because it cannot be demonstrated experimentally that making a sacrifice calms a sea. There could well be instances when this would happen, but this would be coincidence. All the same, making a sacrifice could be rational for people who believed in the reality of Poseidon.

Non-logical action denotes actions for which there is no logical connection between action and outcome. Many of these environments for action are those where prices don't exist, which renders impossible the appraisal of tradeoffs. One recognizable set of human actions involves making charitable contributions to various organizations. Whether one buys an armchair or contributes to a charity, the form of the interaction is the same: there is an exchange of money for service in both cases. With the charitable organization, however, the link between action and consequence is indirect, perhaps vague, and is non-logical in any case (Tullock 1971). In the absence of prices, there is no logical basis for the appraisal of options. A buyer of an armchair has a reasonable basis for deciding whether a more comfortable chair is worth the higher price. A donor to a charitable organization cannot make such a comparison, both because prices are absent and because the services offered are more on the order of credence goods than inspection or experience goods.

Vendors recognize that they operate within an environment where action is predominately non-logical, and modify their strategies to fit the environment. Pareto recognized that one feature of human nature is the desire people have to feel good about their actions. In settings dominated by logical action, that feel-good quality arises as a consequence of being satisfied with market choices. In settings dominated by non-logical action, the direct link between choice and consequence vanishes, which takes with it the ability to feel good about actions through directly experiencing the consequences of those actions. This situation means that the survival prospects of vendors would be weak without some type of compensating action to overcome the absence of experience. One form of compensating action is ideological in character, and entails the purveyance of images that allow the actor to feel good about his or her actions despite the inability logically to adopt that feel-good posture (Boulding 1956) by relating experience directly to action. In this respect, the ability of symbols to evoke strong emotions and actions should be kept in mind.

The entitlements of the welfare state can be summarized by Herbert Hoover's aphorism: "a chicken in every pot." True, this is quite a small entitlement, but it would be easy enough to multiply the level of the guarantee. In his address on the battlefield at Gettysburg in 1863, Abraham Lincoln recognized that the first American constitutional document entitled Americans to life, liberty, and the pursuit of happiness, and nothing more. Chickens in pots and other entitlements came later. Perhaps the most significant quality of the theory of economic equilibrium is its explanation of the interconnected quality of all economic activity within society. Whatever statement that is made in the context of a product market implies some complementary and consistent statement about the factor market that would render sensible that statement made about the product market. Therefore, an entitlement program that offers a chicken in every pot would require an equivalent statement that promised a period of servile labor to staff the chicken farms necessary to put chickens in pots.

Logical action would seek to determine whether the chicken was worthwhile in light of the labor required to work on the chicken farm. Should people apply the same logic to the chicken as they applied to the armchair, they might reject the chicken. But sentiment will dominate reason in this instance because the environment for action does not create a direct link between action and consequence, unlike with the armchair. This environment is still one where people want to feel good about themselves, as is universally the case. Political competition will accommodate that desire by avoiding references to forced labor in extolling entitlement programs. Such programs, moreover, will be conveyed through images of people being deserving of what they receive, for this would fit comfortably with natural sentiments. Widespread references to social contracts and similar images exemplify the creation of images that give a veneer of rationality, as if the program were a product of logical choice. In this there are lessons to be learned from the titling of legislative acts. They all apply a veneer of rationality to what is in no way a logical action. For instance, what recently was titled the Affordable Care Act necessarily must make medical care more costly in the aggregate, but legislation is not titled to summarize some underlying logic of the situation. Rather it is titled to polish the image so as to resonate with sentiments within significant parts of the population. Following Gigerenzer (2008), the substance of rational action depends on the environment within which actors act.

6. THE RECIPROCAL RELATIONSHIP BETWEEN COST AND CHOICE

Choice and cost bear a reciprocal relationship that stems ultimately from the social-theoretic framework for economic analysis. All action involves choices among options. A person faces two options, and must choose one over the other. This situation is faced continually throughout life. It's what economists mean by scarcity. The cost of choosing a particular option is the perceived value of the alternative option that was not pursued (Wicksteed 1910; Buchanan 1969). To choose the more valuable option is the same thing as choosing the less costly option, recognizing that it is individuals who choose, even if sometimes they are choosing for collective entities. Every choice in favor of one option thus involves a renunciation of some alternative action that could have been chosen but which was rejected. In this manner, all actions reflect individual appraisal of the relevant options as those people see them. With respect to such stylized formulations as a consumer moving through a store or Robinson Crusoe alone on his island, the relation of cost to choice doesn't much matter. For many of the other situations in which people pursue purposive actions, however, the reciprocal relation between cost and choice has significant analytical implications that are difficult if not impossible to grasp without recognizing that reciprocal relationship. To see how this is so requires some examination of the different types of environments in which action can occur.

For such actions as a consumer passing through a store, the applicable conventions of private property mean that whatever the consumer buys reduces the consumer's net worth from what it would otherwise have been. The consumer bears the value consequences of whatever choices he or she makes in the store. There are other environments in which people can act where this direct relationship of residual claimacy does not hold. For instance, a club could hold a banquet at a restaurant. As a practical matter in this kind of situation, the banquet would offer a set menu at some fixed price. As a thought experiment, however, suppose the club allowed everyone to choose what they wanted off the menu and then settled the aggregate account by dividing the total bill evenly among the membership. The reasonable expectation in this situation is that the aggregate bill and hence each individual's bill will be larger than what it would otherwise have been. If there are only two entrées, carrying prices of $30 and $50, there would be some mix of the two entrées chosen whenever people paid their bills individually. When the bill is paid collectively under the rule of equal division, there will be some people who would otherwise have ordered the $30 entrée who will order the $50 entrée instead. If the club had 100 members, a member who chooses the $50 entrée over the $30 entrée bears a cost of 20 cents for making that choice, as the remainder is spread over the rest of the membership. In this simple setting, different environments in which people act influence the costliness of their actions. Suppose 80 members choose the $30 entrée under individual responsibility. The aggregate bill would be $3,400 or $34 per member on average, though the average figure is of no relevance under individual responsibility because no one pays that amount. Suppose under collective responsibility, 80 members choose the $50 entrée. The aggregate bill would now be $4,600 or $46 per member which is what everyone pays.

That different outcomes arise under different environments within which action occurs is not news, yet there are numerous instances where this dichotomy between individual action and collective outcome plays out that are less well understood. This distinction arises repeatedly when people refer to aggregate magnitudes accompanied by some suggestion that those magnitudes should induce people to adopt particular courses of action in light of those magnitudes. Someone might claim that extending a subway might save $1 billion compared to building a highway along the same route. Set aside any concern about the correctness of this comparison by assuming it is correct. Yet the highway is chosen over the subway. One could always use that comparison as a basis for complaining about the foolish or even evil qualities of political action. As an explanatory matter, however, it must be the case that the highway was the lower cost option *for those who were able to make that choice*. The aggregate magnitude is just a statistical construction that reflects some projection over a body of people. But action is always taken by particular people in light of the options they face on the ground. If the highway is chosen over the subway, this must mean that the anticipated cost is lower for choosing the highway *for those who are able to make that choice*. The aggregate magnitude is irrelevant because it does not speak to the relevant options for those who make the choice. This is the simple formality of cost and choice. Behind this formality lies the substantive matter of how to give an account of this difference in perceived cost between those who take action and the aggregate magnitude that appears to point in the contrary direction.

Consider a similar situation within a different environment. A construction company has been hired to build a road for a fixed fee. One set of inputs for building the road would require $10 million more than another configuration of inputs. The corporate executive who assembles the inputs does not pay for those inputs because they are charged to the corporate account. Yet the institutional relationships of corporate governance give stronger reason to think that corporations will pursue the less expensive option than would political enterprises due to various features of residual claimacy. Choosing the more expensive option will reduce the value of the firm. There will be some executives whose compensation is based partly on the value of the firm. The carrot of reward and the stick of punishment will both operate in this situation to give good reason for thinking that less expensive options will tend to be chosen over more expensive ones. The difference in choices within different environments has nothing to do with any comparison among projected aggregate magnitudes. To the contrary, it has everything to do with the appraisals that managers on the ground make in face of their understanding of their relevant options. For one manager, the less expensive option might translate into an end-of-year bonus by virtue of the corporation's scheme for executive compensation. For another manager, perhaps a politically based enterprise, there is no market for ownership and hence no share prices, and compensation is independent of any notion of performance. In this instance, an executive who picks the more expensive option must do so because it is less costly to him. Perhaps doing this will lower the claim on his managerial time without sacrificing any end-of-year bonus or risking dismissal for poor performance.

The reciprocal relationship between cost and choice explains that the choice of one course of action entails the renunciation of some alternative course of action. This is a simple fact of life. The ultimate source of scarcity is time (Becker 1965). There are 168 hours in a week, and the more time we spend doing one thing the less time we will have to do something else. By choosing to devote time to one activity we are renouncing some other activity which we could have undertaken, and the value we ascribe to that renounced option is the cost of the activity we chose to undertake. Truly logical action requires some modicum of time to make necessary comparisons in arriving at a choice, whether of an armchair or of anything else. Non-logical action doesn't require much time, and might require none at all. At most, it requires an *ex post* justification that sounds rational.

Market-based firms have enterprise value. Polity-based firms do not. There is a good deal of literature on bureaucracy that examines differences in modes of operation between firms and bureaus, as illustrated by Gordon Tullock (1965), Anthony Downs (1967), William Niskanen (1971), and Steven Richardson (2011). The general thrust of that literature is that bureaus will perform less efficiently than private firms in doing the same tasks. Rarely, however, do they perform truly identical tasks. The existence of firm value provides a framework for employing various market tests, thereby making contract with the domain of human activity that is governed by logical action. A market-based school that introduces a new curriculum or a new approach to evaluating teachers can be subject to market tests. A polity-based school cannot because the absence of transferable ownership forecloses market tests, as no market value can be established for politically organized schools. Polity-based schooling thus makes contact with the domain governed by non-logical action, which in turn is governed by sentimental expressions that resonate with people's desires to feel good about themselves and their activities.

7. HOW SUBSTANTIVE ACTION VARIES WITH ENVIRONMENTS: SETTLING LEGAL DISPUTES

The formal praxeological principle that people seek to be effective in pursuing their chosen actions can lead to different substantive actions across environments. For instance, a sizeable economic literature examines the resolution of commercial disputes, which Miceli (2005) summarizes. The prime interest of that literature is to explain why most commercial disputes are settled without going to trial. Two parties have a dispute in which one party claims the other party owes $20 million, which the other party denies, and the plaintiff files suit to recover the $20 million. The trial will render a verdict in favor of one of the parties. The plaintiff will receive either $20 million or nothing. The defendant will pay either $20 million or nothing. Suppose we further assume each party will spend $2 million pursuing the litigation.

The aggregate litigation expenses of $4 million provide a region wherein the case might be settled without trial. While trial will return a verdict of $20 million, it will do so at an expense of $4 million, leaving a net verdict of $16 million. If both parties agree that the plaintiff has by far the stronger case, perhaps as conveyed by having a 90 percent chance of being successful, a settlement where the defendant pays $18 million could be agreeable to both parties. The expected reward from trial to the plaintiff is $18 million, but the plaintiff would also save $2 million in legal expenses.

For the defendant, the expected loss from going to trial is $18 million, but the defendant would also save $2 million in legal expenses.

The economizing logic of dispute settlement asks whether there are circumstances under which both parties could gain by settling the dispute rather than going to trial. The basic answer that comes out of this literature is that litigation expenses provide the basis for settlement without trial because the parties are residual claimants to their legal expenses. To the extent the parties have similar perceptions of the outcome of a trial, the scope for settlement expands. Furthermore, such legal procedures as the ability of attorneys to depose witnesses and to discover evidence typically will work to reduce differences between plaintiffs and defendants in the probable outcome of a trial. This formulation about dispute resolution fits disputes between private parties; however, it is not directly applicable to disputes where the plaintiff is a political entity because political entities do not operate within the institutional framework of residual claimacy.

Political plaintiffs are not residual claimants to their legal expenses. Practical rationality plays out differently for political plaintiffs than it does for commercial plaintiffs, as Eisenberg and Farber (2003) recognize in their examination of differences between governmental and private plaintiffs. Their analysis, however, treats costs as pertaining to entities rather than to individual actors inside those entities. For instance, suppose the plaintiff is an environmental agency that is seeking to force a builder to change construction plans in a manner that adds $20 million to the cost of the project while adding nothing of value to future customers. The builder refuses to do this and the agency files suit. The market-based calculus of settlement does not apply in this setting because the political entity is not a residual claimant. Economic calculation still pertains to political entities because executives in those entities always face choices, but the context within which calculation occurs is different. As a formal matter, people always choose more of what they value over less. As a substantive matter, however, what they value depends on the context inside of which they act. The logic of practice must relate cost to choice along the lines Buchanan (1969) sketches. Cost is thus the value an actor places on the option that is displaced in choosing the alternative. The cost of choosing to settle a case is the value of the option that the chooser foregoes by choosing instead to go to trial. The relevant cost, however, pertains to a person who faces a choice, and that cost differs between frameworks of private property and collective property, as Ringa Raudla (2010) notes in her treatment of incorporating institutional considerations into the theory of public finance.

With respect to commercial disputants, options for settling the dispute can be evaluated in terms of their probable implications for the value of the enterprise. For collective entities, however, there is no value for the enterprise. Whatever cost the director of such an agency might sense, it will not be connected to some value for the enterprise because there is no such value. The director will still face a cost–gain calculus, but it will be suitable for that particular environment. Where private parties both speak a language of profit-and-loss, this language is not intelligible to a collective party because that party speaks a different dialect, as it were, one framed in non-logical expressions of public interest. For instance, the head of the agency might desire to run for public office. If so, the choice of settlement might influence electoral prospects by virtue of projecting the agency head favorably before a significant part of the electorate. Settlement will not be pursued to reduce legal expenses because those expenses are created as part of a budgetary process. To reduce legal expenses is equivalent to requesting a lower budget, and this outcome is truly rare. Far more likely is the application of a political calculus to the selection of cases. In such cases, legal expenditures can serve as a form of investment in pursuing such a variety of objectives as seeking elected office, gaining an internal promotion, or securing a position with a private firm. These are all logical actions, the pursuit of which will be polished out of view through ideological buffing of a non-logical type.

8.   PRACTICAL ACTION AND THE DECEPTIVE QUALITY OF BEHAVIORAL ECONOMICS

Praxeology is often described as rational choice theory. This is a reasonable description, but it also invites misunderstanding because rationality is often described as a hypothesis and not as a metaphysical principle for organizing observations about people and their interactions. Understood as a hypothesis that is subject to confirmation or rejection, rationality reflects two presumptions: people act consistently and they calculate accurately. In other words, people are logicians and mathematicians. If asked to rank a set of options they will give the same ranking when asked a number of times. When those rankings require calculation and judgment, they will still give the same ranking which implies they calculate accurately. If rationality is treated as a hypothesis and not as a quality of humanity, it becomes something to which people can conform in varying degrees. And if they conform in varying degrees, it becomes possible to entertain the possibility that some external agent can nudge people to make different choices in a manner that the choosers themselves might agree was better (Thaler and Sunstein 2008).

On a superficial level, praxeology and rational choice seem to have the same referent. For people passing through a grocery store this might be so.

But in general it is not. The two parabolas X^2 and $-X^2$ share a common origin; however they point in opposing directions. A similar situation divides rational choice from praxeology. Rational choice imposes a situation on individuals in which an observer presumes to know in advance a correct answer for that situation. Behavioral economists in this respect often speak of designing experiments so as to induce utility functions in their subjects. Having done this, the results of the experiment can be appraised with respect to how close they came to the induced utility functions. Sometimes closeness is found; sometimes it is not. In any case, the experimenter adopts the position of an instructor in a class on logic or mathematics and grades the performances of the participants in the experiment. The experiment, in other words, is not designed to learn something about people that wasn't previously known. Rather it is designed to grade people against some standard the experimenter has constructed. This analytical procedure is the same one that those economists use to posit a model of competitive equilibrium and then ask how closely reality fits that model.

Praxeology embraces a contrary orientation toward people and their situations. To start, praxeology reflects plausible and not demonstrative reasoning, in contrast to rational choice. People are presumed to want to be effective in their chosen actions, given what they have chosen to do. The observer is not there to judge the subject but is there to learn something about the subject. It is presumed that people seek to be effective in their actions, and the challenge is to learn how they truly appraise their situations and construe their options. One might design an experiment in the hope of uncovering some relevant information. Experimental settings in the social sciences, however, are not identical with experimental settings in the natural sciences, as Pareto (1927: 29–101) explains in his discussion of what he presents as the logico-experimental method. What if the subjects in an experiment deviate from what the experimenter had expected based on the utility functions the experiment was thought to induce? One option is to conclude that people are imperfectly rational. This is the method of rational choice approached experimentally. The other option is to conclude that the experiment did not capture fully the mentalities of those who participated in the experiment. This is the method of praxeology.

Much of the effort to treat rationality as a hypothesis stems from behavioral and experimental economics, and with the result of this work generating claims that a good part of human action violates the hypothesis of rationality. Consider the various experiments with ultimatum games surveyed in Camerer and Thaler (1995). This is a game between two people, designated as Proposer and Responder. Proposer is given some amount of money and is instructed to offer some to Responder. If Responder accepts Proposer's offer, Responder gets what Proposer offered and

Proposer keeps the rest. If Responder rejects the offer, neither Proposer nor Responder gets anything. In the standard discussions of the results of these games, it is typically assumed that rational action requires Proposer to offer Responder a modest sum, which Responder should accept because that modest sum would be more than the nothing that would follow from rejection. The experimental results, however, don't follow this pattern. Many of the results show a nearly even division. Those results also report numerous rejections by Responder when Proposer offers 20 percent or less. In this set of experiments as well as in numerous other types of experiments, findings are reported that are widely thought to challenge presumptions of rational action.

The widespread use of the prisoner's dilemma in models of political economy is a cousin to the claims of behavioral economics that people fail to act with full rationality. Formally, the prisoner's dilemma is a bit different because the prisoners are modeled as acting rationally but are unable to secure an outcome that is within their reach without being nudged into this outcome by some outside authority. There is nothing illogical about the prisoner's dilemma, just as there is nothing illogical about defining rationality to entail a transitive preference ordering. To treat a particular setting as illustrating a prisoner's dilemma and then calling for some outside authority to nudge the participants to an alternative and more preferred outcome is, however, illogical because other explanations can also account for the same observation. In this instance, there are multiple logics that could account for the same observation, and there remains an open question of which if any of the possible logics is most plausible.

In this respect, Figure 4.1 illustrates how the prisoner's dilemma model has been applied to support various types of collective nudge for neighborhood development, as illustrated by the widely cited paper by Otto Davis and Andrew Whinston (1961). While the dilemma is illustrated for two people, it is meant to pertain to a setting with a relatively large number of people. Each person can either make an investment in upgrading property in the neighborhood or can refrain from doing so and deploy that capital to some other use. Figure 4.1 shows that if both (or all) parties were to take the same action they would prefer that they all invest in that property over deploying that capital to other uses. Yet each person would most prefer to make no investment in the neighborhood and would least prefer to be the only person to invest in the neighborhood. Many variations on the situation Figure 4.1 illustrates have been used to argue that collective support for urban development is a nudge that would be beneficial to everyone, as illustrated by the superiority of the (2,2) outcome to the (3,3) outcome.

Just because an illustration like Figure 4.1 can be constructed to make a

	B	
	Positive investment	Zero investment
A Positive investment	2,2	4,1
Zero investment	1,4	3,3

Figure 4.1   Prisoner's dilemma applied to neighborhood development

case for collective action does not mean that Figure 4.1 is truly applicable to that situation. For instance, a person who chooses the zero investment option might be pursuing a plan of assembling parcels of land so as to convert the assembled land into some such other use as a condominium, a shopping center, or an arena. Trying to help maintain the neighborhood in its present status would be contrary to this plan. Furthermore, making that plan public would reduce the value of that plan by increasing the price that would have to be paid to assemble the other parcels.

Returning to the ultimatum games, an alternative explanation for those results is that the experiments fail to capture some significant phenomena that the experiments ignored or mistakenly thought they captured, which is a tack that Vernon Smith (2008) pursues. The ultimatum games, for instance, take as a standard of rationality the presumption of what people would do if they were isolated Robinson Crusoes playing on a computer screen and who would never interact with one another. Both players are, in other words, presumed to be solipsistic or narcissistic. If they were, perhaps the expected results would emerge from the experiments. The failure of such results to emerge would otherwise seem to indicate that the experimenter's standard of rationality is not the standard that pertains to the subjects in the experiments.

Mario Rizzo (2015) illustrates the divergence between praxeology and behavioral economics with respect to an experiment that purports to find intransitive preference orderings. An individual confronts three different-sized slices of the same cake and chooses the middle-sized slice. The experimenter then removes the large slice from the set of options, expecting the chooser to reaffirm the choice in the absence of what would seem to be an irrelevant alternative. The chooser, however, now selects the small slice. Choosing the middle-sized slice over the larger slice could be deemed rational on the basis of some kind of tradeoff between pleasure and calories. To remove the large slice from the set of options does nothing to affect the pleasure–calorie tradeoff, so should not affect the choice—if the behavioral economist's view of the situation is accurate. Praxeology, however, would recognize that the economist's view was inaccurate because choosers always select what they perceive to be higher-valued options. In the case at hand, a pleasure–calorie tradeoff may never have been in play. The relevant tradeoff might have been a pleasure–politeness tradeoff. To pick the largest slice available could have been considered impolite, and the chooser was a polite soul. Removing the largest slice was not removing an irrelevant alternative because the chooser possessed lexicographic preferences that precluded actions that were deemed impolite. With the largest slice removed, the polite chooser has no option but to take the smaller of the two remaining slices.

The central claim of praxeology is that all action is rational as a purely formal matter of necessity. Irrational action is intentionally ineffective action, which does not provide a useful foundation for thought. The rationality principle of praxeological action is purely formal, and with the substance of such action emerging in conjunction with the environment in which the actor acts. All action is rational in that it conforms to the praxeological principle. How effective that action might be in a social environment is a different matter, as there are many environments in which people act. Those manifold environments Pareto (1935) collapsed into two with his distinction between logical and non-logical action, mostly because the theoretical framework he was constructing invoked a distinction between economic equilibrium and social equilibrium for which he mapped kinds of action to types of equilibrium. In developing his distinction, Pareto nonetheless maintained that all action was rational. For Pareto, then, the challenge for an outside observer was to understand the actions being observed and not to criticize those actions by suggesting that the observer could improve the actor's situation by nudging the actor in the direction the observer desired the actor to move. For instance, in his wide-ranging examination of Pareto scholarship on the theory of public finance, Mauro Fasiani (1949: 173) notes that Pareto wanted to explain fiscal phenomena while most fiscal scholars wanted to persuade and indoctrinate in favor of particular programs, with Fasiani then concluding poignantly by reciting Pareto's statement that he didn't think it would be good if too many people pursued scientific over sentimental interests because most people lived more by faith than by logic.

NOTES

1. On this point, Stuart Kauffman (2014) asks rhetorically: "how many ways can a screwdriver be used?" His answer recurs to the unlimited potential of human imagination.
2. Some other thoughtful examinations of Schmitt's thought include Gottfried (1990) and Meier (1995).

5. Reason, sentiment, and electoral competition

George Polya (1945) presents a lucid exposition of how heuristic principles can be brought to bear on solving problems in mathematics. Such heuristic principles must invariably come into play when scholars extend their conceptualizations into new areas of inquiry, for theorists seek to extend similarities from familiar material into the new material while taking due account of the differences between the old and the new. It is hardly surprising that electoral competition was originally the focal point of the extension of economic reasoning into democratic politics. It is common to place governments into three categories depending on how political offices are staffed. With democracies, those positions are staffed through elections. With monarchies, they are staffed through some process of familial succession. With authoritarian regimes of various types, they are staffed through some type of primeval struggle to take and keep power. To be sure, there is more to regimes than the methods by which they are staffed, but it is the electoral method that is common to all democratic regimes. Within that democratic category, those eligible to vote can be a small or a large part of the population, elections can take place by district or at large, the rules of election can support two parties or multiple parties, legislative assemblies may have one or two chambers, and there might be a separate election for president in some cases where in other cases a prime minister is appointed from within the legislature.

In light of these various dimensions, in addition to the numerous other possible dimensions that could be added, it is clear that there are billions of particular ways these possible dimensions can be combined to form a democratic system. Yet there will be one commonality among those billions of combinations: some political offices will be staffed through election. It is easy to understand how elections would be approached within an economic approach to a theory of democracy (Downs 1957). Just as firms compete for support from customers, it would seem reasonable to treat candidates as competing for support from voters. Likewise, it would seem reasonable to think of voters as choosing between or among candidates just as they choose among vendors in buying products. Electoral competition has a structural form that obviously is similar to the market-based competition that economists have studied for a long time. It is an intelligible extension of economic reasoning to think of candidates as offering programs that they think will appeal to voters and to think of voters as voting for the candidate whose program has most appeal to them. From this point of departure, the analytical highway separates into two broad avenues of thought. One stresses what is perceived to be similarities between political and economic competition. The other stresses what is perceived to be differences. Both avenues of thought start with competition as a means for selecting winners from among the entrants to that particular competition, which Wagner and Yazigi (2014) explore while distinguishing between formal and substantive properties of different methods of competitive selection.

1.   FORM, SUBSTANCE, AND SELECTION THROUGH COMPETITION

There should surely be little controversy about the principle that using competition to select who will perform a task will tend to select for superior performance compared with prohibiting competition and making that selection through some form of favoritism. While disagreement about the principle of competition will surely be miniscule, there can still be plenty of room for disagreement about the substantive manner through which the principle is put into play. Some competitions will be wholly quantitative, as in who runs fastest over a particular distance, who throws a javelin the farthest, or who lifts the heaviest weight. Even with these kinds of competitions, there can be controversy over such matters as whether that judgment will be rendered after a single competition or after several competitions within a season. If it is several competitions, further controversy can arise if the rankings of the competitors differed among the particular instances of competition. Still, competitions that can be reduced to some single metric will entail less ambiguity in selecting a winner than forms of competition that require qualitative judgments.

In competitions like platform diving or figure skating, qualitative judgments are in play. To be sure, the sponsors of these kinds of competitions invest effort in coaching judges to reduce variation in their judgments. While degrees of difficulty can be assigned to different dives and moves, human judgment can never be abolished. The possibility of such controversy should not, however, be allowed to detract from recognition that competition selects for excellence in any activity. In those cases where a competition cannot be reduced unambiguously to an ordinal ranking among the competitors, controversy can arise over who won the competition. Yet that controversy will be limited to a small number of the potential competitors because most of those potential competitors will have dropped out along the way or never entered the competition in the first place. Hence it is reasonable to claim that competition selects for excellence in the activity to which the competition pertains, though more so when competition is open than when it is closed. For instance, we will never know what kind of record Satchel Paige could have established had he been able to pitch in the Major Leagues from the start of his career instead of having to wait until 1948 when he was already in his 40s.

The generic form of competition is distinct from the substantive context of any particular competition. The ability of competition to select for excellence is a generic quality of competition. Just what talents or capacities are selected through competition depends on the substantive features that frame that competition. It is necessarily the case that competition grades and orders competitors, but the qualities of the competitors that competition selects for depend on the substantive environment that pertains to that competition. There is no sound reason to expect that excellence in one field of competition will extend to excellence in other fields of competition. Someone can be a fine platform diver without being a terrific swimmer. More generically, someone can be a fine athlete without being particularly good at business. Likewise, someone who is good at politics might not be so good at business.

It is easy enough to understand why a good number of economists have concluded that political competition selects for the same qualities of excellence as does market competition (Wittman 1989, 1995; Persson and Tabellini 2000; Rubin 2002; Besley 2006). In reaching this conclusion, form and substance are merged by asserting that pleasing voters is the same type of competition as pleasing customers. Within these kinds of formulations, politicians are treated as ordinary business people who engage in the same kind of activity as other business people. In contrast, this book is predicated on the proposition that politics is a *peculiar* type of business activity. At the generic level, politics is a competitive activity just as is ordinary business. But it is a peculiar and not an ordinary type of business activity and this peculiarity pertains to and emerges from the particular environment within which selection among competitors occurs. To recur to an earlier example, swimming and diving are both water sports, but diving is a peculiar type of swimming.

2. MARKETS, POLITICS, AND SELECTION THROUGH COMPETITION: SOME GENERICS

To denote markets and polities as offering the relevant environments for exploring the qualitative features of selection through competition for a theory of entangled political economy is to work with some average or representative environment for each type of competition. For instance, market competition can operate under wholly private ordering or it can operate with various mixtures of public and private ordering. Moreover, there are many different ways through which the legal arrangements that encase a system of market competition can be constituted. These possible variations are different substantive environments that are covered by the generic designation of a "market economy." Similarly, political competition can operate within systems of single-member constituencies with two candidates competing for election or within multiple-member constituencies where several of the candidates can be elected. Moreover, a democratic system can be federal or unitary. If it is federal, the national government might have independent authority to raise revenue. Alternatively, that authority could be limited. For instance, its revenues might be granted to it by the states acting in the capacity as a legislative conference. Just as it is reasonable to think that market and electoral environments would select for different qualities, so is it reasonable to think that differences in specific environmental arrangements would likewise select for different qualities. The analysis here, however, will keep to a relatively generic level of comparison.

The prime commonality of market and electoral competition is that a set of candidates seek to be selected through some competitive process. Market competition is judged by a "market test;" electoral competition is judged by an "electoral test." Are these tests identical or nearly so, or are they disparate? Both forms of competition declare some entrants into the competition to be winners and the rest to be losers. This doesn't mean that both forms select for identical qualities, any more than it means that a swimming team could be reasonably selected by watching the candidates dive. There is a structural similarity in that in both types of competitive activity candidates pitch appeals to people who select the winner of that competition. While the competitive form is universal, there is also huge variety in the substantive environments within which competition occurs.

Within a democratic system, voters are similar to the stockholders of a corporation. Voters are the residual claimants in political enterprises. If a polity is badly managed, voters as residual claimants will bear the loss either through higher taxes or through reductions in the quality of public services or both. Politicians and other political officials are similar to a company's officers and directors, in that they direct the course of public affairs on behalf of the citizenry. Electoral competition entails candidates for office competing for support among voters. For the most part, scholars of public choice and political economy have treated that competition as occurring through detailed presentations of plans and programs. Simple observation of electoral campaigns should have put the lie to that notion long ago. There is no doubt that campaigns involve candidates trying to sell themselves to voters, or at least to targeted subsets of voters. Those campaigns do not, however, tax the abilities of voters to concentrate or to reason. As a purely formal matter, competition is competition and that is about all there is to the matter. But form does not dictate substance. The substance of competition can play out in numerous distinct environments, and with different environments leading to different qualitative selections.

To illustrate the distinction between form and substance, compare two distinct environments for holding the same competitive process. For the first environment, suppose a corporation has decided to dedicate one billion dollars to constructing a resort. The company's officers and directors decide to hold a contest between two, or perhaps a few architectural firms. The company's officers and directors are asking the competing architects to set forth their visions of what such a billion dollar resort would look like. The architectural firms compete by designing plans for the resort that they think will secure the support of the company's officers and directors. We may be sure that the presentations and designs of the architectural firms will be laid out in considerable detail. Those details will speak to such things as design of the hotel, golf course, landscaping, and the many other details that will contain the firm's plan for the resort. The architects and the company executives and directors all operate in an environment where the stakes are high in the aggregate and, more significantly, the participants in this competition are all residual claimants with respect to their actions. The firm need not be closely held for the officers and directors to be in this position. Even if the firm is publicly held, the officers and directors are likely to hold significant positions in the value of the firm, including compensation through stock options and related forms of remuneration. This intensity of interest on the part of the officers and directors provides the environment within which the architectural firms must deal if they are to be successful in competing for the firm's business. If the executives select a design that proves unattractive to customers, the firm could face bankruptcy and the executives could become unemployed. The architects are in the same position, for they must convince the company executives that their particular designs will keep the resort out of receivership.

At a superficial or formal level, this competition between the architectural firms resembles the competition between political candidates. Both the candidates and the firms will make presentations designed to win over their respective selectorates (Bueno de Mesquita et al. 2003). But form is distinct from substance. It is after leaving this superficial level that the formal similarity ends and the substantive differences begin, in large measure due to differences in the knowledge-generating properties of the different forms of competition, as Somin (2013) explains in his treatment of how political ignorance can expand as governments expand. The presentations of the political candidates will skim the surface and be filled with sentimental generalities and platitudes. Should a political candidate truly seek to develop a programmatic design similar to what one of the architectural firms would develop, we may reasonably expect interest among the electorate to vanish. Suppose a political candidate tried to act like one of the architectural firms in providing great detail across all areas of action. Campaign presentation would become like academic seminars. People would quickly be deluged with far more information and reasoning than they cared to deal with. Why should they want to listen to such detailed presentations that are often complex and always on a high level of analysis? After all, they are not residual claimants to the value consequences of choosing one candidate over the other.

Whatever those consequences might be, they are diffused throughout the selectorate, only in this case pretty much in proportion to the tax liabilities of different taxpayers, many of whom pay little or even no tax. Political candidates must maintain an audience that has but modest stake in choosing between or among candidates. This reality governs substantive content along lines similar to Bertrand de Jouvenel's (1961) analysis of democratic oligarchy where the need to command an audience places limits on the topics that can be discussed within environments where the potential members of its audience are not residual claimants on their actions. However an election turns out, the value consequences will be diffused over the relevant electorate, in contrast to the concentration of value consequences within market competition. This contrast leads in turn to recognition that electoral competition selects for different qualities than does market competition—at least so long as market competition is privately ordered, as distinct from the admixture of public and private ordering that characterizes modern systems of entangled political economy.

3.   MAGIC NUMBERS AND THE COMPETITIVE SELECTION FOR QUALITIES

Political and economic competitions have different "magic numbers," and this difference leads to differences in the qualities selected by the respective competitive processes, as Podemska-Mikluch and Wagner (2013) explain. By magic number, I mean the number of entities that must be included in a model to tell a coherent story about the object being analyzed. Democratic systems of political economy are transactional or catallactical in character. The transactional settings, however, differ as between markets and polities due to differences in magic numbers, and these differences do much work in generating the phenomena of entangled political economy.

For a market economy, the magic number is two. Two is the number of entities that is necessary to illustrate the central concepts and propositions of the economic theory of markets. It takes two people to trade, and two goods to serve as the objects of trade. Production can similarly be illustrated with the magic number two, in this case with a person choosing some mix of two available inputs to produce an output. The magic number two can even be used to illustrate the formation of a business firm. In this case, two people recognize that they can do better by joining forces than by operating separate enterprises. Alternatively, one person could buy out the other person, converting that other person into a supplier of labor instead of a co-owner. In any case, there is very little with respect to the principles of the economic theory of markets that cannot be illustrated with variations on the theme of the magic number two. Even the resolution of disputes can be understood as a variation on the magic number two. Upon entering a commercial relationship, two people can agree upon a third party to resolve disputes if they can't settle the dispute between themselves. The power of the magic number two resides in agreement or consensus as the central operating principle of commercial activity within an institutional framework governed by private property and freedom of contract.

The situation is strikingly different for democratic polities. There, the magic number is three. The principle of majority voting cannot be illustrated by two people. That principle requires three people to convey its meaning and operation. Electoral competition over any particular office divides the world into supporters of the winning candidate and supporters of the losing candidate. When the various successful candidates enter a parliamentary assembly, there will be a dominant majority and a subordinate minority. Elections create winners and losers, both at the level of individual candidates and at the level of parliamentary assemblies where legislation originates. In two-party systems, there will be a winning and a losing party. In multi-party systems, there will be a majority coalition among the parties, with the remaining parties standing in opposition to the majority coalition. The smallest possible model that features winners and losers is one with three people, two of whom are winners. Most political phenomena require the magic number three for their explanation, though it should also be noted that at the level of theoretical principle there are two forms of the magic number three. One form is factional; the other form is consensual. The former has real presence; the latter is more a normative aspiration than a reality. It was in an effort to make reality conform to that aspiration that the complex structure of governance embodied in the American constitutional framework was created. That that framework never fully reflected the consensual principle is well recognized. That consensual principles have increasingly given way to factional principles as the years have passed is equally well recognized.

4.   MARKET CATALLAXY AND THE MAGIC NUMBER TWO

This difference in magic numbers speaks directly to differences in the selection for qualities as between market and electoral competition. Both types of competition involve participants in putting together deals. Figure 5.1 illustrates a central distinction between market competition and political competition, between the magic number two and the magic number three. Panel A, which shall be examined first, illustrates the central framework of liberal market catallaxy. Panel B, which shall be examined subsequently, illustrates the central framework of a Progressivist-inspired democratic form of catallaxy.

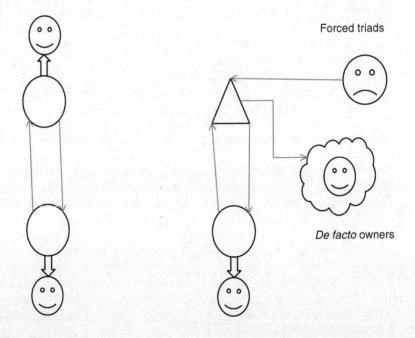

Panel A Pure market   Panel B Political–economic

Figure 5.1   Transactional relationships in political economy

Panel A of Figure 5.1 summarizes the central features of a market catallaxy which can be examined with reference to trade between two people. The two circles connected by the directed arrows on each side illustrate trade between the two parties. The fundamental character of any free exchange is a giving up of what the party values less to receive something the party values more. This formal feature of all exchange covers a wide set of substantive illustrations. Exchange occurs only because each party expects to gain from the trade. This expectation of gain is shown by the small arrows leading away from the circles to the smiley faces. Both parties expect to gain from the trade, and the small arrows leading to the smiley faces convey that expectation of gain.

Panel A is an *ex ante* portrait of a deal within a market catallaxy. Sometimes that deal doesn't work out as one or both of the parties expected. For the spot transactions that garner the attention of most textbook illustrations, this situation is unlikely except for things like defective products that can't be determined on inspection or fraudulent deception of one party by the other. In the case of defective products, sellers typically will make amends because they typically are interested in maintaining a continuing relationship with the buyer that extends beyond the particular spot transaction in question. Fraud is a different matter, and it means that in this situation there was not a genuine meeting of the minds between the parties. That failure to meet, moreover, can come from either party to that *faux* transaction. Most people seem typically to attribute fraud to the seller, as in delivering a product that the buyer knows is not of the quality the seller said it was, only that quality cannot be observed at the time of purchase but can be detected only later after experiencing the product's qualities (or lack thereof). But fraud can also stem from the buyer, who might pay with a stolen credit card or counterfeit currency. Fraud raises issues of law enforcement, and with enforcement being necessary to restrict the expansion in exceptions to the *ex ante* portrait that Panel A shows.

The primary departures from the situation Panel A represents arise in time-consuming transactions where what appears to be a situation of mutual gain when the transaction is initiated appears differently at some later moment. An agreement to build a hotel within two years might have been put together in anticipation that it would be open in time for the city to host the Super Bowl. Subsequently, the location of the Super Bowl is changed, possibly in response to political pressures generated by labor unions seeking to abolish the state's right-to-work character (and which illustrates the infusion of public ordering into a system based on private ordering). The higher expense of the rush job is no longer economically warranted. If construction were to continue as originally agreed, the builder of the hotel would lose and not gain from the transaction.

Typically, however, the parties will renegotiate their relationship because of their interest in further dealings after this piece of construction, in addition to concerns about maintaining good reputations.

Beneath the relationships depicted by Panel A resides the selection for qualities of market participants. Market transactions select for qualities that allow the *ex ante* view of a transactional relationship to be fulfilled *ex post*. Between the *ex ante* and the *ex post* perspectives resides a host of interactions, some of which can work to sabotage the successful conclusion of the transaction. Someone at the planning stage who forgets or neglects to take into account significant details that raise the cost of a fixed-price construction project will sabotage a successful transaction, and these qualities will be selected against through market transactions. Someone who shows up late to work will impede the timely flow of work on the project, and those kinds of qualities will be selected against within the private ordering of a market catallaxy. In other words, selection within a market catallaxy works in favor of qualities and attributes that allow deals to work out as the initiators of those deals planned. Those qualities include such traits and actions as honesty, rectitude, punctuality, team-work, and conviviality, among numerous other qualities. Selected against through market interactions would be the antonyms of those qualities.

5. DEMOCRATIC CATALLAXY AND THE MAGIC NUMBER THREE

It is possible to imagine a political apparatus that does nothing but pre-serve and protect the institutional framework of a liberal market catallaxy. This kind of political apparatus is conveyed by Eucken's (1952) notion of political activities as limited by the requirement that they must be in conformity with the market-generating institutions of property, contract, and liability (residual claimacy). It is also conveyed by Buchanan's (1975b) notion of the protective state which does nothing more than preserve and protect the liberal arrangements of the market order. Whether such a political apparatus has ever existed in its pure form is doubtful, and with this doubtfulness perhaps illustrated by Jonathan Hughes's (1977) examination of the rampant presence of political controls throughout Colonial America. Constitutional arrangements might be crafted in a manner thought to support private ordering of societal interaction, and yet we may reasonably expect the autonomy of the political will to assert itself in the guise of exceptional circumstances (Schmitt 1932), especially as the scale of the polity expands. At small scales, democratic action might be dominated by consensual features. But as the scale of democratic reach expands, consensual action gives way to factional action wherein winners gain at the expense of losers.

Panel B of Figure 5.1 illustrates the transactional character of factional democratic action where the magic number for a transaction is three, because this is the smallest number of participants in a transaction for which a division between winners and losers can be made. Over a century ago, Giovanni Montemartini (1900, 1902) illustrated how the magic number three could explain how municipal enterprises could survive in competition against commercial enterprises. For Montemartini, the explanation ran in terms of the ability of municipal enterprises to practice price discrimination that would not survive free competition among market enterprises. These days many municipalities provide bus services. They don't do that in open competition with other transit providers, for on a head-to-head basis they generally are not able to compete on equal terms with market-based enterprises. Political enterprises, unlike market enterprises, have some ability effectively to conscript customers by supporting those enterprises in part by budgetary appropriations. In this manner, the fares charged to riders are reduced and replaced by budgetary appropriations that come in significant measure from taxes paid by those who don't ride the busses.

Panel B illustrates this situation. Unfortunately, this situation is necessarily more complicated to illustrate than are ordinary market transactions. This is because market transactions take place above ground whereas political–economic transactions must to a significant extent take place below ground and out of sight. Rent seeking and rent extraction bear a cousin-like relationship to bribery and extortion, and the reality of those transactions must be softened or hidden by disguising the character of those transactions. Ideological formulations often play a significant part in creating such disguises, recognizing that we are operating in the realm of non-logical action in any case. One species of such ideological formulation is manifested in claims that riders who choose public transit are imposing external benefits on the remainder of society by reducing congestion and transit time on other modes of transit. The use of budgetary appropriation as a source of finance is thus a way of charging for such external benefits. This claim is not testable through experience, as the alleged external benefit represents a credence good and not an experience good. What matters for the success of the transaction, therefore, is the willingness of the non-riding triads illustrated in Part B to believe the claims of external benefit.

Sometimes market transactions also take place below ground. This is because the presence of political enterprises drives those transactions below ground. In many cases this is because political enterprises seek to impose taxes on market transactions, and moving the transaction underground can allow the participants to escape the tax. At other times public ordering threatens to restrict market transactions that the participants would nonetheless like to make, and so they seek to move those transactions underground. Supporters of political enterprises are aware of the urges to move transactions underground, so they seek to invade the underground to drive those transactions back to the surface. Sometimes they succeed, but at other times they drive those transactions even further underground. All of this movement is part of the continuing drama of life within an entangled system of political economy.

Rent control provides a nice illustration of this phenomenon (Cheung 1975). Imposition of a rent control ordinance creates a situation where more people are seeking housing units at that price than there are units available. The ordinary market response to this situation would be for competition among customers to bid rental prices up, which in turn would create incentives for builders to increase the supply of housing. Under rent control, however, builders have no reason to increase supply. Indeed, they have reason to restrict supply by doing such things as letting units deteriorate or by converting units to condominium status. Setting builders aside, there are still more tenants competing for spaces than there are spaces available. In the presence of this competition, some process of selection will operate. One common method has been the use of tied sales, as when the ability to rent a unit is tied to the purchase of furniture. The price of the furniture would exceed the market price of that furniture, and this higher price would be an indirect way of charging a higher price for the rental unit. Those potential renters who most strenuously wanted a new place to live would be most willing to buy the furniture as a way to obtain the housing unit. The rent control ordinance does little other than to change the structure of transactions, which in turn modifies the substantive operation of selection through competition because someone good at commercial activity in the open might not be so good at such activity when done underground.

Political officials understandably do not like seeing their ordinances being ignored or worked around because doing that undermines the deals that those officials have made. To prevent such undermining, such tie-in sales might be declared to be in violation of public law. This might stop some such transactions, but it also induces people to search for other underground transactional channels, of which there are many possibilities. For instance, some services that had been bundled with a unit could be unbundled. What had been a freely available club room and pool could be unbundled and priced under a separate transaction. What were once free parking spaces could now be priced in a separate transaction. It is the same for storage facilities. A day care facility that had been freely available could subsequently be converted to a stand-alone enterprise, and perhaps even opened to people who resided outside the complex. The central point in any case is that competition cannot be prevented through regulations and ordinances. All that can be done is to change the substantive courses that competition takes, moving transactions into indirect and underground channels.

The complexity of Panel B illustrates this catallactical feature of democratic political economy where the magic number is three. The left part of Panel B is carried forward from Panel A, but with three types of modification. First, the upper circle is changed to a triangle. This change reflects recognition that the transaction is now between a private and a political entity, and with the political entity denoted by a triangle. That simple change from private to political entity sets in motion a train of additional changes that complicate the analysis due to the underground quality of some features of this transaction. For one thing, the political entity is explicitly a nonprofit entity. This doesn't mean political entities don't return profits to "owners." It means only that those profits aren't taken directly from the enterprise in cash. Instead, they are taken through a network of indirect transactions, and it is this indirect feature of that network that generates the transactional complexity, because those transactions can never take place fully in plain sight.

Panel B reduces that complexity to the bare minimum required to illustrate the point. On the far right side of Panel B are two faces, one smiling and one frowning. The smiling face connected to the triangle by a kinked directed arrow shows the payment of "profits" to what are described as "*de facto* owners." The political enterprise generates profits from its activities or else there would be no support for the enterprise. That profit, however, must be removed from the enterprise in indirect fashion as a cousin to money laundering. There are many particular forms through which such profits might be removed, just as there are many particular ways people can contract around rent control. For instance, the political enterprise might require its private counterpart to contract only with unionized labor and to accept featherbedding practices. In this case the *de facto* owners of the political enterprise would be the relevant labor unions and their supporters.

By itself, this arrangement would increase costs on those private enterprises that participated in this kind of deal. To make this participation worthwhile, the political enterprise will have to compensate the private enterprises for their use of this more expensive way of doing business. But where will the political enterprise get the means to do this? The answer lies with the forced triads wearing frowns who contribute to support the political enterprise without receiving anything in return, as Podemska-Mikluch and Wagner (2013) examine. Panel B illustrates the magic number three within a framework of democratic catallaxy.

With respect to the selection for qualities when the magic number is three rather than two, there are both similarities and differences. Obviously, exchanges still take place and the willing parties to the transaction want the transaction to work out as they thought it would. Only this desire is not held as strongly as it is within market catallaxy because of the absence of residual claimacy. When residual claimacy is present in a relationship, the participants have strong reason to execute the transaction as planned or to revise it efficiently if this is necessary. Should the participants fail to do this, they will suffer the losses through a fall in value of their enterprises. Within political catallaxy, however, there is no comparable position of residual claimacy. A private enterprise that contracts with a political enterprise faces a counterpart that does not speak the commercial language of profit-and-loss, as Richard Epstein (1993) explains in his treatment of bargaining with the state.

Political language, moreover, is necessarily a corrupt relative to commercial language, a point that is illustrated in a different though relevant context by Victor Klemperer's (2006) examination of the use of language within Nazi Germany. Commercial practice clearly has instances of fraud, though puffery is more frequent. Yet the basic default setting of commercial practice is openness and honesty as a by-product of private property and residual claimacy. These features of market catallaxy mean that the standard market focus on spot transactions is misleading because participants most of the time are looking for enduring relationships that extend beyond any single transaction. You might cheat someone you don't plan to see again, but you won't if you hope to see them again, and repeatedly, especially in the openly competitive environment associated with private ordering.

Political transactions also entail repeated dealings, only the repetition pertains only to a subset of those implicated in the transaction. Even with respect to *de facto* owners, there can be turnover in political coalitions that will bring to an end the cash flows that were anticipated to continue due to the absence of residual claimacy, and also to the absence of market value for political enterprises. The degree of rectitude present in political catallaxy is surely weaker than in market catallaxy, even among the willing participants to a deal. None of the participants have residual claimant positions in the deal, and many of them are participating on a contingent basis. Should a better deal come along, they will no longer participate in the preceding deal. A *de facto* owner may subsequently become a forced triad to a differently structured deal within the same political–economic catallaxy.

6. ELECTIONS AND THE SELECTION FOR QUALITIES

On the basis of his acceptance of the formal notion that competition selects for excellence in any field of endeavor, Timothy Besley (2006) advances a strong argument that elections select for candidates of high quality and principle. As a purely formal matter, Besley is right; however, such formality evades the substance of the matter. To make contact with substance, we need to dig into the inner workings of political catallaxy to discern the substantive qualities that electoral competition selects for, as Wagner and Yazigi (2014) explore. In a market catallaxy, it is necessary for enterprises to attract participants in open competition with other enterprises. No one is compelled to participate in a market catallaxy, for the self-employment option is always open. The necessity to attract participation leads in turn to personal qualities that are effectively able to explain advantages of participation to potential participants. After such participation has been attained, it will be necessary to continue to attract that participation in a setting where participants are always free to move into other contractual relationships.

Market competition entails degeneracy; electoral competition does not. This difference exerts a significant difference in the competitive selection for qualities. Degeneracy is a network-based concept. It means that in moving between two nodes separated by other nodes, there is no particular node that must be visited (Tononi et al. 1999); there are, for example, many routes someone can follow in driving from New York to Los Angeles. In putting together a plan for a commercial enterprise, degeneracy means that there is no particular entity whose participation must be secured before the enterprise can go forward. This describes the world of mutual attraction within a liberal market catallaxy. Political competition cannot operate in degenerate fashion because political enterprises cannot generally compete effectively with private enterprises in open competition. At base, the lack of explicit capital accounts for political enterprises creates a pattern of activity that renders political enterprises unable to compete effectively with private enterprises on equal terms, as Moberg and Wagner (2014) explain in relating some particular features of municipal bankruptcy to the absence of explicit capital accounts.

The dyadic relationships of market catallaxy are between equals who must continually attract one another in an environment of open competition where there are no entitlements to receive continued support outside of mutual attraction. Within the triadic relationships associated with electoral competition, however, a political entrepreneur can construct a supporting coalition by crafting a transactional structure that entails gainers and losers, while at the same time generating a supporting ideological cover that softens and conceals the redistributive character of the transaction. Electoral competition is clearly intense, just as is market competition. Many political candidates fail to be elected, just as many new businesses fail to thrive and so fold. There is solid basis for thinking each type of competition selects for people who are good *at that kind of competition*. This basis, however, reflects a generic quality of the competitive format. With respect to political economy, it is necessary to move beyond form to substance. With respect to substance, political competition can select for qualities that would have doomed a market enterprise. Similarly, market competition can select for qualities that would lead to electoral failure because such market-inspired qualities as rectitude would be incapable of putting together the political deals that would be necessary for electoral success, largely because of the systemic lying that seems to be necessary for electoral success.

Puffery is an understandable part of market competition as part of an effort to gain initial attention for a product. To be successful within a market environment, however, the enterprise must go beyond puffery to deliver on what customers expect to receive from the product. By contrast, electoral competition is mostly about puffery. In this respect, Pareto (1935) distinguished between logical and non-logical action; this is explored in depth by McLure (2007). Logical action was mainly the province of market interaction where there was a direct connection between the action someone took and the consequences that stemmed from that action. Someone who orders a dinner at a restaurant can soon thereafter expect that dinner to be delivered. The various dinners the restaurant offers, moreover, can be ordered based on a comparison of their prices with the customer's imagination of the qualities of those different items. Market action has clear logical character: if I do A, B will result. This character can be tested through experience.

In contrast, political action has much non-logical character which, as noted earlier, has nothing to do with being irrational but rather speaks to the ascendance of sentiment over reason more so than typifies market action. Consider systemic lying as a feature of electoral competition. It is often noted that unfunded liabilities associated with various American social insurance programs, mainly Medicare, are on the order of $100 trillion. Suppose you state this magnitude in contractual terms. This means there is a discrepancy on the order of $100 trillion between the political promises made to beneficiaries and those made to taxpayers. Obviously, that discrepancy can't persist, and from time to time measures are taken to reduce the discrepancy through various combinations of reducing benefits and raising taxes. Yet those discrepancies are a feature of electoral competition within an environment characterized by Panel B of Figure 5.1.

It was within this kind of setting that Pareto noted the particular significance of ideological articulation as an instrument of political competition. The successful use of the ideological instrument could, Pareto thought, induce people to support measures they might have opposed had those measures been presented within a market framework and open to logical action (Backhaus 1978). With respect to Panel B, ideological articulation works mostly on the forced triads to get them to acquiesce in the measures the political candidates support, or at least to soften their opposition. Since no direct market comparison is possible in any case, all that can be compared are ideologically constructed projections. Those at whom the message is aimed can't do anything to change the outcome in any case, so there is no reason to undertake any effort to convert the message into any kind of as-if logical equivalent, as might be illustrated by constructing a contractual alternative to current social insurance programs. Absent such an effort at construction, electoral choices revolve around the images that different projections create and attach to voter sentiments, recognizing that voters will generally embrace formulations that allow them to feel good about themselves in preference to formulations that result in their feeling badly about themselves.

7. ELECTIONS AND THE SUBSTANCE OF ENTANGLED POLITICAL ECONOMY

This chapter has examined elections as a means for selecting qualities within a framework of political competition. The significance public choice theorists have given to elections was there at the modern beginnings of public choice. That significance also speaks to recognition that elections distinguish democratic regimes from other political forms. All the same, there is good reason to think that the significance of elections has been exaggerated by treating elections as the decisive source of democratic quality. In this respect, V.O. Key (1966) was well known for touting the high quality of democratic electoral politics, as illustrated by the title of his well-known book, *The Responsible Electorate*. In sharp contrast, Brian Caplan (2007) argues that the idea that voters act rationally is a myth, and claims instead that voters act irrationally even if they act rationally as consumers.

The point at issue here is the amount of intelligence that is reflected in democratic action, to recur to some thoughtful musings on the topic that Frank Knight (1960) advanced. Key argues that the intelligence reflected in elections is high; Caplan argues that it is negative and perverse. Most public choice theory has held that elections embody minimal but not perverse intelligence. This holding goes by the name of "rational ignorance." The value to a voter of acquiring information about candidates prior to voting is nearly zero because the probability that a particular voter's vote will determine the outcome of the election is practically zero in anything but truly tiny constituencies. People are observed to vote in large numbers, but those voters are relatively uninformed in comparison with the research they typically undertake before buying houses or cars. The central tenet of rational ignorance is that voting cannot be an instrumental activity through which people select desired political outcomes. In this regard, Geoffrey Brennan and Loren Lomasky (1993) claim that voting is expressive and not instrumental. By advancing this claim, Brennan and Lomasky liken voting to cheering for an athletics team. This claim is a particular illustration of Vilfredo Pareto's (1935) analysis of non-logical action. Within Pareto's framework, candidates are operating in the world of credence and not experience goods, and so compete by creating images that resonate more strongly with the relevant voters than the images offered by other candidates. In the Paretian scheme, voters are acting as if they were cheering for their preferred candidate just as spectators cheer for their preferred team.

Whether voting is approached instrumentally or expressively, voting would seem to be a process that operates with little informative content. In this regard, Gode and Sunder (1993) explain that the logic of market equilibrium tends to create allocative efficiency even if traders operate with zero intelligence. In a similar vein, it might be wondered whether public choice scholars have placed too much emphasis on elections as the source where intelligence is imported into democratic processes. Elections are necessary to maintain the democratic quality of the political apparatus. It does not follow from this necessity, however, that elections govern the types or patterns of intelligence that are at work in democratic systems. Voting can be a low-intelligence activity and yet the democratic process may work outside of elections to reflect high intelligence, even if that intelligence plays out differently when the magic number is three than when it is two. What is called crony capitalism (Holcombe and Castillo 2013; Aligica and Tarko 2014) is a systemic transactional pattern when the magic number is three.

Elections and the associated political campaigns are doubtlessly desired by politicians and their supporters, only not so much for their ability to offer forums for reasoned discussion and clarification of difficult issues, because elections do nothing of the sort. What they do accomplish, though, is to bring increased attention onto political activity. While politicians are a competitive lot and are divided among parties, they are surely united in supporting a larger over a smaller political presence in society, at least when politicians are professional politicians. The real work of politics, however, is surely done outside of elections. Most literature on political economy posits a two-stage sequence. The first stage is where candidates compete for votes by offering programs to voters. The second stage is where politicians implement their programs, or fail to do so as the case might be. The usual presumption is that they will implement promised programs so as to carry a strong reputation into the next election. Within this analytical scheme, the work of programmatic planning is done at the election stage, with the post-election stages being mostly matters of clerical-like execution of plans and programs.

An alternative orientation, the one pursued here, is that it is outside the election period where the real work is done within a system of entangled political economy. Whether voters paid much or little attention to campaigns might make little or even no difference to the substantive content of democratic political economy because it is within the democratic system itself where the genuine work is done and intelligence is brought to bear on that work. It is at this post-election stage where deals are put together or torn apart. Panel B of Figure 5.1 is a highly abstract representation, behind which reside a large number of particular deals that entail relationships and interactions between particular market participants and particular political entities. Reverting to Panel C of Figure 3.2, particular sets of connection between circles and triangles will represent particular deals within the catallaxy of entangled political economy.

A department of forestry might make a deal with a private provider of trailer parks to install a campground on forest land. That deal might have been supported by a significant legislative sponsor of the committee that exercises oversight over the department of forestry. Furthermore, the owner of the trailer park might be a campaign contributor to the legislative sponsor, or, alternatively, might employ a member of the legislator's family, providing a path to access that competitors might not have. In considering these kinds of deals, we enter again into the underground of catallactical interaction within a system of entangled political economy.

8.   SENTIMENTALITY AND MUSCULARITY IN DEMOCRATIC WELFARISM

Earlier in this chapter, I explained how the substantive qualities of competition among architects would play out differently if the selectors were residual claimants to their choice than if they were not. The environment within which competition operates will influence the qualities that are selected. With respect to that earlier illustration, the environment grounded in residual claimacy would select for what can reasonably be called "muscular" qualities among competitors. By contrast, it would select for "sentimental" qualities within the environment where residual claimacy was absent. The selection among qualities is not in the hands of the competitors alone, for it also depends on the interests and desires of the selectors. Selectors who desire muscular presentations will get them. Selectors who don't desire such presentations, perhaps because it will place too heavy a demand on their attention, will get sentimental presentations that tweak their desires to feel good about themselves without having to plumb the depths of complex details.

By democratic welfarism, I refer to a variety of programs and controversies that pertain to what is generally denoted as the welfare state. A century ago, these matters were largely handled through charities and mutual aid societies, as David Beito (2000) explains in careful detail. While charities still exist, their presence within the complex of programs and activities that people have in mind when they make generic references to the welfare state has been dwarfed by the growth of politically sponsored programs. This shift from mostly private to largely public organization illustrates the comparative selection properties of muscular and sentimental environments for competition.

Wagner (2010c, 2011b) distinguishes between raising and leveling as alternative visions for approaching this constellation of issues. The distinction is easy to make even if it is hard to work with. It comes into play in recognition of some observed gap in performance that someone thinks is excessive and who thus seeks to reduce that gap, much as Henry Simons (1938) famously asserted that inequality beyond some degree can become unlovely. For instance, suppose the runners in a marathon were separated by a two-hour gap in their finishing times, with someone further thinking that that degree of inequality should be reduced to a one-hour gap. There are two ways this reduction might be attempted, one sentimental and one muscular. The sentimental approach seeks to degrade good performance by penalizing it; the muscular approach seeks to promote strong performance by encouraging it. With respect to racing, the sentimental approach would give head starts to inferior runners or, equivalently, assign delayed starts to superior runners. In contrast, the muscular approach would do such things as trying to induce inferior runners to train harder or eat better. To be sure, running is a different activity than participating in economic activity. People aren't forced to run, but they must participate in economic activity. All the same, the distinction points in two distinct directions regarding the selection properties of different forms of competition, similar to the different competitive processes for selecting abilities noted above.

Electoral competition tends to select for programs that center on programs of leveling. Market competition among private charities tends to select for programs that center on raising. How do competitive environments relate to leveling and raising? A program of leveling distinguishes between those from whom taxes are taken and those to whom transfers are given. Inequality is presumed to be wholly a matter of chance, perhaps mostly genetic, and has nothing to do with the choices people make, and with this distinction sketched lucidly by Milton Friedman (1953b). An alternative possibility is that people differ in such qualities as attitudes, orientations, and activities, and with those qualities exerting a significant impact on income. Consider a variation on Henry Fawcett's (1871) tale of Robinson and Smith. Each started at the same point in life in similar occupations earning similar amounts of income. Robinson spent all of his income, with a good part of that going to amusement. Smith saved part of his income, and put a good part of the remainder into personal improvement. As the years passed, Smith advanced into higher-paying positions while Robinson stayed pretty much where he started. The incomes of the two diverged increasingly as the years passed. If the two were compared after, say, 30 years, Smith could well be judged to be wealthy and thus taxed to support Robinson, who was poor. Yet the difference between the two is only a reflection of the different choices they made over the preceding years. Robinson could have been less of a spendthrift and saved more in preceding years, as did Smith. Alternatively, Robinson might have been more energetic in his job and hence received similar advancements to what Smith received. However those comparative histories might have unfolded, an observation of comparative income positions in one particular year provides no information about how those people came to hold those positions.

Vilfredo Pareto (1935) explains that a significant feature of political programs is that they allow voters to feel good about themselves. Programs that explain inequalities as consequences of bad things happening to good people within a context where it is presumed that people are universally provident and energetic will generally be easier to sell politically than programs that impose higher demands on the attention space of voters by asking them to work with such distinctions of the past as those between the deserving poor and undeserving poor. This latter type of distinction asks listeners for more attention than any program of leveling requires, for working with this type of formulation requires listeners to bring moral distinctions to bear on different patterns of life, as Gertrude Himmelfarb (1983, 1992) illuminates brightly in her treatments of poverty and as

Deirdre McCloskey (2006, 2010) portrays luminously in her treatments of the civilizing value of bourgeois patterns and styles of living.

The political economy of leveling has emerged while theorists have looked through an analytical window that precludes from view any possibility that the content of the moral imagination can be influenced through social institutions and political programs. This analytical framework means in turn that people individually bear no responsibility for their positions in life, because the conduct of life is a natural talent that everyone possesses in equal degree in light of their genetic endowments. This analytical framework, moreover, is consonant with the orthodox economic-theoretic formulation of people as maximizing given utility functions. To claim scope for societal sources of influence is not to deny the importance of genetics. It's even possible to assign primary significance to genetics while still maintaining room for societal influence. The presumption of a blank slate (Pinker 2002) can be avoided without denying the ability of environmental situations to influence the content of moral imaginations. For instance, it seems to be well recognized that children, young boys in particular, who grow up without fathers present are typically less suited to market activity than other children (Pruett 2000). Furthermore, social arrangements can influence the extent to which children are raised without fathers (Murray 1985).

A program of raising, while making stronger demands on the attention of listeners, would commend a different locus of sympathy and obligation than would a program of leveling. The language of obligation speaks to who owes what to whom. The political economy of leveling holds that those who do well are obligated to support those who don't, under the presumption that people differ only in endowments that are not of their making. In contrast, the example of Robinson and Smith points to a different and more complex locus of obligation because present circumstances are a product of past choices and actions. As compared with Smith, Robinson made choices that led to his standard of living increasingly to sink relative to Smith's. Rather than Smith being obligated to Robinson, it is surely reasonable to ask why Robinson isn't obligated to Smith to avoid becoming a possible burden. A concern with raising and flourishing would surely seek to use Smith and not Robinson as an exemplar for the conduct of lives.

To be sure, the story of Robinson and Smith is only one of many that could be told. Other stories could be told of different initial starting points, perhaps as illustrated by boys growing up without fathers present. Such different starting points are nonetheless consistent with the acceptance of a sense of obligation to conduct one's life in a responsible manner, which would mean in turn seeking to be a positive contributor to life in society.

Difficult circumstances will always be in play, and those circumstances pretty much invariably invoke sympathetic responses through charitable activity.

Self-respect is surely a reasonable quality to find among the members of a flourishing society, and is surely something that is acquired through activity and not through consumption, as Lawrence Meade (1986) recognizes. A society does not attain the quality of being flourishing independently of the actions of its members but rather attains that quality as a result of those actions. Flourishing is a product of activity and not of consumption. It is flourishing that makes consumption possible. What this suggests is the value of an inquiry into the relation between welfare and flourishing because flourishing is a product of activity and the impact of activity on character (Wilson 1995; Shapiro 2007). To speak of self-respect is to bring raising into the analytical foreground; however, raising cannot be accomplished without active participation by the person being raised. Raising requires changes in patterns of conduct, and so involves relationships among participants that are not necessary for leveling, and which are not amenable to effective bureaucratic supervision.

Leveling is a simple program. All that is necessary is for government to tax some people and distribute the proceeds to other people. It is obvious that governments possess the knowledge necessary to do this. Raising is a complex program, one that is difficult even to articulate let alone actually to implement. It is easy enough to state the central idea behind a program of raising: it means helping people to become more effective at making their way in society. While this idea is easy enough to state, it is not easy to implement. A program of raising requires the use of knowledge that is not fully in the possession of any particular person, and involves instead institutionally structured coordination among multiple participants. The knowledge required to level is simple and readily available, so governments are capable of pursuing a program of leveling. In contrast, the knowledge required to raise is distributed throughout a complex network of human relationships and can be put to use most effectively within a polycentric political economy of open competition among ideas and programs (Aligica and Tarko 2012; Aligica 2014).

Among other things, a program of raising requires programmatic distinctions to be made between good and bad choices, and also requires a resolve to act upon that distinction. James Buchanan's (1975a) articulation of the Samaritan's dilemma explains why a central authority is likely to pursue a program of leveling even if it knows how to pursue raising, which it doesn't. While the Samaritan understands that a decision to offer aid now will lead to an increased volume of disability in the future because such aid reduces the cost of bad choices by potential recipients, the Samaritan offers aid anyway. When a position of central authority is present, that authority bears responsibility for the denial of aid and whatever might follow from that denial. It is different in a polycentric system where there are multiple authorities and not a central authority. Polycentricity reduces the force of the Samaritan's dilemma because no single denial is ever a final denial of support. This situation surely lends credibility to requirements by potential donors that potential recipients change their conduct in ways that will improve their ability to support themselves.

Monocentric governments have difficulty making credible commitments about offering or withholding aid because this form of government possesses a grantor of last resort. In contrast, a polycentric system has no position of a grantor of last resort. Credible commitments with respect to offering or withholding aid are more likely within a polycentric system because a rejection of support by any particular donor does not close the door on possible support elsewhere. Hence, the force of the Samaritan's dilemma is likely to be weaker. One Samaritan in a system with many Samaritans will never be in the position of being the last option for a supplicant seeking aid. Since raising requires actions by the recipient as a condition of receiving support, the possible denial of support by a potential donor is a more credible possibility in a polycentric system of Samaritans than in a monocentric system where there exists a Samaritan of last resort.

The distinction between good and bad choices is easy enough to make at an abstract level: good choices are those that lead to flourishing life styles while bad choices lead to debilitation and destitution. But that abstract character leads to numerous difficulties at the level of practical implementation. Early in life, families are the crucible in which the moral imaginations of children are shaped. Some parents pay attention to this and do it well, other parents don't. Political processes aren't at all adept at supervising or policing parental action, and children cannot be said to have chosen their characters or the contents of their moral imaginations. If we ask whether present status is a natural condition or is self-inflicted, as it was for Robinson, the reasonable answer is that both sources are present and with the relative significance of those sources differing among people. Robinson made choices that generated his subsequent condition. A woman who has several children while living on welfare and without a father present similarly had choices. Her children, however, will typically face greatly restricted options regarding the mental and moral orientations they are likely to possess as they enter adolescence and adulthood. As always, there are two types of errors in this situation: one error is to aid the Robinsons when they had the capacity to be like the Smiths; the other error is to fail to aid those Robinsons who had no capacity to be like the Smiths. Furthermore, it is misleading to characterize these errors simply in terms of an amount of aid, for this is the approach of leveling. The aid that accompanies a program of raising involves relationships aimed at promoting the acquisition of orientations and talents that would contribute to flourishing. There is no recipe for perfection in the face of such matters of multi-dimensional complexity.

Leveling is a simple program that can be described by just two elements: (1) a distribution of tax extractions and (2) a distribution of transfers. It is easy to implement leveling. In contrast, raising is a complex program that has numerous components that can be combined in myriad different ways. Each of these combinations represents a different approach to raising. The elements involved in raising can be combined in different ways to generate a huge number of distinct programs. This is a feature of the combinatorial arithmetic that pertains to complex phenomena (Hayek 1967). Hence a program of raising must address numerous elements, each of which speaks to the use of talents and each of which can be combined in numerous distinct ways. For instance, the treatment of fatherless boys is but one of many elements that would have to be combined to comprise a program of raising. But that element has various forks that generate still more options, as does each of the other elements. For instance, one fork might concern whether to treat fatherless boys by leaving them with their mothers or by putting them into foster care. But each of these options leads to other forks in this road of complex possibility. The branch where the boy stays with the mother, for instance, could differ depending on whether the siblings are boys or girls, and also on the numbers of siblings involved. The branch where foster care is the option likewise might differ according to whether the home is proprietary, church operated, or an intact family. In the presence of such complexity, open experimentation is the best procedure we know for generating knowledge, as explained by the essays in Bergh and Höijer (2008). Such openness of experimentation, I might add, has nothing to do with central government grants for local programs, for such grants operate to restrict rather than to promote experimentation because they specify in advance particular branches that must be or cannot be explored.[1]

NOTE

1. This distinction between sentimentality and muscularity is also relevant for such activities as foreign aid and so-called nation building, as Christopher Coyne (2008, 2013) explains in two related books, the earlier one dealing with nation building after wars and the later one dealing with humanitarian aid.

6.   Parasitical political calculation

Look at the organized pattern of activities within a city. That pattern clearly displays organization and coordination. Yet there is no person or office that does the coordinating. It is self-coordinated, or perhaps more accurately, coordinated through polycentric action among numerous independent actors. The pure theory of a market economy is an effort to give an account of that coordination to the extent it is achieved within an institutional framework governed by private property and freedom of contract (Boettke 1998, 2001). The theory of markets does a reasonable job of characterizing those coordinated patterns of activity within the framework of equilibrium theory so as to explain such things as the height of buildings in different parts of a city, the price of land in different parts of a city, and whether particular kinds of activities are spread throughout a city or are concentrated at particular areas within a city. Those patterns also include coordination among different people and activities, as illustrated by coordination between delivery of bread to a restaurant and the preceding delivery of flour to a baker. Economic theory provides a reasonable framework for understanding the generally coordinated pattern of activities we all observe and experience despite the absence of some form of master plan that assures such coordination (Klein 2011). Indeed, one of the central lessons of economic theory is that efforts to implement such planning often bring about mis-coordination.

The theory of markets, however, is incomplete because it doesn't integrate politically sponsored activity into the analysis. The bread that bakeries deliver to stores in the city will be delivered over roads that are built and maintained by political entities. The flours that are used for baking the breads might have been delivered by ship to a harbor at the mouth of a river, and with the harbor dredged by a political agency to keep a channel open so that ships don't run aground. Collective activity appears at numerous places in any complete story of societal coordination. But how is collective activity able to support such coordination? In modern theory, that support is achieved by teleological assumption and not by any scheme of explanation grounded in limited and distributed knowledge. Political agencies are theorized as doing whatever it is they must do to overcome the market failures that otherwise are presumed to impede coordination.

The persistence of this theoretical presumption is perhaps testimony to scholarly inertia dating back to times when collective action was the province of royalty and not something for ordinary people to think about. But we are no longer governed by royalty, and collectively sponsored activities arise through triadic catallactical processes that are not nearly so well understood as are dyadic catallactical processes (Podemska-Mikluch and Wagner 2013). The analytical challenge for a theory of social economy is to incorporate collective action within the same non-teleological scheme of thought as economists have long used in their development of market theory.

For market relationships, prices play an essential role in coordinating activities, through both the knowledge they generate and the incentive they supply. We can thus understand the quantities of different types of bread that are produced and how coordination is achieved among the various complementary activities: for instance, the baking of bread is coordinated with both the delivery of flour and the appearance of trucks to deliver the bread. We can understand all this even if we couldn't actually plan it, as Leonard Read (1958) explains for such a simple product as pencils. But how about maintaining the highways or dredging the harbors? There is no direct exchange of service for money. To be sure, there are a number of broad assertions that polities operate by exchanging protection for tribute, of taxation as being the price of civilization, and of political campaigns as writing the script that successful candidates follow until the next election. These kinds of formulations, however, are just aggregate teleology that recognizes the explanatory problem and then evades it rather than trying to face it.

It would always be possible to imagine a market-based organization of road construction and maintenance and of harbor dredging. Getting a pothole filled in your neighborhood would be similar to getting a dental cavity filled. In both cases, the transaction would be directly catallactical. Getting a harbor dredged to prevent boats from running aground would likewise be an ordinary catallactical transaction. But roads aren't produced and maintained in this manner, and yet they are produced and maintained—and in pretty much the right places and kept generally decently repaired even if some might dispute just how decently. The analytical challenge is to explain the operations of such political agencies as those that maintain roads and maintain rivers and harbors from within the triadic catallactical orientation of entangled political economy. Economic calculation must be present in deciding which roads to repair and which channels to dredge. That calculation, however, cannot be directly dyadic because political agencies don't receive their revenues directly from sales to customers, and so that calculation must be triadic in some fashion.

Within the spirit of entangled political economy, market-based and polity-based activities are coeval and both limited by the principles of localized and specialized knowledge. How to theorize in this fashion is the distant objective at which this book aims, with the more immediate objective being to take a few useful steps in this direction. In this respect, I call upon Maffeo Pantaleoni's (1911) long forgotten model of parasitical political pricing to provide an analytical point of departure, some aspects of which Wagner (1997) discusses. Pantaleoni set forth a model based on two distinct price systems, one a system of market prices and the other a system of political prices. He conceptualized these systems as operating within separate bazaars. Within the market bazaar, vendors charged what Pantaleoni called economic prices, by which he meant prices equal to marginal costs. Within the political bazaar, prices were parasitical attachments to market prices and were determined through taxation. For instance, income taxation at a flat rate would generate a set of discriminatory prices that varied directly with a person's income, and with Buchanan (1964, 1967: 160–68) reflecting a somewhat similar scheme of thought in setting forth conditions under which a flat tax on income would lead everyone in a collectivity to choose the same amount of public output.

Pantaleoni's model of two bazaars was a form of additive political economy. Contrary to Pantaleoni's formulation, entangled political economy recognizes that a single system of pricing exists within any society. That system of prices, however, is not generated within an institutional framework governed exclusively by private ordering. Public ordering is also infused throughout the societal catallaxy. There is only one system of pricing within a society, but that system has different characteristics within a framework of wholly private ordering than it has within a framework of entangled political economy. Political enterprises can't generate market prices, yet they necessarily must use those prices in various ways. Some of those ways include actions to modify the pattern of those prices along various margins. Political enterprises need market prices to provide navigational guidance, and so operate by making parasitical attachments to those prices.

1.   COLLECTIVE ACTION AND ECONOMIC CALCULATION

Political enterprises and market enterprises are identical in that they all face a continuing parade of choices they must make. Each of those choices entails options among which one will be chosen. The cost of the chosen option is the value the *chooser* places on the most highly valued of the unchosen options (Buchanan 1969), recalling that cost pertains to the valuation of options a *chooser* faces and not to some aggregate magnitude that might be associated with that choice in someone's mind. This is the simple logic of cost and choice as Chapter 4 noted. Choice requires valuation of options. For commercial enterprises, market prices facilitate economic calculation by allowing options to be appraised with the assistance of market prices. Market prices are typically not the final word with respect to economic calculation, but they are a significant word from both *ex ante* and *ex post* perspectives. The *ex ante* perspective pertains to deciding among possible future courses of action, as illustrated by such possible activities as initiating a new enterprise, buying another enterprise, or expanding the existing line of products. In these kinds of situations, enterprise officials must reach a determination of whether the new activity is likely to increase the enterprise's net worth.

The *ex post* perspective pertains to the retrospective valuation of past decisions. Were there choices made that turned out to decrease net worth even though the *ex ante* belief was that net worth would increase? If so, perhaps the damage should be undone by reversing that earlier choice. But the past can't be undone. Past experience might offer instruction, but nothing can be done about it. All action is aimed at the future, necessarily so because the past is dead and the present is simply a proverbial knife-edge between past and future (Shackle 1961, 1968, 1972). One might conclude that to this point an earlier choice has not worked out well and yet stay with that choice because there is good reason to think that doing so will increase the enterprise's value going forward as compared with the relevant alternative. While all action is aimed at the future and unavoidably entails economic calculation, such calculation can also be applied to the resultants of past choices. However, to attribute a negative outcome to some past choice does not imply that that choice should be abandoned, though it might.

Money is often described as a medium of exchange, and it is surely that. But it is also a commercial language that brings into focus what would otherwise be a vast array of incommensurable items and activities. Any commercial plan will entail the bringing together of many activities. Buildings will be leased, people hired for various jobs, agreements made with vendors, and customers located. Without prices these particular items cannot be compared in anything but some arbitrary manner. While commercial plans can be rich in detail, they can also be summarized by constructing monetary comparisons of probable sales and expenses projected over various intervals from the present. A drug manufacturer, for instance, might be considering whether to undertake the research to create a new drug. The interval for evaluation might run 20 years and involve such concrete activities as hiring scientists and equipping laboratories, later running various types of experiments both on animals and on people, and still later, if the former steps were successful, hiring sales personnel and undertaking the various other activities necessary to sell the product. All of these particular activities can be brought into common focus by appraising all those activities through their prices. To be sure, those prices are projections of future prices and not current prices, and so economic calculation requires judgment and is not a simple matter of arithmetic. Still, any choice requires economic calculation, though such calculation can be done well or badly.

The prime interest in this book is calculation by politically established enterprises which typically do not sell products and services directly through market transactions. And yet such enterprises must calculate just as do market enterprises, unavoidably so. Where a hortatory theory of political activity might offer instruction as to how those enterprises should calculate, as illustrated by benefit–cost analysis, an explanatory theory starts from recognition that such enterprises already calculate in some fashion, and the analytical challenge is to uncover the grammar of such calculation. With respect to grammar, we can distinguish between direct and indirect calculation. Direct calculation pertains directly to the object of choice. Indirect calculation pertains to some indirect but complementary object as a kind of proxy for the object.

Consider a simple oceanfront illustration. Within a market setting, vendors might be free to establish food stands along the beach, hearkening back to a simple model by Harold Hotelling (1929) that became the inspiration for the spatial voting models that became prevalent in public choice (Enelow and Hinich 1984, 1990). Any particular vendor has to decide where on the beach to locate, as well as whether to locate there at all. The vendor also has to decide what kind of products to stock and offer for sale. The vendor faces many options, the comparison of which is facilitated by market prices in conjunction with the sales information associated with those prices. Sure, the vendor will also have to use intelligence in determining what items to stock, which is not a simple matter of calculation. Still, calculation in money facilitates generation of the pattern of location of vendors along the beach, so the social organization of beachfront vendors is directly amenable to economic analysis.

But where does politically sponsored activity fit into this overall pattern of organized activity? This is where the challenge to theoretical analysis arises. The beachfront is a small ecology of activities. The location of people and vendors along the beach is directly subject to economic explanation. But the beachfront also features participation by politically sponsored enterprises, and those activities also call for theoretical explanation, both as activities on their own and with respect to coordination among market and political enterprises within the entire beachfront ecology. The value people place on visiting that particular beachfront depends on its quality. The willingness of vendors to locate there depends on the number of people who use the beach. Suppose further that the beach is subject to erosion at a significant rate, so the sand must periodically be replenished by dredging sand from the ocean and putting it on the beach. As a conceptual matter, it would be possible to transform this situation into one of ordinary commercial calculation by assuming that the beach is privately owned. In this case the owners of the beach would support replenishment as guided by economic calculation. To do this, however, is to evade the theoretical challenge for entangled political economy.

In some fashion a politically based enterprise would handle beach replenishment. There are two basic organizational methods by which this might be done. One would entail the creation of some special district to handle beach replenishment, and perhaps some complementary activities. Special district governments are numerous in number and relatively infrequently studied (Fink and Wagner 2013). They generally are established to provide a narrow range of services, as illustrated by beach replenishment and mosquito control. Sometimes, however, they cover large areas, as illustrated by water districts and flood control districts. In all cases, they have governing boards and have governmental powers of a limited nature. They are perhaps closer to market-based enterprises than are general purpose governments. Still, their revenues are typically derived from taxation, often as an attachment to a real estate tax, and not from prices charged to customers.

The other organizational method would fold beach replenishment into the activities of some political bureau or agency, such as a Corps of Engineers. The Corps of Engineers operates through budgetary appropriations, behind which reside complex catallactical processes. It is surely the case that agency actions with respect to its budget will influence future budgets because any one agency is in competition with all other agencies. Budgetary processes, however, are not directly catallactical because there is a peculiar relationship between agencies and customers. Stated alternatively, there are two categories of customer: nominal customers and real customers. The nominal customers are those who furnish the revenues with which the agency operates. These are taxpayers. The real customers are the subset of citizens who have commercial-like dealings with the agency. Within this indirect setting, the social organization of beach replenishment lies unexamined on the analytical table. One significant question concerns the amount of discretion existing at the agency level. Some discretion there will always be because unforeseeable contingencies will arise throughout the year. There will be general rules or principles of procedure, along with allowances for discretionary activity. Beach erosion somewhere may be faster than normal and a major holiday weekend is approaching. Will the beach be replenished out of phase with the normal work schedule, or won't it?

Catallactical principles are in play for both categories of action, but those categories raise different issues for explanation. One category is the recurring or normal patterns of activity. In this respect it is reasonable to recall the time-saving character of administrative rules and procedures, for they economize on administrators' time. In this respect, Hebert and Wagner (2013) set forth a two-stage model of taxation in a similar vein. They start from recognition that there is surely some modicum of desire for collective activity within a society, along with recognition that the best tax is always one that someone else pays. This base recognition leads to a simple flat tax, the return for which can be filed on a post card. At this point, fiscal politics enters to generate the proverbial flood of exceptions and exemptions that creates a tax code so large that no one can read it and which generates nearly a unique tax liability for each taxpayer. As Carl Schmitt (1932) explains trenchantly, and which Bolsinger (2001) amplifies, the autonomy of the political within society is bound up in the ability of those who hold political power to act on and grant exceptions to rules and to act on and reinforce distinctions between friends and enemies. It is in the exceptions that generate thousands of pages of tax codes where the autonomy of the political resides and which is of primary interest here, and not in the general rules and principles which would yield but a page or two of tax code.

The other category concerns exceptions from normal routines. Parliaments face economic calculation throughout the gamut of their activities. They create bureaus and agencies to administer the enterprises they have chosen to sponsor, and they confront unavoidable problems of economic calculation due to scarcity. Parliaments have limited ability to support the various enterprises they have chosen to sponsor. The bureaus and agencies seeking parliamentary support likewise face scarcity in that they must choose among ways to operate the programs they have been created to operate. For instance, a parliament will have to decide how much support to give to a recreation department relative to a police department. A recreation department will in turn have to decide how to organize its activities and what kinds of activities to organize. These issues include such matters of how much land to devote to playgrounds relative to how many and what kinds of buildings to construct on that land. It will also have to decide what kinds of equipment to install on the playgrounds. For market-based enterprises, economic calculation is straightforward in principle even if it is not so easy in practice. It is not so straightforward for polity-based enterprises, but it is unavoidable all the same. What makes economic calculation straightforward for market-based enterprises is private property and market pricing. Collective property doesn't generate market prices and political enterprises don't have market value, yet political enterprises must calculate and evaluate the options they face. To a significant degree, political calculation must operate through parasitical attachment to market prices and transactions. After all, without market transactions and prices, there would be nothing to offer guidance for political calculation.

2. PARASITICAL CALCULATION AND PUBLIC SQUARE CATALLAXY

Valuation and calculation are actions of individuals. Collectivities can't value or calculate, nor can they choose for that matter. What is typically described as collective valuation or choice is a shorthand type of expression that pertains to the product of some institutionally governed interaction among some set of participants. If no one in the collectivity wanted to replace eroded beach sand, replenishment wouldn't occur. At least one person must support replenishment if it is to occur. It is not, however, necessary for a majority to support replenishment for it to occur. What happens with respect to replenishment, or any other object of collective action, depends on the institutional framework that governs collective interaction, or what was described as the framework of public law in the earlier discussion with respect to Figure 3.3.

For instance, all items set before a parliamentary assembly might be subject to approval through a referendum. That referendum might stipulate that the cost of any project be distributed equally among all citizens. If majority approval is required, it might be thought that motions would be approved only if a majority thought the program was beneficial. This wouldn't be a reasonable conclusion, however, under other approaches to financing the project. Nor would it be a reasonable conclusion if the cost of voting is taken into account and approval requires only a majority of those voting and not of everyone. For instance, 10 percent of the residents might use the beach and value replenishment highly. The other 90 percent might make little or no use of the beach, but the cost they would bear if the motion passes does not make it worthwhile for many in this position to vote. To pick yet another illustration, the ballot might contain a number of motions rather than having separate ballots for each motion. This situation would likely elicit a higher turnout of voters, yet again changing the outcome of the proposal.

There is no standard of preference revelation independent of action within some type of institutional regime. Whatever the character of that regime, however, the logic of economizing action asserts that people will select that option they value most highly. For some, this will mean going to the polls and voting in favor of replenishment. For others, this means they will not go to the polls even if such people might vote against replenishment if the polls were brought to them. In the face of such analytical complexities, it is perhaps easy to understand why conventional political economy invokes different principles to explain political and market activity. Doing this reflects what Mitchel Resnick (1994) calls the centralized mindset, in which observed order is attributed to some specific ordering agency when it really arises spontaneously through some process of self-organization. Once it is recognized that polities are likewise self-organized, because there is really no other option to self-organization for contemporary levels of social complexity, invoking the centralized mindset short circuits any effort to bring society fully within the purview of economizing action writ large. However this might be done, all relationships in society are transactional in nature and governed universally by incomplete and divided knowledge.

In addition to Pantaleoni's (1911) recognition of the parasitical quality of political pricing, the theory of tie-in sales offers another potentially useful analytical tool. One use of tied sales is to avoid price controls. The classic illustration is a rent-controlled apartment that can be leased only by also buying furniture from the lessor at a price that exceeds the market price. The rent control creates a situation where there is a shortage at the controlled price. Thus demanders seek to gain a competitive advantage, which they can do by paying more in secondary market transactions. In some cases ordinances can seek to prevent such tie-ins, which in turn would set in motion a further search for ways of competing for apartments when competition through price is not allowed.

Getting a road repaired or a harbor dredged is particularly valuable to enterprises whose operations depend on those facilities. We may think of the demand for marina services as a variable that depends on the quality of beach and harbor maintenance. In an open market a marina owner would purchase the amount of such service that obtains the maximum value for the marina. But these services are not directly priced. Public–private interaction must still be catallactical, only this must be indirect and involve secondary markets, as with tie-in sales. Indeed, we can think of road and harbor maintenance as available at zero price, which is below the market-clearing price.

What we should thus expect to find are other types of transaction that operate equivalently to the sale of furniture in cases of rent control.

As a conceptual matter, we can say that such channels must exist for harbors to get dredged and in orderly fashion, with some people getting dredging done more quickly than others. What can't be determined is the particular transactional channel that might be used. Indeed, there could be and probably are multiple channels in use. Some channels could be quite venal, as in bribery. Other channels would be less so, as illustrated by contributions to political campaigns. Both of these channels are relatively direct and not too far removed from the exchange of service for money.

It is easy to imagine yet other channels that are less direct still, and yet which can be intelligible features of efforts to gain competitive advantage. The marina might take out a full page advertisement for a high school dramatic production where the relevant bureau chief has children attending school, or possibly even in the production. We are dealing with an open range of possibilities here, all of which are intelligible as efforts to gain competitive advantage. There is a deep intertwining achieved between polity and economy, as a comparison of Panels A and B in Figure 5.1 illustrates. Panel A illustrates a simple market catallaxy as this is explained in the theory of markets. Panel B illustrates the less direct and more complex pattern of catallactical interaction in the presence of political enterprises. The politically organized provider of service is illustrated by the triangle. It can receive no profit nor does it carry a market value. Yet it faces scarcity and must make choices, just as must market participants. People will compete for scarce services just as they will compete for products sold under price controls. Panel B is meant to portray some of these catallactical ideas. The cloud with the smiling face extending from the triangle illustrates that the political enterprise yields gain to someone or else it wouldn't exist. The sad face above the cloud illustrates that public enterprises also receive support from taxpayers who may well place no value on the enterprise's activities.

Publicly sponsored firms compete both with one another and with market-based firms, while at the same time fabricating networks of cooperative and mutually supportive relationships. Budgeting isn't a top-down, hierarchical process; it is an interactive, polycentric process, as such authors as Ostrom (1973), Wildavsky (1975), Primo (2007), and Wagner (2012c) explore. For instance, publicly sponsored firms advertise as a method of garnering support. Much of this advertisement is denoted as public relations, but it also extends to such things as assisting market-based firms in producing movies and television programming. It also includes such activities as providing speakers for a wide variety of civic forums. A marina owner might not only contribute to political campaigns, but also belong to civic clubs that invite speakers from particular public agencies, while also contributing selectively to charities that in turn have connections that impact positively both the marina and the relevant public enterprises.

3. CALCULATION, VALUATION, AND POLITICAL ENTERPRISE

Let me now return to the setting of the town with a marina and some shops, hotels, and restaurants, all of which are organized through market interaction. By assumption, the maintenance of roads and the dredging of river channels are supplied by the town rather than by market enterprises. Each of these collective activities is subject to scarcity, which means that choices among options are necessary. To make those choices, calculation is necessary. For instance, there are multiple qualities of materials with which roads can be paved. Furthermore, roads may be allowed to fall into varying degrees of degradation before repairs are made. Similarly, channels can be dredged to varying depths and with variable frequency, and with the depth and frequency influencing the number of instances when boats run aground.

It is easy enough to describe how road maintenance and river dredging would be accomplished within the context of market interaction. Firms would compete to offer maintenance and dredging services. They would offer qualities of services at prices that the owners calculate will maximize the present value of their ownership rights. Customers, moreover, would choose among enterprises according to which proffer they prefer. There is no need to invoke some god's-eye presumption in any of this, for what we have is a process of spontaneous ordering where the standard equilibrium conditions are emergent qualities of interaction within the market frame-work and not something that is imposed through direct calculative planning or theoretical stipulation (Alchian 1950).

Only now, road maintenance and river dredging are supplied through town enterprises, commonly called bureaus or departments but enterprises all the same. Town enterprises, just as market enterprises, need to attract revenue sufficient to cover their expenses to make the enterprise a going concern. One problem with working with this illustration is its small scale, for it is easy to think that with a small channel to be dredged and a few miles of road to be maintained, it would be a simple matter of planning to undertake these activities. To do this, however, would be to bring in the god's-eye presumption through the back door. To the contrary, the object of this thought experiment is modern democratic government of sufficiently large scale and complexity that the presumption of a god's-eye perspective is clearly nothing but an evasive fable.

I start from recognition that the demand for collective activities is derived from the demand for market activities. The demand for road maintenance derives from the demand for the services of marinas and hotels; similarly, the demand for river dredging derives from the demand for the various water-related activities that are organized within the marina. All of the market enterprises have alienable ownership, and so have market value even if some of those enterprises are not publicly traded. After all, someone can always advance a proffer to buy a closely held enterprise, so that enterprise has a value even if it is not rendered visible through market trading of ownership shares.

The value of those market enterprises depends on the quality of the collective services that are complementary to the activities undertaken by the market enterprises. Channels that fill with silt cause boats to run aground. The boat owner loses revenue because the boat is not earning revenue while it is stuck in the river, and the owner loses still more revenue because it is necessary to take another boat out of service to rescue the stranded passengers. Even more, such bad experiences can decrease future business. Clearly, the value of river-related enterprises varies directly with the quality of the dredging services. It is the same for road maintenance. Poor maintenance increases the time required to visit restaurants and shops in the town, and may also increase the wear and tear on cars that use the roads. In consequence, patronage may move elsewhere.

Road maintenance and river dredging are of value to enterprises in the market economy, but they are provided free of direct charge. This simple setting creates numerous problems and challenges for an explanatory theory of entangled political economy. The public enterprises do not have owners whose fortunes vary directly with the willingness of other people to acquire shares of ownership. Public enterprises acquire their revenues through a budgetary process and not directly through the sale of services to customers. Those who receive the services provided by public enterprises, moreover, do not pay directly for those services but pay instead through some system of taxation combined with a process of budgetary appropriation.

If the god's-eye sleight-of-hand is to be avoided, it is necessary to create some invisible-hand form of theorizing that allows coherence to be brought to bear on the complex of collective activity in modern societies. Only in this way can the conceptual antinomy be bridged. It is here where I think Pantaleoni's insight about parasitical pricing comes into play. Parasitical pricing operates through attachment to market transactions. Not simple or neutral attachment, however, but attachment that modifies the pattern of market transactions in the process of attachment. In this respect, what is the meaning of calls for "reform" these days but changes in patterns of market prices? Some reforms seek to change the prices that particular sets of people receive as suppliers of inputs. Other reforms seek to change the prices that particular people pay as demanders of outputs. So parasitical pricing does not operate in some neutral fashion, such as commonly portrayed in notions of lump sum taxation, but operates in non-neutral fashion. Political enterprises do not become ordinary market enterprises and yet can't operate without market enterprises because parasites require hosts.

Parasitical political pricing means that political enterprises must acquire information from relevant market participants, and with that information having some degree of complementarity to the market pricing that could have been practiced under some alternative institutional environment. The economic theory of tied sales suggests one path along which such a treatment might be explored, though other paths could also surely be blazed. One use of a tied sale is to price something when direct pricing is prohibited. Rent control is the classic example of this. To be sure, the rent control illustrations pertain only to price ranges above the controlled price. But nothing of significance would be changed if the price were controlled at zero. This situation could reflect an arrangement where apartments were financed through budgetary appropriation, and with the recipients of appropriations being precluded from charging positive rents.

The rent control doesn't eliminate scarcity, but only changes how scarcity plays out in particular settings. At the controlled price of zero, the demand for space exceeds the space that is available. Those who desire space will compete among themselves, and with the resulting full price of the tied package tending to clear the market. The relevant example, however, is not apartment rental but river dredging or road maintenance. Dredging is produced under conditions of scarcity. In any one day, week, or any other period there is more desire for dredging than there is capacity to dredge. The dredging enterprise must establish priorities and those who desire dredging seek to receive higher rather than lower priority. This initial situation mirrors the rent control situation. But how might it play out in a way that is relevant for an explanatory theory of political economy?

There are multiple forms of parasitical pricing, and these can be ordered according to their degree of venality. The most venal form is bribery, which effectively restores market pricing despite the surface appearance that pricing is absent. In this case, people pay a positive sum for the right to receive something at a zero price, which is what Cheung (1975) described as "key money" with respect to rent control. While bribery clearly exists, in western democracies as well as elsewhere, it seems plausibly to be less in the democratic lands than elsewhere. The absence of open venality, however, does not prevent the operation of competition among those who compete for priority, but only changes the form which that competition takes.

Whatever particular form that competition takes, it will conform to the general template of a transaction: a demander will undertake a costly action that he or she thinks will improve his or her position in the queue. Contributions to political campaigns comprise one well-cited channel. Political activism is another. Membership in civic clubs where bureau officials are hosted is yet another. Support for charitable activities and even advertising in public spaces can serve the same function, though seemingly with decreasing degrees of venality. As long as public bureaus and agencies can exercise discretion over such things as which channels to dredge and how deeply or widely, competition for position in the queue will be present (Buchanan and Congleton 1998). The existence of such competition is an analytical implication of scarcity and the necessity of choice. The particular form such competition takes, however, is a matter of historical contingency that is a subject for empirical-historical and not theoretical inquiry.

4. COORDINATION WITH PARASITICAL CALCULATION

Tribes can act in generally coordinated fashion without alienable property and the markets and prices that emerge when property is alienable. Great societies, however, can't operate within a framework of political property alone because that framework can't generate the market prices that are necessary for economic calculation. All choices require some framework for ranking options. Market prices are indispensable for arriving at such rankings, even if calculation requires judgment in addition to the information that prices provide. Collective entities face the same necessity for choice as do market entities, only interaction among collective entities within what might be called a collective economy cannot generate prices. Hence, collective entities must develop parasitical attachments to market entities or transactions. The value of political activity can be calculated only in light of how that activity is refracted through market activity. The internal economy of the polity cannot generate prices. Prices can arise only within that part of society where property is alienable, and which is denoted as the market. Thus in a technical sense a polity must act parasitically upon a market economy, as recognized both by Maffeo Pantaleoni (1911) and Joseph Schumpeter (1918). Political entities must use market prices as calculational aids even if they make incomplete use by staying within the polity as against joining the market.

Attilio Da Empoli (1941: 91–136) notes that there are two snares that an explanatory theory of collective economic action must avoid. One snare is to treat the polity as acting apart from economy, as illustrated by the "hailstorm tax" (*imposta grandine*) treatments that characterize theories of optimal taxation and also by treating electoral competition as the forum within which a policy plan is chosen. The other snare is to treat the polity as an ordinary participant within the division of labor in society, perhaps as reflected by that engraving about the headquarters building of the IRS: "taxation is the price we pay for civilization."

The image of a parliamentary assembly as a *peculiar* form of investment bank is one way to avoid both of these snares. This assembly could not be a simple investment bank, for this would be to fuse the taxing and spending sides. Yet it is an arena within which the conflicting desires of people for programs are intermediated. In many respects, a parliament is like a partnership of investment bankers, in that it intermediates between the political enterprises that supply services on one side and the citizens who provide revenues to support those enterprises on the other side, as explained in McCormick and Tollison (1981; Leibowitz and Tollison 1980).

As an investment bank, the legislative partners seek to develop connections between people who have enterprises for which they are seeking support and people who have the means available to support political enterprises. To say they have the means of support does not imply that they turn it over voluntarily, for if they did that the polity would be a regular investment bank and not a *peculiar* investment bank. It is almost surely the case that there is complementarity between decisions about the support of enterprises and the ability of legislatures to generate revenue, which provides a budgetary bridge between the two sides of the fiscal account, provided only that people who are attracted into the legislative form of investment banking prefer to do more business rather than to do less.

A bridge always exists that connects sources of revenue provided by citizens to sources of service provided by political enterprises. To be sure, political enterprises do not operate by the same rules that govern market-based enterprises, but the connection between revenue and service must be there all the same. It would always be possible to make that connection as direct as it is with ordinary commercial transactions. Knut Wicksell's (1896 [1958]) well-cited formulation articulated one particular approach to doing just this. In Wicksell's formulation, the legislature would serve explicitly as an intermediary to connect those who supply services with those who demand them. The organization of legislatures along non-Wicksellian lines does not deny the connection between service and revenue, but it does render that connection complex and ambiguous, and something to be explored and illuminated. A good deal of that complexity comes about because of the large number of political enterprises that run some of their financing through the legislature, along with the large number of revenue sources that legislatures tap.

As Wagner (2007: esp. 125–54) sketches, a society contains numerous enterprises distributed across public and market squares. Some of those enterprises are supported through a legislative process and so operate with inalienable ownership. These enterprises bear a parasitical relationship to the system of market pricing (Pantaleoni 1911): they don't generate prices and yet must use prices to guide economic calculation. All of the enterprises are seeking to expand their custom, only with the different forms of enterprise governed by different rules of organization that in turn generate differing patterns of conduct. Zones of conflict and cooperation would arise among different enterprises, and the political arena would expand or contract depending on the particular organizational efficiency this peculiar investment bank is able to attain. Government would be a factor of production in society, and its operation within society would radiate throughout society in thoroughly oblique and knotted fashion. Governments would be participants within the complex adaptive system that society represents, not necessarily all to the good by any means but there all the same as social phenomena to be explained.

5. POLITICAL ENTERPRISES AND THE CAPITAL STRUCTURE OF PRODUCTION

As a purely formal matter, political enterprises face the same organizational problems as all other enterprises in society, in that they have to survive as going concerns in the presence of competition from other enterprises that face the same problem. With respect to substantive practice, however, political enterprises operate within a different environment than other enterprises in society. These environmental differences lead to different patterns of conduct, due mainly to differences in capital accounts. To be sure, political enterprises typically are not conceptualized in terms of their capital accounts, and yet the capital account of political enterprises has significance in several ways. For political enterprises, the distinction between a *de jure* capital account and a *de facto* account has significance that does not exist for market-based enterprises where that distinction has no relevance. As a *de jure* matter, capital is provided through taxation, and each citizen can be regarded as having supplied capital in proportion to his or her tax payments in support of political enterprises. In contrast, the *de facto* perspective pertains to the distribution of gains from an enterprise's operation. The recipients of those gains are the *de facto* owners of the political enterprise, and it is they who are in competition with the *de facto* owners of other political enterprises. To speak of the aggregate of political enterprises and the people as the owners of those enterprises is to embrace a piece of ideology that may be important in raising the public acquiescence in political activity but which all the same has nothing to do with understanding the processes that undergird some such formulation as that depicted by Figure 3.3.

Political enterprises require capital for successful operation, and that capital must be obtained in competition with other uses for capital in society. What is relevant in this competitive process is always individual enterprises and their *de facto* owners, and not some aggregation of enterprises as represented by aggregate statistics and macro-level variables. Political enterprises can conscript some of their capital through taxation, and yet in democratic polities, and probably in all polities, those enterprises must also have some willing supporters. To speak of a capital structure for political enterprises means that those enterprises compete for capital with other enterprises, and with that competition being continuous. With respect to any particular political enterprise, that competition occurs along two margins: (1) there is competition for capital among political enterprises and (2) there is competition between political and commercial enterprises. As a formal matter, there is a tendency always for the owners of capital to shift their capital from where it yields less to where it yields more. Within the pure theory of a market economy, it is easy to imagine how this process by which a structure of capital forms and undergoes change plays out (Lachmann 1956). The form of the theory is changed not one bit by introducing political enterprises into the societal ecology of enterprises, for everyone acts always to replace what they value less with what they value more. The substantive content of the theory, however, is changed considerably through changes in the environmental context of human action.

Within a framework of private property, people can use their rights of ownership to establish proprietorships and corporations, and the value consequences of such establishment rest with the *de facto* owners. Within a democratic polity, however, political enterprises must be corporate in form because those enterprises are established through and operate within forms of public or political property. A proprietorship acts according to the volition of the proprietor. For political enterprises, however, enterprise action must always entail concurrence among some plurality of people who direct the enterprise. Hence, all political entities are corporate in form, whereas many commercial entities are individually owned. To speak of a plurality of owners is, however, to speak only in a purely formal manner, for plurality means any number greater than one. One piece of democratic ideology asserts that political enterprises organized through democratic processes entail concurrence among everyone, as illustrated by references to "we the people." Other pieces of ideology assert that concurrence is required among at least a majority within the relevant unit. Yet other lines of argument assert that concurrence may be confined to minority segments within the relevant population. In any case, it is straightforward to sense how a democratic polity can be reasonably conceptualized as being similar to a market economy in denoting an order of enterprises and most certainly not a single enterprise.

One must in this respect be careful to avoid being led astray by a direct reading of some constitutional parchment, for the reality is often different from what the parchment states (Runst and Wagner 2011). This recognition pertains to the ecology of political enterprises that constitutes a democratic polity. That ecology contains numerous enterprises, typically characterized as agencies, bureaus, or departments. However they are characterized, each of those agencies has particular clientele to which it supplies services, has particular champions within the peculiar investment bank denoted as the relevant parliamentary assembly, and operates within an openly competitive environment where an enterprise's continued survival requires that it seek continually to cultivate support for its activities to withstand the similar competitive efforts of other enterprises. To be sure, it is possible to place all enterprises within a model of static equilibrium, in which case it is meaningful to speak of the stasis of profit maximization. Within an evolving framework of emergent dynamics, however, there is no stasis, and any apparent stasis is nothing but a reflection of offsetting expansionary efforts among enterprises.

As corporate bodies, political enterprises have capital accounts even though they are not typically conceptualized in this manner. As with the reference to constitutional parchment above, it is reasonable to distinguish between some parchment-based notion of the capital account and a genuine notion grounded in real action within an openly competitive environment. A parchment-based notion would say that "the people" are the owners of the political enterprise and would further say that politicians and agency executives bear a fiduciary relationship to "the people." While such notions are repeated often, that repetition does not witness the accuracy of those notions.

With respect to political enterprises and their capital accounts, we can distinguish between the initial entrepreneurial establishment of an enterprise and various practices that subsequently are undertaken to enable that enterprise to operate as a going concern (Commons 1934). At the stage of enterprise inception, an entrepreneur must sell a plan to supporters or investors. With respect to market-based enterprises, that selling is reducible to projections of net returns to investment. Political enterprises nominally are nonprofit organizations, and yet no enterprise would be established unless its sponsors sensed that they would gain by establishing the enterprise. In this respect, Pauly and Redish (1973) explain how a hospital organized as a nonprofit enterprise has a capital structure that returns what are effectively profits to physicians. A spectrum of venality comes into play in this respect. That gain, moreover, must pertain to the micro or action level, even if the enterprise might puff itself in ideological fashion through macro-level statements about public or community interest, reducing in the process a polity to a representative agent who supports the political action in question.

One significant aspect of constructing an enterprise is the design of its capital account. A corporate charter is a type of constitution, for it governs relationships among those who supply capital to the organization. The literature on agency notes the several ways in which the compensation of management is tied to indicators of the market value of firms. A good portion of executive compensation, for instance, is tied to changes in the market value of firms through stock options. Political enterprises are different in this respect because they have no market value; therefore, they are neither subject directly to the take-over processes that a capital market allows nor can executives be compensated through arrangements that vary directly with changes in firm value. All the same, all enterprises, however organized, face the problem of becoming going concerns in a setting where capital can always be deployed to other uses.

6. UNANIMITY, AGENCY, AND CORPORATE CAPITAL ACCOUNTS

Any publicly organized corporation, commercial or political, confronts problems of agency that arise because the suppliers of capital are more numerous than the subset of people who will direct the organization. The potential is always present for corporate managers to siphon corporate capital into their personal accounts in several forms, any of which reduces the net worth of the firm while increasing net worth of managers. By now, a great deal of literature has explored agency within commercial corporations. The general finding of this literature is that the transferability of shares of corporate ownership operates to mitigate though not eliminate the ability of managers to siphon off corporate capital, and with several strands of thought converging on this same theme. The most significant of those strands is the ability of transferable ownership to create unanimity among the owners regarding more valuable and less valuable corporate actions, provided that voting is weighted in proportion to shares of ownership. In the presence of transferable ownership, firms will have market value (De Angelo 1981; Makowski 1983). The establishment of market value induces a common utility function among corporate shareholders, with utility varying directly with firm value for all shareholders. Indeed, it is this common utility function that makes it meaningful to speak of agency among multiple parties.

Without transferable ownership, as is the case with political enterprises, agency might exist in a purely formal sense (Besley 2006), but the form of agency will lack substantive content. A corporation, commercial or political, faces at any moment a menu of possible activities. It would be normal to expect differences of opinion to be in play about the value of those activities. But those differences operate to different effect when ownership is transferable than when it is not. With transferable ownership, a corporation's vector of activities is reduced to a scalar measure of firm value through the market for ownership. In contrast, no such reduction is possible in the absence of transferable ownership, for all that exists is a vector of activities along with perhaps some statistics associated with each activity, but without those statistics being expressible as some market value.

With transferable ownership, it is reasonable to think that discussion among corporate governors about options will be genuine and logical. In contrast, there is good reason to think that such discussion will become eristic and non-logical in the presence of nontransferable ownership. The very transferability of ownership would seem to promote genuine discussion, in contrast to the eristic quality that would seem often to be promoted when ownership is not transferable. The source of this difference resides in the ability of transferable ownership to create a common utility function with respect to the actions of the enterprise. Without such a common utility function, the possibility of a disinterested test of claims vanishes, leaving only eristic references to public interest.

The reasonableness of working with a common utility function does not deny possible differences of opinion over possible corporate activities. It says that those differences are of the nature of scientific judgments in the presence of irreducible uncertainty. For instance, the executive board of a chain of franchised restaurants might be considering changes to its menu, whereby some items would be added and others deleted. It's easy enough to imagine differences in opinion among the members of the board because what is at issue is the effort to project future responses to current actions. About those responses people can reasonably differ, and there is no good reason to think that discussion will lead to agreement on a single projection even though there is agreement that higher value for the firm is better than lower value. To avoid the situation of Buridan's ass, however, at some point the motion must be called and a decision made. In this setting majority rule has much in its favor because there is unanimity about the desired direction of movement combined with uncertainty about how to get there.

The situation is different once capital can be conscripted, as it typically is with political enterprises. Without unanimity, no universal content can be assigned to the distinction between more and less. What is more and what is less will depend on who is asked to answer the question. The assessment of options among the members of some committee can no longer be arrayed along the real line in the absence of transferable ownership and the resulting existence of enterprise value. What exists rather is a vector of activities without some set of prices to reduce those activities to a common value.

To be sure, more than transferable ownership is involved. In the early days of commercial corporations, it was common for each owner to have one vote rather than each share to have one vote. So long as the number of owners was small and the various owners supplied similar amounts of capital, the differences between the two voting schemes were probably minor. But with growth in the number of owners and with dispersions in the amounts of capital invested among owners, the differences intensified and voting weighted by shares replaced voting by person with respect to commercial corporations, save for municipal corporations.

Cities are commonly described as municipal corporations, and these typically operate with unweighted voting, though at an earlier time votes were sometimes weighted in proportion to taxes paid. Municipal corporations face the same kinds of situations as commercial corporations, only they operate within different institutional environments. Both types of corporation might supply recreational services. Both periodically will face questions of retiring old equipment and adding new equipment. The governing board of the commercial corporation can be reasonably construed as seeking to maximize the value of the firm, and to choose the replacement equipment in a good faith effort to do so. It should perhaps be noted that what makes this construal reasonable is not some preference for venality by members of governing boards but rather is an openly competitive environment that compels such action in an effort to continue as a going concern. This is not to deny that agency problems might arise. For instance, a member of the governing board who chairs the committee on replacement equipment might skew the presentation to favor a supplier owned by his brother-in-law. While such activities happen, they are clearly recognized as corrupt in light of the obligation to seek to maximize the value of ownership shares.

Should the corporation become a municipal corporation, the environmental setting is changed. There is no longer any common standard of value against which options can be compared. Rather than firm value as a standard, some such virtual standard as "public interest" or "social justice" takes its place. There is, of course, an unavoidable ambiguity in references to firm value that arises because all actions are necessarily taken prior to the subsequent revelation of the value of those actions. Action is always based on projections of future results, and the *ex post* evaluation of action can differ from the *ex ante* projection in which that action was based. What transferable ownership accomplishes, and all that it can accomplish, is to inject some sense of sober realism into commercial discussion. Within the environment where commercial options are examined and chosen, there would seem to be a strong selection bias in favor of rectitude. When those options are examined and chosen within political enterprises, the institutional environment would seem more fully to select for misdirection and posturing, due simply to the absence of transferable ownership and the discipline this imposes on the making of claims.

7. COOPERATIVE AND POLITICAL ENTERPRISES AND THEIR CAPITAL ACCOUNTS

Political enterprises are organized as forms of cooperative enterprise, save that membership is acquired by geographical residence rather than through explicit request to join the enterprise. Like the standard form of cooperative association, political enterprises are of the nonprofit form whose operations are overseen by a governing board. For both ordinary cooperatives and for political enterprises, there is a tying together of the conceptually distinct capacities of being an owner of the enterprise and being a consumer of the enterprise's services. Municipal corporations acquire capital from residents and provide services to those residents (MacCallum 1970; Foldvary 1994). Informational processes, however, work differently for municipal corporations than they do for commercial corporations, both as those processes pertain to people as owners of assets and as they pertain to consumers of services (Wagner 2011a).

While the residents of municipal corporations supply capital to the corporation, they receive no explicit return on that capital. Yet capital always has an opportunity cost in terms of the return that could have been obtained from some alternative use of that capital. As a first-order approximation, it is surely reasonable to assert a general tendency for capital to expand in areas of activity where it offers relatively high returns and to contract in areas of activity where it offers relatively low returns. The end state or static representation of this tendency is equalization of marginal returns between capital deployed to commercial and political enterprises.

To describe this state as a first approximation is not, however, to signify that this approximation is close in a plausibly objective sense. The reference to first approximation pertains only to the counter-factual presumption that commercial and political enterprises operate within the same institutional environment, which means in turn that there is no effective distinction between commercial and political enterprises within the social ecology of enterprises. Yet there are significant differences between the institutional environments. Political enterprises are not subject to transferable ownership, which means in turn that people can't specialize in ownership. With respect to political enterprise, many people are forced and not willing suppliers of capital.

For commercial enterprises, the capital account can be meaningfully depicted in aggregated fashion because each shareholder has a *pro rata* share in that account. This is the quality of unanimity noted above, and which makes it reasonable to reduce the capital account to a representative account holder, for statements that pertain to one pertain to all. For political enterprises, however, the capital account cannot be so reduced, at least if that capital account is to be used to derive meaningful statements about an enterprise's operation. For political enterprises, it is necessary to distinguish between *de jure* and *de facto* capital accounts. By *de jure*, I mean the common representative agent reduction as reflected in statements of "we the people" or "we owe it to ourselves." By *de facto*, I have in mind the analytical implications of recognizing that a political enterprise will be operated for the benefit of a subset of those who supply its capital and consume its services.

Referring to an earlier discussion about Amtrak as a political enterprise, Amtrak seems clearly to be a going concern, or at least it has exhibited such characteristics to this point. Once we recognize the future to be open and hence uncertain, it becomes necessary to recognize that what appears to be a going concern today might not be so recognized tomorrow. Still, from today's vantage point Amtrak is a going concern in that it is able to generate revenues sufficient to pay its suppliers. While Amtrak receives more than $1 billion annually from Congressional appropriation, it would not have received that appropriation had it not provided service that some significant members of Congress valued more highly than other possible objects of appropriation. The governing boards of commercial corporations typically have large representation from large investors and creditors. It would seem reasonable to expect something similar for political enterprises. The cooperative nature of political enterprises, moreover, means that value cannot be extracted through the capital account and rather can only be extracted either through input supply or product purchase. By input supply, I refer to enterprises whose commercial profitability is increased by Amtrak. By product purchase, I mean large consumers of

Amtrak services who otherwise would pay for costlier substitutes. In the background of this illustration resides a general point about the capital accounts of political enterprises. Those enterprises must yield anticipated returns to whatever set of supporters is sufficient for that enterprise to operate as a going concern. That set of supporters, moreover, will be far narrower than the nominal owners of the enterprise. Those genuine owners, moreover, will reasonably expect to gain from the activities of the political enterprise as compared with the absence of that enterprise.

Commercial enterprises operate under different institutional arrangements than political enterprises, and these differences all center on the presence or absence of explicit enterprise value. Management in commercial corporations is compensated to a significant extent in terms of changes in firm value through stock options, along with various types of bonuses. Management in political corporations cannot be compensated in this fashion, at least not directly, though indirect forms of compensation might operate through occupational mobility. An executive in a political enterprise has opportunity to demonstrate future value to executives in private enterprises. In this instance, service in public enterprises can serve as a path of entry into complementary market enterprises. In this manner, performance in political corporations might lead to recruitment into commercial corporations.

With respect to recruitment into managerial positions, a literature has arisen which asserts that the recruitment of executives operates in tournament fashion where people compete for future managerial positions. There are even headhunting firms that operate in this specialized market. It is plausible to think that such firms seek to order candidates according to the contribution to firm value they are thought likely to bring to the firm. Political enterprises likewise need to recruit managers, and yet those enterprises have no information about the possible contributions of candidates to enterprise value to guide their efforts or order candidates. Yet ordering is necessary as a prelude to making choices. A school district, for instance, will have a Superintendent along with Principals for however many schools the district has. Districts, moreover, will vary greatly in size and compensation. The same situation characterizes police and fire departments, recreational services, and the gamut of politically supplied activities. To continue as going concerns, political enterprises as well as commercial enterprises must have ways of selecting systematically for managers who will continue to promote flourishing enterprises. The degree to which the qualities selected within the different corporate environments converge or diverge is a question worth further examination. For instance, it might seem reasonable to think that military promotion might reflect operational success in combat. Dwight D. Eisenhower never engaged in combat and yet became commander of all allied armies in Europe in World War II. In contrast, George Patton saw much successful combat going back to World War I, and yet was subservient to Eisenhower. Military advancement, just as advancement within public schools, police departments, and commercial corporations can all be analyzed as forms of tournaments, only what makes for success in such competitions varies across environments in which that competition occurs.

8. COMPETITION, CALCULATION, AND SCALE-FREE POLITIES

Competition is a vital facet of economic calculation, for competition provides an institutional check on economic calculation. Any claim that a commercial activity is worthwhile is put to a test through competition. That test is passed so long as people are willing to put their capital into the enterprise. Calculation for political enterprises must confront the weaker quality of economic calculation in two respects. One respect, noted above, is the absence of direct pricing for political services and the absence of market value for political enterprises. The other and possibly more significant respect is that political enterprises seem to be scale free, in contrast to the scalability of market enterprises. This scale-free quality would seem to generate a form of increasing return to the use of political power. Size brings advantages to political enterprises that it does not bring to market enterprises. If there is any case to be made for breaking up large enterprises, it surely applies more strongly to political than to market enterprises.

Sure, there can be economies of scale to enterprise size outside of the varieties of regulatory control that typically favor large enterprises. But those economies are still limited by competition and freedom of choice. As enterprises expand and problems of managerial control intensify, room expands for the operation of smaller enterprises. It is common to find producers of all sizes engaging in commercial and industrial activity. A firm that becomes so large that it faces increasing difficulty in managing its internal operations smoothly will at the very same time be creating opportunities for smaller firms to capture commercial space, provided only that they are free to do so and not precluded from doing so by politically created shelters for large corporations. The commercial world is largely scalable. This means that there is little significant difference between large and small firms other than size. At the relevant margins, all sizes of firms will offer the same products at roughly similar prices and will have roughly the same degrees of consumer satisfaction.

The same thing can't be said about political enterprises because of the scale-free quality those enterprises face. In other words, significant differences should be observed between a town of 10,000 people and a city of 100,000 people, and even more significant differences between either of these and a nation of 100 million people. This difference, moreover, reflects the inherently oligarchic character that overcomes democracies as they expand in size. A town of 10,000 can be governed by a Council with ten members, each of which is selected by a constituency of one thousand. It is reasonable to think such a Council member could know something about a thousand people, and would also have chance conversations with many of them in grocery stores, at the movies, or at high school theater productions or athletic events. The Council could have official meetings conducted by Robert's Rules, yet much of the business would be conducted informally and ratified pretty much by previously established consensus. Such a town probably wouldn't be a lot different from a club.

The situation changes a bit should the town grow tenfold to become a city of 100,000. If the same scale of representation is kept, the City Council would have to have 100 members. Precious little Council business could be done informally through conversations among members. The City Council would become the locus of doing collective business. But 100 people can't participate effectively in conversations. There will have to be limits on collective deliberation, both on who can speak before the Council and for how long. The ability to make such determinations is a position of oligarchic significance, as Roberto Michels (1962) and Gaetano Mosca (1947) explained carefully and which Bertrand de Jouvenel (1961) illustrated with lucid brevity. Alternatively, the size of the Council could be kept at ten. In this case, however, each member of the Council would represent 10,000 citizens. It is impossible for one person truly to know 10,000 people and to have random encounters with them. There would still exist a network of connections between Council members and citizens, but a graph of that network would no longer be random.

As size is increased from 100,000 to 100,000,000, those oligarchic tendencies would surely increase. At this scale, few people would have any direct connection with representatives. A graph of the pattern of connections would be distinctly non-random (Barabási 2002). This pattern is a simple reflection of the scarcity of time. With a constituency of 1,000, someone who has ten random encounters a day will have on average four such encounters with each citizen within a year. When the constituency size increases to 10,000, the limited time of the representative still gives time for but ten random encounters per day. Over a year, this representative will have but one random encounter with one-third of the constituency. And when the scale is increased to one million constituents per legislator, the chance that any citizen will have a random encounter with the representative will fall to less than four chances in ten thousand. Oligarchy is an inescapable product of large-scale democracy due to limits on time. A graph of legislator–constituent interactions will have power-law features where the preponderance of people has no direct connection, and with nearly all connection occupied by a few, a few, moreover, that have multiple sources of power and influence behind them. An individual who has four random encounters in a town might have a similar frequency of indirect encounters in a nation as a result of being a member of some organization, but that very observation speaks to qualitative changes that result from the size of democratic polities.

Federalism is a form of government that in principle can operate to curb the oligarchic tendencies of democracies, as explained in such works as Vincent Ostrom (1987), Michael Greve (2012), and Richard Wagner (2014c). For that potential restriction on oligarchic tendencies to be effective, it is necessary that the federalist system operate in an openly competitive manner. This system of genuine federalism, however, easily gives way to a form of spurious federalism (Eusepi and Wagner 2010). Within the US, the direct election of federal senators in conjunction with the creation of the federal income tax did much to cartelize what had been a reasonably competitive system of federalism where states and local governments existed in a more openly competitive environment than they do now, even if the openness of that competition was not as open as it could have been. Yet the shift from a relatively competitive federal system to a relatively cartelized system was itself a product of political entrepreneurship wherein people continually seek options they value more highly than those they currently experience. As Ben Franklin noted, the creation of a republican form of government is not itself reason for that form to persist. Whether it does persist or how long it persists or the manner in which it erodes is itself a systemic and emergent quality of social interaction. The energy to propel those interactions is supplied by economizing efforts of individuals as they participate with others within a complex constellation of institutional arrangements where there is no puppet master though there are many people who participate in pulling strings in one direction or another.

7. Societal tectonics and the art of the deal

Within a democratic polity an election selects a set of political officials who collectively oversee governmental actions. Reality presents us with many particular forms of parliamentary assembly. Some of them are quite small, as illustrated by councils for small towns that might have but a handful of members. Others have several hundred members. There is plenty of reason to think that much of significance resides in the size of a parliamentary assembly due to the scale-free qualities of democratically structured interaction. Parliamentary assemblies of all sizes resemble financial intermediaries and not industrial firms. Parliaments don't produce goods and services for customers, but rather serve as intermediaries between people who are seeking support for their enterprises and people who have the means to support those enterprises. It is in this setting that parliamentary assemblies are *peculiar* forms of investment bank, in that a good deal of parliamentary intermediation is forced and not voluntary. Donald Trump's (1987) *Art of the Deal* is a lucid description, written from the subjective orientation as a participant in making deals pertaining to real estate transactions within a system of entangled political economy.

Maffeo Pantaleoni (1911) set forth a related line of analysis, only written from an objective orientation where he treated parliamentary assemblies as forms of bazaar that feature many enterprises selling their wares. Political activities are organized through networks of transactions and so are catallactical in nature, only the institutional arrangements that frame parliamentary activity are peculiar when compared against those that frame ordinary market transactions. Members of a parliament are engaged in putting together legislative deals that will attain concurrence among a relevant set of parliamentary members, starting with the relevant committee and then extending to the full assembly. Those deals are made on behalf of people who are seeking parliamentary sponsorship for enterprises they are promoting. Those deals are undertaken in a context where choices must be made because scarcity and competition are as much a fact of life inside the parliamentary bazaar as they are within the rest of society. To support a higher appropriation for one enterprise requires supporting lower appropriations for other enterprises, or else either supporting higher taxes to be imposed on some people or supporting increased borrowing, which is a different way of raising taxes. In contrast to the dyadic character of ordinary investment banking, deal making within the parliamentary investment bank is triadic. This triadic relationship sets up a parade of societal tectonics (Young 1991), which is the social equivalent of earthquakes. Through such tectonics, democratic politics, especially at a large scale, operate more as sources of turbulence than as sources of stability (Wagner 2012d).

1. TRIADIC TRANSACTIONS AS TEMPLATE FOR ENTANGLED POLITICAL ECONOMY

Entangled political economy entails the claim that all processes associated with political economy have a transactional or catallactical character (Commons 1934). The economic theory of a market economy is completely catallactical, but so too is the political, only those transactions are triadic and not dyadic (Podemska-Mikluch and Wagner 2013). Entangled political economy seeks to overcome the conventional theoretical antinomy wherein economy is treated as organized through market transactions while polity is organized through teleologically guided planning, and with candidates competing by setting their plans for action before voters (Persson and Tabellini 2000; Besley 2006). Entangled political economy starts from recognition that property rights are not absolute and invariant, but rather denote social relationships that are subject continually to margins of contestation and potential change (Bowles and Gintis 1993). At any instant, a social order will contain a collection of enterprises that have been organized by different sponsors under different institutional arrangements. Among the enterprises denoted as schools, for instance, some will be organized as profit-seeking enterprises, others as nonprofit corporations, and still others as politically sponsored enterprises. Those different types of schools will have different capital accounts which in turn will generate different patterns of conduct with respect to deploying the art of the deal. Contracting between profit-seeking enterprises will typically play out differently than contracting between profit-seeking and politically sponsored enterprises, as Richard Epstein (1993) explains. Within a social order, the partially decomposable subsystems denoted as polity and economy each contain many organizations within their precincts, and with those organizations interacting among themselves in both cooperative and antagonistic ways.

While all organizations are oriented teleologically through plans, the resulting order emerges spontaneously through interaction among participants (Aydinonat 2008). Within polity there is no one organization that denotes polity, for polity is plural and not singular with respect to its organizational pattern. Neither a president nor a parliamentary assembly represents a polity but rather they denote particular organizations inside polity. This recognition is reflected in the treatment of a parliamentary assembly as a *peculiar* form of investment bank that operates inside a polity. This analytical framework treats budgetary configurations as emerging in largely bottom-up fashion through complex networks of transactions. The core of this theoretical effort entails dissolution of the theoretical antinomy between polity and economy. Both polity and economy contain numerous enterprises, each teleologically oriented, but with all such enterprises operating within a non-teleological order. To recur to an earlier illustration, society is a pedestrian crowd and not a parade. That pedestrian crowd, moreover, contains an admixture of organizations that are by no means oriented on and reducible to a common objective function.

The economic activities of human societies have ecological character. A society contains an intertwined set of enterprises, some commercial and others political. Those enterprises don't operate independently of one another in separate ponds of activity. They are intertwined in a complex human ecology. Prices emerge through commerce, which is possible only with alienable property. Economic theory has largely been concerned to explain how alienable property rights operate to promote social cooperation through competition among commercial enterprises. Complex forms of social organization are made possible by the information that is created by the market prices that arise from commercial transactions. Those prices provide navigational aids that promote the growth of complex commercial ecologies.

Market-based cooperation, however, is only part of the story of societal coordination. A complete analysis of societal coordination requires political enterprises to be brought into the picture, and without resorting to systemic teleology as distinct from the local teleology that accompanies the activities of individual entities within the societal catallaxy. Within the complexity of modern societies, the ecology of enterprises must necessarily rest heavily on alienable private property. Hence, commercial enterprises occupy the foreground and political enterprises the background of a healthy social ecology, for the value of politically sponsored activity is generally derived from market-based activity, even as the politically sponsored enterprises operate to modify market-generated patterns of activity. The value of a marina and of commercial activity generally is determined directly by the willingness of people to support the marina. The value of the highways and the dredging that support the marina, and of political activity generally, are subordinate to and derived from the desires for the marina. People don't support dredging services for their own sake, but do so only in consequence of their desire to visit the marina; the demand for collective services is derived from the demand for market services.

All models of political economy treat an economy as a complex organism that is self-organized through interaction among people in the presence of private property. To say something like "the market works" is to engage in metaphorical and not material speech. There is no market that does anything. "Market" is an abstract noun that is used to denote processes of commercial interaction. When it comes to polity, however, orthodox political economy commonly treats the state as a person or enterprise. This is the state as a mechanic who tunes the social engine. To be sure, orthodox political economy contains extensive debates over how competent the mechanic-state might actually be, but those debates occur within the presumed antinomy between polity and economy.

Entangled political economy treats political entities as operating on the same plane as economic entities. The polity, just like the economy, contains multiple participants who differ both in what they know and in what they desire and yet who operate within the same social order. It is just as metaphorical to assert that the state does something as it is to assert that the market does something. What we denote as state activity, as with market activity, emerges out of complex patterns of interaction, the properties of which remain largely to be uncovered. Whatever that uncovering might reveal with respect to particular details, the dyadic and triadic transactional forms will be seen at work in giving particular shape and tone to a society.

2. SMOOTHNESS, ROUGHNESS, AND THE ORGANIZATIONAL MARGINS OF ACTION

Methodology is not independent of substance. The two interact. A model allows some questions to be examined more deeply or fully than otherwise would be possible. At the same time, however, any model prevents other questions from being addressed because those questions don't fit within the model's framework. The theory of the firm with which economists mostly work illustrates this interdependence between method and substance. The standard theory of the firm can be modeled on a smooth, twice-differentiable surface. Doing this allows precise answers to be given to some questions while preventing other questions from being asked. For instance, tectonic clashing created by collisions between differently constituted organizations cannot come to life on smooth surfaces, save for navigational error, as it were. To explore these ideas requires a rough surface, as illustrated by non-integral or fractal geometry (Potts 2000), wherein tectonic clashing can become a systemic quality of interactions among differently constituted enterprises. Conceptualizing the action arena as resembling a Koch snowflake with its sharp and ragged edges offers a framework to accommodate tectonic clashing; conceptualizing that arena as some smooth surface cannot. While this point about interdependence between methodology and substance is a general one, to maintain contact with this book's analytical scheme I shall limit elaboration of the point to the theory of the firm.

Most economic models treat firms as producing a single product. Pantaleoni's (1911) model of parasitical political pricing from which I have drawn strong inspiration was based on a model of a single-product firm. His analytical point of departure was the theory of a single-product firm operating under free and open competition. Hence, he defined economic prices as prices that were equal to marginal costs. Doing this allowed Pantaleoni to create an unambiguous starting point against which to compare his conceptualization of a system of political pricing. The condition that price equal marginal cost is the standard theory of the firm, with a great deal of welfare economics revolving around violations of this condition. Indeed, the standard theory of public goods is a variation on violations of this condition. In Samuelson's (1954, 1955) contributions, production of a public good had positive fixed cost and zero marginal cost. Even though a way might be found to price such goods, the standard Pareto-efficiency conditions would be violated so long as the positive price prevented anyone from consuming the good. This conceptual situation was an adumbration on a model of a single-product firm modeled on a smooth surface wherein a fence around the public good prevented entrance to people who nonetheless had positive value for the good. This formulation leads instantly into second-best types of analyses within the context of a single-product firm (Wagner 2015b).

As a descriptive matter, it is reasonable to wonder just how many single-product firms there are in reality. There might be a few, but they would surely be rare. Perhaps two eight-year-old girls selling punch in front of their home on a summer Saturday might comprise a single-product firm. But even this would change if they added cookies or brownies to their product line. Bringing these girls into the discussion in this way illustrates the point that there is effectively no such thing as a single-product firm. A good part of the reason for this situation is surely the absence of anything even remotely approaching full knowledge of what people would like to buy. With reasonable presumptions about possessing only limited knowledge, wise commercial conduct resides with those who offer a line of products. One might like to say that people will want to buy bread, and so bakers bake bread. But to say this is to impose the model of the single-product firm upon the world rather than letting the world share its features for theorists, and with those theorists then seeking to articulate the underlying coherence of those features.

Actual bakers bake numerous types of breads, in addition to baking cakes, rolls, muffins, and other flour-using items. As an accounting artifact, it would be possible to construct a concept of marginal cost as pertaining to an artificially created composite good, which would allow reduction of a multi-product firm to a single-product firm. But customers don't buy composite goods. They buy real goods. In thinking about the real situation that bakers face, marginal cost is ill-defined. Production is too heavily involved with common costs and joint costs for marginal cost for a single product to be definable in anything but an arbitrary accounting manner, as many of the essays collected in Buchanan and Thirlby (1973) explain and which Marburger and Peterson (2013) illustrate in concrete detail. Still, to remain a going concern the baker must earn revenues above expenses. For a multi-product firm, however, relevant action occurs along numerous margins and not just a single margin denoted as output or even composite output, and with those margins resembling the roughness of a Koch snowflake and not the smoothness of a circle.

In most settings where a theory of the firm is used, the distinction between a single product and a multi-product firm does not do significant work. All it does is complicate the analysis, which warrants use of the single-firm model in those cases. When it comes to political economy, however, a multi-product notion of a firm can open into insights that a single-product notion precludes by the very construction of the model. The multi-product firm has numerous margins of action, in contrast to the single-product firm where the only margin is output. The same claim can be made with respect to input markets. The single-product firm is accompanied by two generic inputs, labor and capital. The equivalent construction for a multi-product firm would recognize a multiplicity of inputs. The single-product firm involves continuous variables; the multi-product firm involves discrete variables.

The question at issue is: what difference does this make for understanding the art of the deal within a system of entangled political economy? The generic answer to this question is that it brings into the open the myriad margins that are necessary for putting together the triadic deals that are the *sine qua non* of a system of entangled political economy. A number of bakers of various sizes and with various typical product mixes might be organized within the market. Within the polity there might be regulatory agencies that deal with safety and credit, and with those agencies in turn having different champions within the legislature. Within this miniature ecology, various deals are explored and made. Some bakers might have access to some source of genetically modified rye that is not approved for use, and which in any case would not be available to other bakers because of the limited supply of this rye in conjunction with durable contractual commitments. Those bakers might face a reluctant regulator, and seek to induce a champion within the legislature to prod the regulator. That champion, in turn, is trying to reduce resistance among other legislators to amending a bill favored by a manufacturer of billiards tables located in his district. Multiply this partial glimpse of a deal a good number of times, and we begin to peer into the substantive playing out of the art of the deal within a system of entangled political economy. To deal with that substance analytically requires recognition that reality is filled with margins of action wherein the art of deal making concerns understanding which margins to move forward along, and which to leave alone.

3.   POLITICAL MONEY LAUNDERING AND THE ART OF THE DEAL

The discussion surrounding Panel B of Figure 5.1 explained that triadic transactions within a system of entangled political economy had an underground character relative to transactions within a dyadic arrangement. The dyadic arrangement is the ordinary commercial relationship where buyers and sellers exchange pieces of their property, typically a product, say a loaf of bread, for money. The triadic arrangement has underground features to soften what would otherwise be a clear display of venality. While money is the language of commerce, there are many dialects through which that language can be spoken. At any instant in any society, there will be some implicit ranking of those dialects along a spectrum of venality. Direct bribery, as with a baker giving money directly to a regulatory official to get a favorable ruling on genetically modified rye would head the list of dialects of venality. At the other end of the spectrum would reside such activities as the baker taking out a full-page ad in a high school production in which the regulator's daughter had a leading role. The challenge for putting together deals in any case is to create paths of connection when most people have no such paths available to them in large-scale democracies, even though they might in small towns.

   To recur to Pareto's (1935) distinction between logical and non-logical action, to describe deal making within a system of entangled political economy as a form of money laundering is to adopt an objective and not a subjective point of view. From the subjective point of view, there are just different ways of putting together deals, with deals between private parties being put together differently than deals between some mix of private and public parties, as Trump (1987) notes in his discussion of various real estate deals, all of which involved participation with public agencies. There are different ways of putting together deals, and this is just one of those facts of life. People working on the ground level understand this and deal with it. There are pitfalls involved in dealing with public agencies that often require choices of whether the trouble is worth the gain (Epstein 1993), but such peculiar business transactions are transactions all the same. In a small town or even a modest-sized city, connection between political figures and citizens is relatively open and easy. It is in relatively large scale democracies that networked relationships take on significantly non-random features. It is ultimately the scarcity of time that gives an oligarchic tenor to democratic arrangement of large scale. Those arrangements and their venal qualities likewise are discrete in nature and feature myriad margins of action. In any case, from a subjective orientation deals are put together under institutional conditions of varying complexity, but deals are still just deals.

From an objective point of view, different patterns of deal making would be observable in societies with high entanglement as compared with societies with low entanglement. Only some of those patterns would be reducible to a direct exchange of a product or service for money. In other patterns, an exchange of service for money could be inferred, but that inference would fall within the domain of plausible reasoning. In some cases that inference might be easy to make, while in other cases it might be on the order of difficulty of Jerzzy Neyman's (1950) analysis of making a judgment about a lady's claim that she could tell whether in making a cup of tea it was the milk or the tea that was put first into the cup. Whatever the degree of difficulty in arriving at such inferences, it is surely reasonable to describe these indirect transactions as forms of or cousins to money laundering. Someone spends money on an activity in anticipation that some desired outcome will result. A baker takes out an ad in the anticipation that he will get an audience with a regulatory executive to get an exception to an existing regulation. This kind of deal has an element of speculation that ordinary commercial transactions don't have. All the same, the principle of following the money is surely wise counsel to invoke in any effort to develop explanatory theories of fiscal catallaxy. Without doubt, some people will object to such analytical efforts on the grounds that people attracted to political activity have weaker interest in venal matters than people attracted to commercial activity. This proposition is far from obvious. Public employees show at least as much concern with their pay and benefits as other employees. Prominent legislators who leave the business often stay in the capital city and sell their services to people seeking to make deals. People who seek political positions may have a stronger interest in wielding instruments of power than do people who seek positions in commerce and industry, but it is difficult to find notable differences in attitudes toward the venal side of life. Granted, it is easy to find politicians who complain about greed and thereupon seek to raise taxes—and yet what finer exhibit of greed is there than to advocate taking from people who have earned something so that those who have earned nothing can spend it?

4. PARLIAMENTARY TECTONICS

Deals made within a framework of political catallaxy should generally be less durable than ordinary commercial deals, and with the difference in durability expanding with the size of the political unit. With reduced durability comes increased turbulence. This proposition about political sources of turbulence is, of course, sharply contrary to orthodox macroeconomic theories which hold that political action can calm societal turbulence. This orthodox claim on behalf of macro stabilization is a wholly hortatory proposition that is not grounded in any coherent framework that is suitable for continually evolving societal ecologies, as Wagner (2012d) explains. The orthodox proposition about political action is incoherent because it fails to take into account the properties of emerging systems of political economy that operate under different institutional settings.

With respect to the pure market catallaxy described by Panel A of Figure 5.1, there is solid reason to think that durability is the default setting of that form of catallaxy. This setting is a feature of the relational nature of market contracting in conjunction with the fixed costs that accompany the creation of new relationships. Even such a simple activity as changing a grocery store will encounter a fixed cost of getting familiar with the different layout of the new store, which will increase the time required to shop until familiarity has been attained. To describe durability as a default setting is not, however, to invoke a presumption of equilibrium. To the contrary, the conceptual framework used throughout this book is of a non-equilibrium or ecological framework. Creativity and change are ubiquitous in social systems of the modern type. Entrepreneurs continually inject new plans and enterprises into society. Some of those succeed and others fail. Either way, a healthy societal ecology will be characterized by turbulence, and with that turbulence in no way indicating that something is wrong that might call for correction, in contrast to the common presumptions of orthodox macro theory. The commercial world will have some degree of natural turbulence.

Setting aside the natural turbulence that is a by-product of commercial creativity and entrepreneurial action, the most significant source of societal turbulence surely resides in political catallaxy. That turbulence, moreover, intensifies as the domain of the political grows within society, as well as intensifying with the size of the political unit. Within the pure market catallaxy described by Panel A of Figure 5.1, both the creation and failure of enterprises inject turbulence into the societal ecology. With respect to creation, new enterprises must fabricate new commercial relationships. Doing this will disrupt some commercial relationships already in place, which in turn will elicit further adjustments due to the interconnected quality of the social order. With respect to failure, commercial relationships will be disrupted, and with those disruptions leading in turn to disruptions of other commercial relationships. While disruptions to commercial relationships cause turbulence, all participants are residual claimants to their activities and contracts and so have strong reason to seek other relationships in an efficient manner. The legal framework of private ordering, moreover, supports efficient disruption by allowing breaches of contract subject only to the condition that the breaching party compensates the other party for reasonable losses of expected profit.

Within the dyadic catallaxy, the owner of a failed plan has strong reason to liquidate the enterprise and redeploy those assets to what now appear to be their most highly valued uses. The situation is different within the triadic catallaxy described by Panel B of Figure 5.1. The owner of a failing plan can seek additional support from a political sponsor. Political sponsorship of that failing enterprise might be accompanied by logical-sounding remarks about the enterprise being too big to fail, but this statement reflects rationalization of a non-logical sentiment. The legislative sponsor of that enterprise will have to secure that increased support in competition with other legislative sponsors of other enterprises, which renders the resulting outcome a product of complex catallactical interaction accompanied by some degree of money laundering to square the accounts.

This sponsorship of a failing enterprise would by some measures appear to reduce turbulence. The enterprise that receives added support will continue as a going concern. That continuation, however, will be accompanied by other adjustments in the catallaxy as other relationships are readjusted to make room for the additional support for the enterprise in question. What if the enterprise in question had been allowed to fail? Most likely, it would have been reorganized under new management. The old management did not do such a good job judging from observation, so there are good grounds for thinking that successful managerial bidders to operate the enterprise will do a better job with the enterprise. These kinds of consequences are clearly in play within a continually evolving ecology, even if any effort to assess their significance would entail speculative judgments.

Within legislative assemblies, moreover, deals are less durable than within a dyadic catallaxy due to significant institutional differences. Within the framework of equilibrium theory, market outcomes will be invariant so long as preferences and knowledge are invariant. In contrast, a triadic catallaxy does not have an equilibrium position defined for invariant preferences. Even if preferences and knowledge are assumed to be invariant, outcomes can change within a triadic catallaxy. This quality of political catallaxy is often described as cycling. William Riker (1962) explained that successful political coalitions tended to be of minimal winning size because that was the size that would maximize the gains to the winners. One thing this situation means is that there will be no equilibrium defined in preferences. Consider a simple majority game of two against one, where a new game is played at some regular interval. Each member of the winning coalition gets one dollar while the loser pays two dollars. There is no logical reason why this coalition will persist in future periods. For instance, the loser might offer $1.50 to one of the winners to form a new coalition. The person who previously lost $2 will now gain 50 cents, a clear improvement.

The general point of this illustration is that any majority rule outcome established for one period can be revised the next period, with this logic having no end. There are, it should be noted, institutional arrangements that curb the range of majority cycling. One of those arrangements is the organization of parliamentary assemblies into parties. These institutional arrangements operate to reduce the fluidity in coalitional patterns, but they do not eliminate that fluidity. Hence, legislative deals will have less durability than the deals made within market catallaxy. The hortatory pleadings of orthodox macro theory for political action to calm catallactical volatility run contrary to the explanatory analysis of the comparative properties of dyadic and triadic arrangements.

5. HOW MUCH MONEY IS THERE IN POLITICS?

From time to time someone advances a claim that political campaigns should be more expensive than they actually are if common presumptions about the significance of rent seeking are accepted. Gordon Tullock, the founder of the rent-seeking idea in Tullock (1967) published a later work (Tullock 1989) where he wondered why the amount spent on seeking rents through political favors wasn't higher. If a sugar quota is worth something like $500 million annually to producers, why isn't something like that spent to maintain the quota program to stave off predators who might shift those rents to other activities? The simplest equilibrium model of rent seeking leads to complete dissipation of the rents. Two risk-neutral parties with equal chance of securing a rent valued at $10 billion will each spend $5 billion to secure that rent. While political campaigns are expensive, they are not nearly as expensive as would seem to be suggested by the models of rent seeking. Perhaps the significance of rent seeking has been exaggerated. But perhaps it hasn't, and what has happened instead is that people have been looking in the wrong places for evidence.

This long-standing question about the implications of rent seeking for the amount of investment in political campaigns has been framed within a model of additive political economy. Within this model, an election is the point where future policies are chosen, and so an election is the fulcrum where rent seeking is elevated through campaign contributions. People compete for political favor by contributing to campaigns, and receive returns through rents after the election. Under exact dissipation models of rent seeking, aggregate campaign contributions would approximately equal the aggregate value of rents. It is plausible to locate the election campaign as the locus of rent seeking within a model of additive political economy where a periodic election is the moment where rents are awarded for the next election period.

The situation changes within a framework of entangled political economy. For one thing, political and economic activities are continuous. For another thing, an election is not the locus where future policies are chosen but is only an arena where some of the participants in the creation of future policies will be selected. It is, moreover, misleading to speak of policy as being *chosen* because it really emerges through *interaction* among various interested participants—and with the character of those interactions shaped by some framework of rules and conventions. Little substantive work is actually accomplished through elections and political campaigns. The substantive work is done outside electoral politics, and entails the interactive elements necessary for constructing and maintaining deals. Once this situation is recognized, it should become apparent that the realm of what we denote as "political" is not confined to elections and their associated campaigns.

Look at movies and television shows. What is the subject matter? What kind of activity is being portrayed? And how do such things fit into the processes through which political activity proceeds in society? Political agencies advertise their programs just as do market-based firms. Political agencies have public affairs offices just as do market-based firms. Political agencies engage in such outreach services as providing speakers at various events. Look at the content of newspapers, and consider changes in the distribution of space over the years. If you ask where you will see the political, is not the answer "everywhere?" As for how this situation has come to pass, must not the only economically sensible answer be that the process through which this has happened offered gains to significant players along the way?

6. PARLIAMENTARY ASSEMBLIES AS PECULIAR INVESTMENT BANKS

Within the spirit of Pantaleoni (1911), Wagner (2007, 2012c) treats parliamentary assemblies as forms of investment bank, peculiar forms to be sure. A regular investment bank intermediates between people who have funds they wish to save rather than to consume and people who have enterprises for which they are seeking support. The officers of the investment bank are intermediaries in this process of bringing together the two sides of the saving–investment relationship. Within this framework, a parliamentary assembly would be the officers of the investment bank and the outcome of the assembly would be a budget in conjunction with orders and regulations imposed on market entities.

While the parliamentary assembly might be divided into teams or parties, it should not be presumed that the harmony of Nash equilibrium prevails there. The people who populate such assemblies are energetic, ambitious, and intensely competitive, with nearly all of them striving for greater prominence than they now have. Competition is surely as severe among the members of a party as it is between parties, even if that competition manifests itself differently between the settings. Prominence is achieved by bringing business to the bank, only the funds are supplied largely through forced saving. Pantaleoni worked under the assumption that all income was taxed at the same rate. Suppose a parliament operated under the rule that whatever enterprises it chose to support, the resulting budget would be financed by a flat tax applied to all income without exemption or exclusion. This represents one particular system of political pricing. There are an indefinite number of systems of political pricing corresponding to the indefinite number of particular ways a particular magnitude might be extracted from some given set of people.

The parliamentary investment bank is a hub for making deals. Urban transportation, both historically and contemporarily, provides numerous illustrations of material that would seem amenable to analysis within the motif of the peculiar investment bank. Early in the twentieth century, jitneys were a market-based form of mass transit (Eckert and Hilton 1972). People who owned cars would carry people downtown in the morning and back in the evening, for a fee. Jitney service was competitively organized and it reduced traffic congestion from what it would otherwise have been.

Despite its successful qualities jitney service succumbed to hostile regulation as well as giving way to streetcars and busses. More recently, streetcars have been gaining political advocates, though now with streetcars rebranded as light rail. While a good deal of hortatory writing surrounds urban transportation, the investment bank motif would seem to offer a potentially fruitful template for explanatory analysis regarding triadic political economy.

If we take two snapshots separated by some time interval, one might show a scene with people riding in jitneys while the other shows a scene with many people riding in municipal streetcars or busses. Suppose, along the lines of the analytical narratives collected in Bates et al. (1998), we were to try analytically to construct the missing frames that connected the first scene to the second scene, thereby converting the snapshots into a movie. One thing that must be recognized in facing this analytical challenge is historical contingency. At any moment there can be several possible paths forward, with one of those paths being a product of parliamentary deal making in that session. This is the nature of the setting in theorizing about open-ended and emergent phenomena.

If we start with jitney service which seems to be working well, we must ask how political involvement in urban transportation comes into play. The formal answer must be the standard answer of some entrepreneur seeing an opportunity to make a deal (Kirzner 1973, 1979), only one that seems more salable to a parliamentary assembly than to some private investors. One question always to ask about political entrepreneurship is how does the entrepreneur capture profits from his activities? Perhaps he is seeking to get the city to create a streetcar enterprise, which he would operate for a while and then convert that position into a higher-paying position of an executive of a company that manufactures streetcars. There are many possible avenues of entrepreneurial gain in a world of historical contingency.

For the entrepreneur to be successful there must be people who are unhappy with current jitney arrangements and the options to those arrangements, probably taxis. Jitneys paralleled residential density and also main traffic arteries, as well as mostly following the ebb and flow of the normal work day and work week. While many people clearly had convenient jitney service, not everyone did. For instance, people who worked at home or in the neighborhood and who wanted to go downtown for only short periods would probably not be well served by jitneys, and perhaps would prefer not to pay taxi fares. There would seem to be a latent demand for some alternative transit arrangement, only one that would not be supported by investors acting through normal commercial channels populated by real investment banks. Perhaps the peculiar features of a parliamentary investment bank would generate support for a municipal enterprise.

Rather than engaging in extended speculation about how support for such a deal might be generated within the parliamentary investment bank, suppose it is done and a municipal bus enterprise is created. That enterprise will have a *de facto* capital account that pertains to those who receive cash flows through the enterprise that they would not otherwise have received. After all, if no one expected to gain from creating the enterprise, it would not be created. It is not necessary that everyone gain or even that most people gain. It is, however, necessary that at least some people gain. One significant facet of the art of the deal in this case is putting it together in such a manner that the gains go where the sponsors intended. Another facet concerns how to bring non-logical sentiments into play in support of the deal. Yet a third facet concerns how possibly to increase the price to competitive sources of transit, which in turn would increase demand for the municipal service. For instance, a tax could be placed on parking garages or limits could be placed on parking spaces allowed in new construction. In these and numerous other ways, the explanatory challenge is to bring politically sponsored activity into the same explanatory rubric as market-based activity, making due allowance for institutional details regarding the putting together of deals in different environments.

7. TAXATION, ENTANGLEMENT, AND THE SIZES OF FIRMS

It has long been noted that the distribution of firms by size is highly skewed, however those firms are classified. In large measure, that distribution is treated as a natural product of a market economy, as illustrated by Simon and Bonini's (1958) early treatment and Luttmer's (2007) recent treatment. These efforts seek to explain features of recognizable market processes that would account for the highly skewed distributions that persistently are observed. The data on which these observations are based come from periods of high entanglement between polity and economy. Recognition of this situation brings into analytical consideration the extent to which the observed size distribution is a quality of dyadic ordering and to what extent it might be a quality of triadic ordering. It is easy enough to model the sizes of firms as resulting from a stochastic process where at any instant each firm faces equal chances of expanding and contracting by some percentage of its previous size. This scheme would generate a skewed distribution with many firms stacked near the origin and with a few very large firms that had experienced the equivalent of a long run of heads on a coin flip.

But observed economic interactions are not governed wholly by the institutional framework of free exchange and private ordering. Governance rather involves considerable latitude for restricted exchange and public ordering within a framework of entangled political economy. Is it not reasonable to think that the observed size distribution of firms might differ within a system of entangled political economy from what it would be within a pure market economy? While it might not be easy even to define how this question might be addressed, or even whether it is decidable (Chaitin et al. 2012), it is nonetheless something worth exploring in light of continuing controversy over whether contemporary troubles are economic or political in character when we have no contemporary experience with a pure market economy.

To illustrate this question, compare what might be described as a nation of shopkeepers, where the preponderance of economic activity is organized through proprietorships, with a nation where the preponderance of activity is organized through corporations. Political enterprises derive their revenues through taxation and not directly through sales to customers. Might not tax-financed political enterprises tend to favor corporations over proprietorships, and perhaps large corporations over small corporations, because large corporations provide more nourishment for political parasitism? The preponderance of modern taxation is collected for governments by corporations. Income taxes, social security taxes, and sales and excise taxes are all collected in this manner. The only exception is the property tax on real estate, and even this is only a partial exception. People who own houses without mortgages pay real estate taxes by writing checks to the relevant governmental unit. In the case of those who have mortgages, however, which covers the bulk of residential real estate, taxes are collected largely through the lenders who put funds into escrow accounts and transfer the payments to the relevant governments.

It is surely plausible to think that the corporate form of enterprise in conjunction with its elaborate procedures for record keeping facilitates tax extraction within a society by obviating the need for governmental entities to reach directly to individual citizens. A point of individual contact is still necessary as the collections passed on by corporations undergo a final verification and reconciliation, but the bulk of the work in tax collection is done by commercial corporations. In this setting there are reasonable grounds for thinking that parliamentary assemblies would be able to arrange a larger volume of deals in an economy where much activity is organized through large firms than when it is organized as a nation of shopkeepers, due to the position of firms as agents of tax collection. This type of causation would run from firm size to polity size.

The alternative direction of causation also seems plausible. Suppose a political enterprise can contract with a single large firm or a dozen small firms to yield the same outcome. The political enterprise will have to monitor the firms with which it works so as to ensure that those firms do their part in upholding the politically sponsored deals that parliament ratified. Suppose there is a fixed cost of establishing a monitoring relationship, along with a variable cost that is proportionate to the amount of activity monitored. Under this assumption, the variable cost to the political enterprise of monitoring transactions is the same, whether the relationship is with a few or with a large number of firms. The fixed cost is perhaps a dozen times higher when contracting with the set of small firms than when contracting with the single large firm. The political enterprise is not a residual claimant, so there is no one who can capitalize directly on reducing fixed cost. Differences in fixed cost, however, still have implications for the choices of agency managers and interested political sponsors. Fixed costs in this case speak to the use of managerial time. Reduction in those costs might increase managerial free time. Alternatively, reduction in those costs can allow managers to undertake activities they value more highly but which would be precluded by having to deal with many small firms, especially in light of recognition that the work accomplished by the dozen small firms is identical with the work accomplished by the large firm.

8. REGULATING MONEY AND CREDIT TO COMMAND THE SOCIETAL HEIGHTS

Within a capitalist system, entrepreneurship is the locus of leadership in society. It is through entrepreneurial activities that the substantive forms of life differ in the future from what they were in the past. Where in the past people washed their clothes on scrub boards, as time passed they came to use washing machines. And rather than hanging the clothes on lines to dry, they dried them with clothes dryers. Along with these kinds of changes in the substantive ways that people lived, there were also associated changes in the features of commercial enterprises. As the growth of automobiles made it possible for people to travel longer distances over any period of time, chains of hotels and restaurants emerged, doubtlessly giving a sense of familiarity while being away from home. Within a capitalist system, entrepreneurship is at the forefront of generating the changing societal configurations that people will experience. Finance is a vital facet of entrepreneurship. While it is possible for entrepreneurs to finance their plans from their own wealth, such plans can be multiplied by bringing wealth from other people into the entrepreneurial ambit. Finance allows this to be done, and in several ways. Finance can occur through equity or debt. Politics is also involved in bridging present and future. With respect to parasitical politics, credit provides a commanding height for a program of political domination within society.

On conceptual grounds, there are strong grounds for thinking that free banking and private ordering dominate central banking and public ordering in systems of government by distributed and local knowledge (Selgin 1988; Selgin and White 1999; White 1999, 2012). Yet the political investment bank continually returns support for public ordering and central banking. There must be patterns of cost and gain to particular people that return this result as a durable feature of the deals made within an entangled system of political economy. The literature on public choice and political economy has identified two strands of thought that work in this direction. One strand concerns the possibility that electoral competition will generate economic instability in an electorally systematic fashion, provided only that there is political control of money and credit, as illustrated by the essays collected in Willett (1988). The other strand notes that collectively undertaken counterfeiting masquerading as "monetary policy" can serve as a form of taxation, provided only that the creation of outside money is the province of political authority, as Selgin and White (1999) explain. Both of these strands of thought locate a direct link between political control and economic impact.

Indirect links seem also plausibly to be present. By indirect, I mean the ability of control over money and credit to increase the private demand for regulation within the real economy. Money and credit would seem to represent a commanding height in modern economies. Nikolai Lenin advanced the image of a commanding height from which a program of economic control can be employed. Lenin, however, thought in terms of heavy industry such as mining and manufacturing supplying the heights from which the remainder of the economy could be controlled (Bolsinger 2001). Alternatively, the commanding heights might be located not within the real economy but within the realm of finance capital. Within a dictatorial political system it is perhaps reasonable to locate the commanding heights within the real economy to the extent a dictator can insert power wherever he chooses. Within a democratic system, however, there is no such position of outside insertion. Power emanates from inside the system, and must to some extent be invited by some subset of people to do its work within the broader society.

Central banking, and credit regulation more generally, can serve as a source of state revenue, but it should also be remembered that pretty much whatever can be accomplished through budgetary appropriation can also be accomplished through regulation. For instance, an appropriation for public schooling can be pretty much eliminated by requiring that parents send their children to approved schools. Regulation can thus expand the influence of governmental entities beyond what budgetary magnitudes might indicate. With respect to regulation, might not the regulation of finance serve to leverage regulation into what are normally designated as real activities? Consider the common distinction between real assets and financial claims on those assets. As a point of analytical departure, suppose you start with a desire to implement a progressivist program of exerting governmental presence throughout a society. One approach to doing this would be to take on the challenge industry by industry, by forming contractual relationships with those enterprises while also imposing conditions on the market entities that join in those relationships. For instance, a government agency might contract for the delivery of trailers, but make as a condition of fulfillment that the company hires only union labor. Some companies will refuse to enter into such a bargain, but others will accept (Epstein 1993) and will be snared by that bargain. This procedure would be a type of conquest through commercial bribery financed by taxation.

Might not the regulation of finance reduce the cost of promoting an expansion in the business done by politically sponsored enterprises? Instead of pursuing regulation across *n* distinct groupings of real activity, regulation could be concentrated more on finance. The groupings of real activity would self-enlist in regulation through the financial channel, leading to finance capital serving as a commanding height in society. By regulating the terms of credit that lenders can extend, those lenders would seem to be in a position of enforcing regulatory requirements indirectly. The reference to commanding heights fits the progressivist program of subjecting society to thoroughgoing political control within a spirit of totalitarian democracy where there is no principled limit on the reach of political entities (Goldberg 2008). Nearly all entrepreneurial activity requires outside finance. By controlling finance, the real economy can perhaps be subjected to political control with less resistance than would have been encountered by direct efforts to exert control over real activities.

There will always be more requests for financial support than there will be ability to provide that support. Within the free-market vision of a credit market, individual creditors will decide which projects to support, with the aggregate of such projects being the outcome of what is denoted as the credit market. Cannot regulation applied to credit transactions be used as leverage to extend regulation to real activities? For instance, might not financial regulation that requires lenders to hold a balanced portfolio defined in terms of, say, old and new technologies for energy supply advance a program of real regulation more effectively than efforts directly to exercise that control? Energy companies would no longer face a political adversary. They would face a market of financial suppliers, each of whom faced regulatory standards. But these suppliers would not be adversaries, but would rather be commercial entities that could not fulfill all demands. Political control over finance will enlist suppliers of finance in the service of administering a program of real regulation. Doing this would seem to project political figures more centrally into positions of prominence with respect to being in the foreground and not the background of evolving commercial activity. A system of free competition in money and credit would seem to entail a more passive role for political enterprises in determining the substance of entrepreneurial experiments than would a system where processes regarding money and credit are subject to extensive public ordering.

9. CREDIT AND SOCIETAL LEADERSHIP IN A SYSTEM OF ENTANGLED POLITICAL ECONOMY

As a qualitative matter, credit stands apart from typical transactions in goods and services. Those typical transactions are connected with past economic decisions and technologies already in place. Buying a phone, a car, a pair of shoes, or nearly anything else is a transaction that is rooted in previous entrepreneurial choices that have generated the menu of goods and services from which people can choose in the present. The abstract theory of consumer and producer choice refers to choices among presently available objects. For those objects to be available, they must have been objects of entrepreneurial action at some earlier moment. Among other things, entrepreneurship bridges present and future. Presently observed commercial configurations are emergent products of past entrepreneurial activity. Today's entrepreneurial activity will transform those configurations into what will be experienced tomorrow and the subsequent string of days after tomorrow.

Joseph Schumpeter (1934) explained that entrepreneurship is the locus of leadership in a capitalist society. Entrepreneurship occupies the foreground where the transition from present to future occurs. Starting from now, it would be possible to imagine a set of parallel universes, with the different universes corresponding to different selections among possible entrepreneurial projects. Those universes would have a common point of origin, but they would diverge as time passes due to differences in entrepreneurial projects selected. To be sure, this possibility is typically obscured by presumptions that knowledge is fully possessed prior to action. Once it is recognized that action is a source of learning, along with recognition that learning and knowledge are specific and not general, the choice among entrepreneurial projects influences the structure of knowledge at work within a society.

Credit markets are thus implicated in the determination of numerous specific features of the life we will come to experience. Much of this will be small in scale, as illustrated by the types of breakfast cereals that will be available. But some of it will be larger in scale, as illustrated by the types of medications people will take or the attributes of the cars they will drive. Entrepreneurs are thus competing among themselves to seize the future. Successful entrepreneurship offers both fame and fortune. Within an institutional framework of free banking and private ordering of credit transactions, the future qualities and characteristics of a society are an emergent feature of this market process.

While a good deal of entrepreneurial activity is self-financed, credit is also a significant source of entrepreneurial support. At any instant, we can distinguish between entrepreneurial experiments that were set in motion in the past and entrepreneurial experiments that just now are dreams and not actualities. So long as scarcity prevails, the amount of support for future projects desired by incipient entrepreneurs will exceed the amount of funds available to support those projects. Within a system of free banking, the division between projects selected and projects rejected will be an emergent quality of this system of financial intermediation.

Free banking and the private ordering of credit transactions is obviously a fragile arrangement, and this fragility perhaps attests to the deep truth that Carl Schmitt (1932) articulated in his treatment of the autonomy of the political. Credit markets are centrally implicated in the transformation of the present into the future, though, of course, more than credit markets are involved in this transformation. Private ordering of credit transactions would seem to have relatively weak survival value within democratic systems. The weakness of this survival value can be seen by asking about the sources of support for injecting public ordering into credit markets. Those sources would seem to fall into two broad categories. One refers to entrepreneurs who are dissatisfied with how they think they would fare within privately ordered credit markets. The other refers to political figures who want to catapult themselves from background to foreground in the cosmic drama that is human society. Private ordering consigns political figures to the important but still secondary task of being stagehands to assist the actors who are the prime carriers of the drama. Public ordering allows those officials to move to the center of the stage, as it were.

These two categories together operate to insert public ordering into credit markets. On the demand side are market participants who think they could gain through public ordering. These can be people who might have been denied credit, who were granted credit but on less favorable terms than they had hoped to receive, or who had been executives of failing enterprises who were given a new lease on their executive life styles by receiving support from a political agency. For instance, someone might have wanted to build a solar powered car but could not find sufficient support to allow the enterprise to move forward. Alternatively, someone might have received a small loan for a pilot study of a new process for building storage batteries that might support solar powered cars, only the borrower found the lender asking repayment when the borrower had hoped for an extension of the loan along with an increase in the amount lent. In the presence of these and many similar circumstances, it is easy to see how a latent demand for public ordering might be converted into a deal within a political investment bank.

To activate that latency requires political figures who sense that such expressed unhappiness with private ordering offers a platform that can help those figures move into positions more in the foreground of the cosmic drama. The move from private to public ordering is facilitated by the replacement of what Pareto (1935) described as logical action by what he described as non-logical action. The gist of Pareto's 2,000 pages is presented luminously by Raymond Aron (1967: 101–76), with McLure (2007) elaborating the fiscal sociology of Pareto and his Italian compatriots.[1] Non-logical action operates when there are no prices or choices to be made, with this situation leading to rationalization based on sentiment and ideology. For instance, ideological articulations about how alternative power might provide a cleaner environment might resonate favorably with the sentimentality of many people, thereby breaking ground to facilitate the insertion of public ordering into the market for credit.

Just how that public ordering might be inserted can take any of several forms. It could result through budgetary operations, perhaps by establishing an enterprise that would offer favorable loans to enterprises that worked with different technologies for powering cars. Alternatively, it could result by imposing requirements on market-based lenders that, say, 10 percent of their loans must go to enterprises dedicated to exploring new ways of powering cars. As such requirements expand, the credit market increasingly becomes dominated by public ordering. Through such extensions of public ordering, it is possible to arrive at a situation where tie-ins are created of the type that for some given volume of loans with positive expected profitability for the lender, some volume of politically favored loans with negative expected profitability for the lender must be made. Yet that component of expected negative profitability cannot offset the component with expected positive profitability, for if that happened the deal would not go forward. A tied arrangement is created through regulation, wherein deals with positive expected profitability are combined with deals that have negative expected profitability. Such deals are likely to be accompanied by secondary guarantees, possibly accompanied by language about being too big to fail. In any case, the triadic transactions of entangled political economy will have different substantive qualities than what would emerge within a credit market governed exclusively by private ordering. It would still be reasonable to speak about a credit market, only its operating properties would differ as between a setting of wholly private ordering and a setting where credit markets are governed by some admixture of private and public ordering as befits a system of entangled political economy.

NOTE

1. During his career, Aron treated Pareto several times in various ways, and with Campbell (1986) identifying four distinct versions of Pareto in Aron's work. It should be noted that those four distinct versions reflected changes in Aron and his set of concerns as the years passed, for Pareto's body of work had been completed by the time Aron started writing about Pareto.

8. Moral imagination and constitutional arrangement

The preceding seven chapters have been concerned with explanatory topics that arise in treating politics as a peculiar type of business practice within a context of entangled political economy. Hortatory topics have surfaced on occasion, but the focus has been on genuine explanation of interactions among political and economic entities. By genuine explanation, I mean the avoidance of resorting to such teleological fictions as postulating a social welfare function, treating "government" or "state" as denoting some action-taking entity as against denoting a congeries of interdependent entities, or positing that collective outcomes are the mechanical execution of commitments made during political campaigns.[1] To the contrary, I have approached my explanatory task by embracing the setting posed by the fable of the blind men of Hindustan, and doing so without resorting to the *deus ex machina* of a sighted person who sees the entirety of the situation. There is no sighted person or philosopher king who sees the entirety, though there are many who seem to claim to do so, probably as a reflection of the enduring competition for attention space (Collins 1998) that is an indelible aspect of human nature. While that competition for attention will understandably promote various claims of being sighted and thus seeing the relevant entirety, such claims all exemplify what Hayek (1974 [1989]) described as the pretense of knowledge. That pretention, moreover, is abetted by the framework of general equilibrium theory which allows reduction of a society to a representative agent whose optimizing plans are disturbed from time to time by exogenous shocks. In the aftermath of this common methodological move, society is eviscerated and the autonomy of the political and the work it does disappears, and with the raucous quality of a pedestrian crowd transformed into a placid parade.

While the primary interest that has informed the construction of this book has been explanatory, economics is also a science of general social significance because it concerns the qualities of human interaction and living together in close geographical proximity. Humans have a reflexive quality through which we can escape the moral straitjacket imposed by orthodox presumption of people having given preferences. Ross Emmett

(2006) captures beautifully this reflective quality and its possible implications for economic theory when he asks what Frank Knight would have thought about George Stigler and Gary Becker's (1977) claim that economists should assume that preferences are invariant across time and place. With Knight having died several years before Stigler and Becker published their remonstrance, Emmett's essay was an imaginative reconstruction of a debate that never happened but which poses starkly the implications of the reflexive capacity of humans for theories based on a denial of such a capacity. Just as individuals have the ability to view themselves reflectively, they also have the capacity to recognize that they are caught within some social system wherein the object denoted as society is pretty much observationally equivalent to the object denoted as God (Durkheim 1915).[2] God and society are both externally given objects that variously place demands on people, make impositions on them, and can help them to order their lives. This reflexive quality points toward political economy as a form of societal agriculture that lies between science and moral philosophy. As science, it recognizes that people and societies exhibit law-like qualities that are open to discovery and articulation but are not open to repeal. As moral philosophy, it seeks to bring that science to bear on uncovering the various terms of the Faustian bargain that the use of political power injects into societies (Ostrom 1984, 1996).

The book opened by referring to Benjamin Franklin's remark at the conclusion of the American Constitutional Convention in 1787 that the Convention had created a republic, but whether it would be kept was for the future to tell. It's clear that it hasn't been kept, as the original creation has morphed into something else through a process of piecemeal evolution, a crisp account of which is Richard Epstein (2014), and which I refract through public choice theory in Wagner (2014b). The first seven chapters of this book have set forth explanatory ideas that can help to give an account of this evolutionary process. This observed record also elicits hortatory-type questions. Has the observed evolution been a good and unavoidable adaptation to changing conditions? What is unavoidable is inevitable, in which case there is no point in asking about its goodness. But perhaps at any instant divergent paths were available, and some of the paths not taken might have been better. But that was then and this is now, and today those rejected paths might no longer be attainable nor might they seem so good. The emergence of political parties might have undermined republican principles even if that emergence might have taken a century or so to do its work. The emergence of industrial gigantism in the nineteenth century might have altered the political landscape so severely that genuine republicanism could not survive. Perhaps the emergence of electronic communication and social media, with its replacement of reading with video, did the actual work that Franklin saw only as possibility. However the historical pattern might be explained, the narrative could be one of always beneficial societal adaptations to changing conditions, in which case people always live in the best of the attainable states of the world.

Alternatively, those rhapsodic claims and beliefs might just be noise made to sound good through ideological blinders that lead people to see and embrace what is not there, much as Pareto (1935) saw non-logical action. Victor Klemperer (2006) in his study of *The Language of the Third Reich* explains that language is much more than a means of writing and thinking, for it also governs sentiment and feeling. It is easy, perhaps natural, for scholars to exaggerate the power of reason. After all, reason can only work with what feeling and sentiment give it to work with (Dennett 1978). Perhaps the language of contemporary life has constructed a "we" out of nothing by expanding the sharply limited domain to which "we the people" originally pertained. After all, if someone kidnapped you and a friend, took you to some dark parking lot, and robbed and beat you, you would not later tell police investigators that "we went for a ride." You and your friend would comprise a "we," but the two of you plus the kidnapper most certainly would not. To use "we" properly requires consensus among those whom the "we" covers.

The language of welfare economics and economic policy, for instance, treats all political entities as all-encompassing instances of "we." The notions of social welfare functions and conceptual unanimity reflect this encompassing "we." Perhaps such ideology repeated again and again comes to be accepted. If so, the stage is surely set for an expansion of the reach of the political within society. In this respect, we may wonder what the reach of the political would be if there were general recognition of Pareto's response to claims on behalf of using political action to maximize social welfare: "how can you maximize happiness when happiness for the wolf requires eating the lamb while happiness for the lamb requires avoiding being eaten?" So, yes, language matters in its ability to govern feeling and sentiment, for it is these that are largely responsible for what particular matters people choose to reason about. In other words, methodology and substance are not separate endeavors that can be added to generate Truth. To the contrary, method and substance are entangled, which means that what our theories allow us to see depends on the methods we adopt to examine our material.

1. THE ENTANGLED QUALITY OF METHOD AND SUBSTANCE

All social theories refer to objects that no one can apprehend directly. No one has ever seen a society, a polity, an economy, or other similar objects to which social theories repeatedly make references. Those objects are creations of prior theoretical construction, and with social theorizing proceeding in the aftermath of that prior construction. Once this situation is recognized, it becomes immediately apparent that there are different ways of constructing the objects that social theories are subsequently employed in examining. The substantive statements that are generated within a social theorist's mind thus depend on the methods he or she uses to construct objects which the theory examines. Method and substance are entangled. This situation poses, in turn, questions regarding the usefulness or helpfulness of different conceptual frameworks to use in apprehending societal reality.

Arthur Lovejoy (1936: 7) explains that the nominal features of theories rest on and reflect "implicit or incompletely explicit *assumptions*, or more or less *unconscious mental habits*. . ." (Lovejoy's italics). With respect to these habits of mind, Lovejoy distinguished between two within the western philosophical tradition, both present in Plato. One was a simple and other-worldly scheme of thought that appears robustly in Enlightenment-style thinking, and which posits a vision of societal perfection to be pursued through the acquisition of knowledge. The other was a complex, this-worldly scheme of thought which replaced fables about perfecting reality with emphasis on vigorous action within this life. With respect to Erik Reinert's (www.othercanon.org) distinction between two canons for economic theory, Lovejoy's this-worldly scheme of thought would fit within the Renaissance canon, which is a non-equilibrium scheme of thought suitable for capturing the turbulence of a crowd of energetic pedestrians pursuing their myriad and distinct plans.

As Lovejoy explains, alternative unconscious mental habits channel social theory in different directions, each bringing different material into the analytical foreground. The Enlightenment mental habit is the predominant habit within contemporary economics. This scheme of thought is other-worldly in that it compares an imperfect reality with some vision of perfection, which in turn often leads to the advancement of suggestions of how power might be used to nudge society closer to some imagined state of perfection. This unconscious mental habit has led to the generation of various schemes of thought that reflect that mental habit. General equilibrium theory, particularly of the stochastic sort, is one such reflection. This scheme of thought sets forth a vision of perfection in conjunction with recognition that reality falls short of perfection and so requires the insertion of power to move society closer to perfection. The stochastic quality of the theory is necessary to explain why perfection is never attained, which in turn means that the insertion of power into society will always be warranted.

The non-equilibrium scheme of thought this book embraces reflects a this-worldly orientation where a directional belief in progress is replaced by a non-directional belief in experimentation and change. Within this mental habit, there is no source for the injection of power into society because power is always resident within society. Hence, polity and economy refer to autonomous features of societal interaction wherein people are continually engaged in activities that are generating the reality they will live with and experience, and with no end in sight for this process. It is worth noting that change is present in either scheme of thought. Within the other-worldly scheme, change is the consequence of those reflexive characters who seek to remove sources of imperfection their theories have identified. In this case, the "their" refers to some intellectual vanguard who must bring society along with their plans and schemes toward greater conformity with some external image, as befits the Progressive vision of political leadership. In contrast, change within the this-worldly scheme is the activity of everyone as they act in their various ways and precincts. People are naturally curious and inquisitive, and they experiment in numerous ways, some small and others large, all of which contribute to societal change. Some people might change their patterns of consumption, as in shifting from meat to vegan diets. Other people might develop new products or enterprises. The full range of such change promotes on-going societal evolution in bottom-up fashion.

2.   AGREEMENT, ACQUIESCENCE, AND IDEOLOGY OF SOCIAL CONTRACT

The notion of a social contract is often used in political economy as a type of Paretian derivation to express the sentiment that people should accept this or that use of political power because . . . , and it is in continuation of this sentence that analytical problems arise. The standard sentiment expressed by claims of social contracts is that people have agreed in advance to whatever outcomes the political process generates. The idea of a social contract is thus wrapped inside the shell of commercial and personal contracts with which people have actual experience. People know what it means to agree to do something. They know what it means to keep their promises, and they recognize that breaking those promises is generally a bad thing. Most people, moreover, have experience in collective, club-like settings where they participate in group decisions, and sometimes a decision is made that runs contrary to the choice they wanted. By joining the club and agreeing to its procedural rules, people can reasonably be described as having made a form of social contract. With club-like settings, people are always free to leave the club, but so long as they remain they are obligated to support club decisions because they said they would do so by the fact of their joining the club.

This club-like setting grounded in human experience is typically extended to political entities, surely not because some act of logic commands that extension but rather out of some underlying sentiment that resonates with human nature and the pursuant recognition that we are social creatures. It is on this basis that Wagner (2007) claims that both polities and markets are grounded in human nature. One facet of that nature requires accomplishment and autonomy which market-governed relationships support. The other facet recognizes interdependence with others which supports relationships grounded in collective action of some sort. To accept the assertion that no man is an island is not, however, automatically to embrace the orders issued by particular collective entities. A person can acquiesce in a situation without accepting or embracing it. One can recognize that the notion of a social contract is a fiction or myth or derivation, but this recognition changes nothing but the language we use in describing a situation, which can be quite significant all the same (Klemperer 2006).

There is a categorical difference between agreeing to a situation and acquiescing in it. The former leads to notions of social contract. The latter does not. Look at the American Constitution and the republican form of government that was established in 1787. Obviously, some people agreed to that. But not everyone in the land agreed. Those who did not can be said all the same to have acquiesced in the new Constitution. For one thing, a good number of people wanted to remain British and had no desire to secede. Some of these people did not acquiesce in the Constitution and moved to Canada, but many of them did acquiesce and remained. Of those who remained, many opposed the Constitution. It took two years to marshal sufficient political support to get legislatures in all 13 colonies to ratify the Constitution. About a third of the participants at the Constitutional Convention withheld their support for the Constitution. While the essays collected in *The Federalist* are well known today for their support of the Constitution, the writings by the anti-federalist opponents of ratification were likewise numerous, thoughtful, and impassioned (Storing 1981).[3]

Agreement is easy to recognize, both subjectively and objectively. Subjectively, individual participants will recognize when they have agreed to participate in a collective process that generated outcomes that were not of their liking. Objectively, a third party can collect various observations through such means as transcripts and interviews to determine whether it is reasonable to infer that the parties accepted the need to make some collective decision, even if the actual decision made is contrary to what they would have liked. This type of observation, it should be noted, accords with a two-part procedure for undertaking collective action. The first part addresses whether the participants agree that the body should undertake some collective action in response to a situation, regardless of the substance of that action. The second part begins only if the first part has been answered affirmatively through a consensus among the membership. To be sure, political decisions are not made in this manner, probably because fewer such decisions would be made. For instance, a polity that does not presently provide medical insurance would first have to secure consensus on the desirability of some collective provision before moving on to deliberations over how actually to do that. Otherwise, it cannot be reasonably claimed that collective provision became part of a social contract because the desirability of collective provision was never put to a reasonably consensual test. For it to be put to such a test, it would first be necessary to have a decision on whether there was agreement that some form of collective provision should be instituted, and with the implementation of any such program subsequently left to ordinary political processes.

One can acquiesce in collective outcomes without agreeing to them. This is surely a reasonable distinction to make, and it leads thought along a different path than it would follow if it pursued the social contract path. Under social contract ideology, all collective action is *ipso facto* warranted because it was all warranted by the social contract. For instance, there can be no violation of the Fifth Amendment if one truly embraces the social contract ideology. At the end of the day, that ideology must declare that all collective action is warranted because all participants agreed to the procedures through which collective action emerges. One might object that a particular taking is for private use and not public use. Such a person can try to seek legislative or judicial reversal. If those efforts fail, however, the taking must *ipso facto* have been for public use because the social contract ideology allows no other option.

Acquiescence is a different matter. It is possible and meaningful to acquiesce in a situation without choosing or embracing it. For social creatures there is no option but to live in society, and with everything that this brings in its train. Even near-hermits who live in out-of-the-way places in Alaska occasionally catch a train to go to town for supplies and a bit of conversation. One can picnic in a park while having no desire to associate with anyone else in the park. Some associations can be embraced while others are avoided. Civic associations are volitional. Political associations on such a small scale as a town might be similar, but as the size of political associations rises they become increasingly grounded in conflict due to the operation of triadic processes where losing parties have no satisfactory ability to escape being losers in those processes. On a small scale, one can acquiesce without rancor because one can also recognize the value of living in society. As political entities expand in scale and scope, the demands placed on what might be called the ethics of acquiescence increase, and surely bring in their train increased political rancor within political entities from which there is little or no reasonable option for exit.

3.   VALUATION, COGNITION, AND THE CONSTITUTION OF THE POLITICAL

Alexander Hamilton opened Federalist No. 1 by asking "whether societies of men are really capable or not of establishing good government from reflection and choice, or whether they are forever destined to depend for their political constitutions on accident and force." The task of securing good governance through reflection and choice requires the exercise of both the cognitive faculties and the moral imagination. The moral imagination speaks to what makes for a good polity, recognizing with Carl Schmitt (1932) that any polity will have autonomous features. For instance, is a good polity one where its members are able to support themselves in an independent manner? Or is it one where significant numbers of people are apparently unable to do so, and thus depend in significant ways upon politically dispensed largesse? And do not think that such dependence pertains only to people with relatively low incomes. There are also a good number of corporate executives who owe their positions to their ability to arrange deals with political figures to avoid bankruptcy and the reorganization that would have resulted. The recipients of such largesse are likely to be compliant voters in supporting politicians who support largesse. Independent persons are surely less dependable in this respect. The cognitive faculties come into play because the operating properties of any political arrangement will fall within the purview of economic law, and that arrangement may work to undermine what would be regarded as a good polity. In the face of such a conflict between cognition and valuation, either constitutional modification will be necessary to recapture the good, or the existing arrangement will continue to play out in contrary fashion. Political economy as societal agriculture thus involves both appropriate valuation regarding goodness in systems of governance and accurate cognition regarding the ability of particular constitutional arrangements to support or undermine what is thought to constitute goodness in governance.

Government necessarily involves a form of Faustian bargain, as Vincent Ostrom (1984, 1996) explains. Government injects an instrument of evil, force and violence, into human relationships, under the presumption or hope that the weight of the evil forestalled or prevented is even heavier. Whether this hope is borne out is a different matter. Ideas from the theory of statistical decision making are relevant here. The central idea from that theory is that perfect decisions are impossible because errors will be unavoidable. Any decision procedure operates as a form of filter that allows some actions to go forward while preventing other actions. There is no such thing as a perfect filter, any more than there is such a thing as a universal solvent. Filters can err in two ways. They can let pass items that should have been filtered out, and they can keep out items that should have been allowed to pass.

The Fifth Amendment to the American Constitution can be used to provide substance to the idea that decision procedures operate as filters. That Amendment allows government to take private property subject to two conditions: (1) the taking is for public use and (2) it is accompanied by just compensation. It is easy to see that the Fifth Amendment is a reflection of the classical liberal foundation of the American republic (Epstein 1985, 2014). That Amendment starts from recognition that the taking of private property can be for good public use, with the assembly of land to build highways being a common illustration. The requirement that just compensation be paid reflects the classical liberal basis of the Constitution. The first American constitutional document, the Declaration of Independence, asserted that governments derive their just powers from the consent of the governed. Hence, private property comes first, normatively speaking, and people use their rights to property to establish governments to preserve and protect those rights. While the Fifth Amendment allows governments to take property, that taking must be for public use which means in turn that it will be of general use to the citizenry. The requirement of just compensation means effectively that governments should act as if they were engaging in market transactions when they take property. Any way you look at it, the Fifth Amendment seeks to have governments act in congruence with the private law principles of property and contract, all the while acknowledging that governments have powers that ordinary citizens lack.[4]

Having such powers, moreover, means that they can be abused as well as used in a manner consonant with the classical liberal foundations of the Constitution. Whether those powers will be used or abused, or the extent to which they will be, depends on the working properties of the constitutional filter through which the Fifth Amendment works. Any framework for decision making will be plagued by the two types of errors. With respect to cognition, one well-recognized principle regarding collective action is that no person should be a judge in his or her cause. This is a principle that is easy to state and hard to implement. For instance, it is represented in the practice that someone who complains about some state action can file a complaint in federal court. Symmetry within a federal system would require that a complaint about federal action could be adjudicated in a state court. But this isn't the case, and our federal system contains this among several systemic biases that operate to give a cartelizing drift to what began as pretty much a system of competitive federalism (Greve 2012). In similar fashion, numerous executive agencies act in a legislative capacity in creating rules that people must follow and act again in a judicial capacity in adjudicating complaints they have filed against those same people. The underlying principle of liberal constitutional governance is concurrence among differently situated people, for such concurrence is the only effective or pragmatic way for determining whether some principle has been followed or violated. But does the principle of concurrence give sufficient guidance when humanity is fabricated from crooked timber?

4.   LIBERTY, SERVILITY, AND THE MORAL IMAGINATION

What is the cost of liberty? What is the value of servility? And what are the tradeoffs between the two? It is often taken for granted that people want to be free. But is this really so? Living free imposes conditions and restraints on people. Basically, people must live as independent people who make their way in the world as governed by the private law principles of property and contract. Being independent does not mean living in isolation, not at all. It means participating in society through relationships governed in congruence with the principles of property and contract. Myriad forms of cooperative association emerge when people live freely in close geographical proximity, as David Beito (2000) explains in his examination of mutual aid societies prior to the coming of the welfare state. Participation in cooperative association, however, requires that people pull their own weight (Wagner 2011b). Responsibility for one's conduct is a concomitant of liberty, and it's conceivable that some people will regard the cost of responsibility as too high relative to the value they place on liberty, and so opt for servility (Buchanan 2005). It's equally conceivable that some people like to think of themselves as guardians who shepherd, herd, or nudge people who seem to those guardians to be incapable of conducting their own lives in a good way.

In June 1959, for instance, I entered the American Army under a program where recent high school graduates could discharge their military obligation by serving on active duty for six months, followed by three years of reserve training one weekend a month and two weeks during the summer. A good number of people who I knew at that time liked army life more than civilian life. Civilian life was mostly a liberal life where you had to make your way by employing your talents in providing services that other people valued. In civilian life you were pretty much responsible for yourself and the circumstances of your life. Army life was mostly a servile life, particularly at the level of an enlisted recruit. You were told when to wake up and when to go to sleep. You were told what to wear and what to eat. You were cared for comfortably so long as you did what you were told. You weren't free, but neither did you have cares that went without attention. If you became sick you received medical care. If you couldn't see well, you would be fitted for glasses. Materially speaking, it was a fine even if not a luxurious life, but I didn't know luxury at home either so I didn't miss anything in that respect. But I wasn't free, knew it, and didn't care for it. But many of the people I knew during those six months of 1959 did like it, or at least said they did.

James Buchanan (2005) pondered the possibility that significant numbers of people have become afraid to be free. There might not be any conscious sense of fear to be in this state. There could just be a sense of comfort in knowing that if you didn't want to drive a car or hire a taxi, you could enlist in a public program that would provide van service from door-to-door. Or, alternatively, rather than enduring the arthritic pain your job continually reminds you about, you can be granted a disability pension. These simple examples could be multiplied many times to generate a long list of activities that are provided through bureaucratic agencies that substitute for what would otherwise be activities that people would have to organize through their practice of free association. This situation might not be an active fear of freedom so much as it is an exchange of the responsibilities of living freely for whatever comfort it is that servility offers. One long-standing aphorism declares that "when the going gets tough the tough get going." Quite obviously, this aphorism is practiced by many people. Equally obviously, however, many people embody the aphorism "when the going gets tough, find a place to rest."

Robert Frank (1987) asks "If homo economicus could choose his own utility function, would he want one with a conscience?" The point of Frank's paper was to argue that a conscience could be a valuable means of pre-commitment, which in turn suggests the value of an affirmative answer. Frank's formulation takes for granted that conscience, or morality generally, is an object of choice. It is a strategy that one selects to achieve what one wants. There is no doubt that strategic considerations can influence actions. It is doubtful, however, that such actions reflect what people mean when they speak of conscience. Thieves act strategically in selecting their targets. But thieves typically don't steal from one another, for conscience mostly leads to honor among thieves. One cannot choose among moral precepts in the same manner as one chooses among books or shoes. The mind is not a *tabula rasa* onto which a particular morality can be placed or erased as the owner of that mind chooses.

Morality is surely not an object of choice that exists on the same plane as ordinary consumer goods, as Graham Walker (1990) explains in his treatment of the reality of the moral. Lexicographic orderings and not utility functions are surely a more accurate and useful way for thinking about morality in relation to action. An adult did not have the option to choose a morality because that morality was implanted during childhood, for better or for worse. Morality was implanted through practice within some social context until the moral sentiments became habits outside the realm of conscious thought or reflection (Elias 1939 [1982]).The existence of conscience, or the substantive structure that conscience entails, is not an object of choice but rather is something that has been generated through practice starting with childhood. Within a framework of lexicographic ordering, conscience operates to influence the valuations a chooser places on the particular options for choice the chooser faces.

This is not to say that morality remains invariant after leaving childhood. It is only to assert the primacy of practice as the means by which the substantive conduct that constitutes morality is acquired or extinguished. A system of bourgeois commercial relationships rests upon a legal order of property, contract, and liability. These legal institutions create the central governing framework for a market economy. These institutions also reflect a particular form of moral imagination (McCloskey 2006, 2010). These legal institutions can be given a reasonably accurate representation as moral injunctions. The legal principle of property maps reasonably well into a moral injunction to refrain from taking what is not yours. The legal principle of contract maps reasonably well into a moral injunction to keep your promises (or to secure the permission of the aggrieved party before breaking a promise). The legal principle of liability maps reasonably well into a moral injunction to make good the wrongs you do to others.

A market order operates more effectively in the presence of people who possess such moral imaginations. At the same time, a market order tends to reward practice that conforms to that morality. For the most part, commercial activity that is consistent with the moral order that, in turn, is complementary with the legal order will yield higher commercial returns than will conduct that runs contrary to that moral order. Such traits as being reliable, energetic, and trustworthy will tend to bring larger commercial return than such traits as being unreliable, lazy, and dishonest.

Hence, commercial practice tends to reinforce its supporting morality. To be sure, it is possible for children to reach adulthood within environments wherein the habits of heart and mind that have taken hold within them do not yield high return within a commercially oriented society. Recognition of this situation recurs to the closing section of Chapter 5 regarding the distinction between sentimentality and muscularity with regard to issues concerning mutual aid and the welfare state.

What happens when political enterprises and their economic activities enter the picture? To address this question, it is necessary to look first of all to the kinds of practice that political entities sponsor. This is because the crucible within which the moral imagination is shaped and reshaped is primarily the world of practice and not the world of theory or conscious reflection. To pose the question in this fashion is to ask whether political enterprises call forth the same, or at least complementary, kinds of practice as do commercial enterprises (Wagner 2006b). The Fifth Amendment sought to place political participants in the same kind of practical setting as market participants. Political parties were not envisioned at the time of the American constitutional founding, and politics was mostly a temporary service activity and not a profession. Within this earlier setting it would be reasonable to think that politicians were similar to random draws from the population, in that they would share the same interest in independence and liberty as the rest of the population. People would carry those values with them in executing their offices, and even the autonomy of the political would be expressed with those values lurking nearby. But what were those values? How might they be characterized?

5.   MORAL SENTIMENTS: GLOBAL VS. LOCAL

Political economy necessarily touches upon moral sentiments in some manner. Additive political economy does so in a global or top-down manner. It asks what constitutes goodness where society is an object that can be manipulated at will to conform to some moral stipulation. The additive approach to political economy maps into a theoretical framework where people write the first draft of the manuscript of social life through their various civil and market activities. When that draft is judged against some normative scheme, it is found to be deficient in some way. Perhaps the distribution of income or wealth is thought to be too unequal. Perhaps too many trees are being cut down or too much coal is burned in furnaces. Whatever the particular list of normative faults, the polity is seen as the agent that perfects the manuscript of social life. Moral discourse thus reflects a global or top-down orientation. The characteristics of a good society are first determined through some abstract scheme of thought. This determination imposes one singular judgment on the entire system of actions and relationships that constitutes a society. One of the best known of these formulations is due to John Rawls (1971), wherein inequalities are warranted only to the extent that they redound to the benefit of the least advantaged person in society. This approach to morality is the natural complement of a scheme of additive political economy.

One particularly notable feature of this common scheme of thought is its presumption that all relevant knowledge can be assembled in one mind. Such hypothetical formulations appear in a most peculiar light when they are examined against a background of limited and distributed knowledge. There is an alternative approach to morality that is grounded in the limited and distributed knowledge that is suitable for a scheme of entangled political economy. It is a local and not a global morality. To see what this means, consider the central legal principles of the market economy: property, contract, and liability. These legal principles frame what we denote as a market economy. So long as social relationships are governed by these principles, a market economy is in operation. Those legal principles of a market order also comprise a good part of a complementary moral order. For instance, the legal principle of private property can be stated alternatively as the moral principle to avoid taking what is not yours. Similarly, the legal principle of contract can be stated pretty much equivalently as the moral principle to keep your promises. The legal principle of liability, moreover, can be translated as the moral principle of making good the wrongs you have done unto others.

This local morality plays out within a network of relationships and interactions. It is a bottom-up morality. It is also a morality that is understandable and intelligible, as against being hypothetical. It asks people to act in the world as they experience it as guided by their natural sentiments as these are conveyed by the title of Budziszewski (2003): *What We Can't Not Know*. The central theme of the classically liberal tradition of political economy is that flourishing will arise to the extent that people manage to live within the contours of this moral framework. This tradition does not ask people to imagine that they know nothing about their personalities or their histories while knowing everything about the laws of production and distribution. There is no lawgiver but rather every person is a carrier of law. It is a morality of the good neighbor that is propelled through networked relationships and interactions. It is a systemic approach to morality. The moral tone exhibited within a society emerges out of the myriad interactions within that society.

The classical approach to moral education recognized that it is through practice that right conduct moves from becoming an object of conscious deliberation to becoming a central default setting of the psyche. Wrong practice would, in turn, promote wrong conduct through its ability to generate an ill-ordered psyche. It is reasonable to ask how various institutional arrangements might promote or extinguish notions of normativity through the kinds of collective practice they encourage or discourage. To go down this path is not to embrace a pure moral conventionalism, for one can think that our natures limit the range of moral belief while nonetheless recognizing that those natures can accommodate a wide variety of conventional practice, a point that is articulated nicely in Ekkehart Schlicht (1998).

Consider the common textbook illustration that demonstrates the equivalence of a tariff and a quota. These illustrations are always provided in a highly generic fashion. For instance, there may be a generic market for shoes with a tariff placed on imported shoes. The tariff increases the price of shoes and reduces the amount of imported shoes. Showing this is a simple blackboard exercise. An equally simple exercise is to show that a quota on the importation of shoes could achieve the same outcome. For whatever tariff might be imposed, there is an equivalent quota that would have the same effect on market price and quantity. This blackboard equivalence, however, is not the same thing as equivalence in real life because the quota creates different forms of social relationships and institutionalized practices than does a quota. A tariff imposes a tax on transactions, but leaves those transactions within the domain of private ordering, provided the tax has been paid. A tariff makes a product more expensive, but otherwise does not disrupt ordinary market processes. How much of that product is sold in the aggregate, and how that aggregate is distributed among different vendors, are governed in decentralized fashion through open competition and interaction among buyers and sellers. With a tariff, people are still free to work out commercial arrangements among themselves through private ordering, subject only to the surcharge that the tariff represents. To be sure, a tariff can become sufficiently high as to encourage smuggling, inducing secondary actions by political entities to contest such smuggling.

In contrast, a quota disrupts ordinary market relationships from the start. A quota creates a qualitatively different regime of human governance. With a quota, the distribution of sales across vendors and the specific types of products sold through market transactions are not determined through ordinary commercial arrangements. Rather, they are determined through a political process where those who hold offices of political power are able to award allotments to the particular vendors that those holders of power choose. A quota necessarily injects venality, inequality, and hierarchy into political practice and changes the character of effective commercial conduct. What economists refer to as rent seeking (Tullock 1967; Rowley et al., eds. 1988) and rent extraction (McChesney 1997) will flourish under quotas, and such activities may eventually come to comprise new norms for commercial conduct.

A low tariff pretty much maintains the legal principles of property, contract, and liability, along with their supporting normative sentiments. With market-conformable institutional arrangements (Eucken 1952; Liepold and Pies 2000), commercial practice reinforces the normative complements to the private ordering principles of property, contract, and liability. In contrast, the quota generates a different form of practice, one that is part of a hierarchical, status, or caste society and the values that support it. For no longer is everyone free to enter the competition for market share. Only those who receive a quota allotment can do so. Those in a position to award allotments hold a position of privileged status, as do those who receive allotments. Furthermore, a quota will generate incentives for people to evade the quota. State officials know that quotas have this effect, and to curb this evasion they will employ undercover agents to spy on people and to entrap them into evasion. Where the ordinary liberal institutions of property and contract spread trust and friendship throughout a society, the quota, and all policy measures of its type, promote suspicion and distrust, thereby generating a structured hierarchy of relationships within society.

A quota is, of course, but one particular outcome of a democratic process. Many similar outcomes can emerge, as illustrated by the vast and expanding literature on rent seeking and rent extraction. Democracy may clash severely with liberal market governance and its accompanying moral imagination. To illustrate, consider a small town with only three residents. Primo and Secunda like to play tennis, Terzo does not. Within the market framework of private property and freedom of contract, Primo and Secunda could readily finance from their own funds the building of a court on which to play tennis. However, they also comprise a voting majority, and could play tennis more cheaply if they were to declare the provision of tennis courts to be a town activity. Democracy allows Primo and Secunda to do this by incorporating tennis courts into the domain of public policy, perhaps accompanied by derivations to the effect that playing tennis promotes the public good due to complementarity between exercise and mental acuity. Hence, the taking would be for a public use, for which something like two-thirds compensation might be just.

There is a potentially deep cleavage between democratic ideology and democratic practice. The ideology treats government as an institution of common benefit that people create to promote their common interests. The practice, however, seems often to clash with the ideology. There are two approaches to limiting the clash. One looks to the cultivation of virtue within the populace, so that majorities would not exploit their voting power. The other looks to auxiliary measures that would limit the domain of democratic governance, as illustrated by a variety of constitutional provisions to limit and structure the exercise of governmental power. To the extent such constitutional limits are established and operate successfully, the governing regime becomes something other than purely democratic, possibly taking on classical republican qualities.

6. PUBLIC POLICY AS NODE-BASED SEARCH FOR PROFIT

Conventional linguistic usage refers to political officials as "policy makers." It is reasonable to wonder for whom they make policy. In most discussions that use this language, it is presumed that policy makers make policy for everyone. Is this a statement about reality? Or might it be a fanciful or sentimental statement? To claim to be a policy maker is to claim nothing outside the ability to move people to do something different from what they would otherwise have done. Someone might announce that he or she is a policy maker. But do people jump in response to that statement? Or might they ignore it? Suppose we look not to what people say but to what people actually do. We could determine the identities of policy makers by looking at how much change people are able to inject into various precincts in society. If we did this, we would find many policy makers inside society, with only some of them being political officials.

Consider one of the earlier network illustrations of societies as ecologies of political and private enterprises, either Panel C of Figure 2.2 or the bottom part of Figure 3.2. Take any node in that network and have it announce a change in its pattern of action. That announcement will have some effect on adjacent nodes which might elicit further changes at other nodes. In most cases those changes would be slight, whether those nodes were private or political entities. In some cases the effects would ramify throughout society in significant fashion, whether those nodes were privately or politically organized. These days, it is difficult to walk down a sidewalk without seeing and hearing people talking on phones as they walk. It wasn't this way 20 years ago. The world changed by some acts of policy by private entities that created cell phones.

The polycentric orientation this book pursues does not eliminate the position of policy maker in society, but rather recognizes that that position is potentially open to everyone. Entangled political economy recognizes that polity is an order of organizations inside society. Within an order, policy arises not from one source but from many, a situation that in turn raises questions regarding the relationship among those sources. Policy arises from many nodes within a society. If you ask who is responsible for preserving lawful and orderly relationships among people, the common answer these days would probably be something like police or state. An alternative answer, which takes us to De Tocqueville's (1835) science of association that Ostrom (1997) probes, is that everyone in society bears this responsibility, with police being specialized helpers in maintaining law, but with maintenance of law being everyone's bailiwick and not that of police alone.[5]

To state the case differently, theories based on emergence and spontaneous order do not affect the actual practice of public policy. Conventional theories that portray political entities as acting immediately to change society as a unitary object pertain to a fantasy world and not to reality. Entangled political economy tries to develop a theoretical framework that locates public policy within the world in which we actually live, which is a polycentric world of emergent interaction. Practice is guided by theories we hold pertaining to the situations in which we find ourselves. Inapt theories will lead to practices that don't accomplish what those theories would lead someone to expect. Much of this is passed off as error terms and unintended consequences.

Orthodox public policy is articulated in global and not in local terms. By this, I mean that the object denoted as economy is treated as a single entity that is subject to modification through top-down policy. In contrast, entangled political economy approaches public policy in local or bottom-up terms, though I would also note in this respect that local does not mean small. Rather it means only that policy is an activity that emerges within an order and is not some outside insertion into an order. Policy arises in polycentric fashion at particular nodes within the polity and subsequently spreads in a manner that is variable and also subject to explanation. We can still distinguish between the causes and the consequences of policy, but the underlying conceptualization differs from the orthodoxy and with the larger difference probably pertaining to causes. For an order, moreover, there isn't really any alternative. Before turning to these differences, I should perhaps note that spontaneously generated orders are capable of generating outcomes that most if not all participants might regard as inferior to other outcomes that could have been attained. Thomas Schelling (1978) gives a number of such illustrations. Both Carl Menger (1883 [1985]) and Friedrich Hayek (1973), moreover, argued that legislation might sometimes be necessary to correct deficiencies that accompanied such spontaneously generated processes as common law.

The creation of policy is just another name for the search for profit, and with the search for profit not eliminated by nonprofit status but only transformed: gain, betterment, improvement—these are synonyms for profit for actors who operate in nonprofit settings. In thinking about these matters, I take it as axiomatic that people who rise toward the higher levels of any firm, agency, profession, or similar social setting will stand relatively high in terms of such categories as ambition, energy, and wit—social life does not run on lassitude and lethargy. As an equilibrium condition pertaining to the end of history, we should require that the return people believe they can obtain from investing in promoting reform should equal the return they believe they can obtain from ordinary commercial activities; indeed, reform is just another commercial activity (Tollison and Wagner 1991).

One thing this formulation suggests is that policy is active and not reactive, in sharp contrast to the standard corrective-state formulations in orthodox theories of welfare economics and public policy. In this respect, one significant difference between rent seeking and rent extraction is that rent extraction entails politicians who are more active and entrepreneurial than they are portrayed by the notion of rent seeking. Most economic theorizing about policy treats policy as reactions to alleged market failures. To the contrary, politicians are like ordinary business people in always looking for and open to profitable business opportunities. A polity contains numerous enterprises, so policy can arise from many sources. Without doubt, there is enormous variation in the size and reach of political enterprises, just as there is with market enterprises. Still, policy is an on-going activity that arises from multiple sources within a society.

Benefit–cost analysis, for instance, is typically treated as a way of securing greater rationality in the articulation of public policy. In the US, every President since Richard Nixon has issued an Executive Order calling for express benefit–cost analyses to accompany significant policy proposals. The benefit–cost framework adopts a hypothetical framework of Kaldor–Hicks efficiency, and postulates an unobservable standard of societal profitability, in contrast to real profitability (Makowsky and Wagner 2009). Benefit–cost analysis is hypothetically conducted from the vantage point of someone who is seeking to maximize some aggregate value over the entire catallaxy. An alternative and I believe reasonably realistic orientation would make those calculations from the vantage point of particular nodes whose principals are in the position to take action and bear cost.

To illustrate, consider the examination of the mid-State project by Hanke and Walker (1974). This was a project sponsored by the Bureau of Reclamation to divert water from the Platte River in Nebraska, mostly to provide irrigation. Where the Bureau of Reclamation claimed that the ratio of benefits to costs would be 1.24, Hanke and Walker's alternative estimation provided several ratios ranging from 0.87 to 0.23. I raise this illustration not to champion benefit–cost analysis, but to illustrate the point about how policy arises from particular nodal points of action within an order, and the relevant considerations in explaining policy, as against exhorting about it, are surely the costs and gains as perceived by the occupants of those nodal positions.

Hanke and Walker could well be right in their critique of the Bureau of Reclamation. But why might this matter to a Bureau of Reclamation? If you haven't seen that oft-duplicated cover of *The New Yorker* that illustrates the view from Manhattan looking to the west, you should take a look. That is the type of view that appears from every node looking out into the world. What I would say in this respect is that all public projects are undertaken because returns are expected by the *relevant* people to exceed costs. I realize this statement begs the question of just who are those relevant people. One thing for sure is that it is not some aggregate entity called The People, nor for that matter would it be some theoretical creature called Median Voter. Rather it would be real people doing the best they can to promote what they think they are about; those people may well advance what Pareto (1935) designated as derivations or rationalizations when asked to explain what they were doing, as an alternative reflection of the point that an indefinitely large number of functions are capable of fitting any set of points. As Pareto summarized his theme, there is an endless supply of derivations that can be advanced for particular actions, but the residues that are truly responsible for those actions are nonetheless pretty much constant.

7. PARCHMENT, GUNS, AND THE CONSTITUTION OF ORDER

It is widely thought that just as a market economy is an expression of liberty, so is a democratic polity. A market economy and a democratic polity would combine to form a constitution of liberty. In this respect, the renowned constitutional scholar Charles McIlwain once asserted that "constitutional government is by definition limited government" (McIlwain 1947:21). Without some explanation as to how it is possible truly to limit government, however, this common formulation is perhaps more sentimental than realistic. The task of giving that sentiment some grounding in reality is a difficult one that raises some knotty issues regarding the relationship between liberty and democracy, both as fact and as value.

The very idea of limited government implies that government is not the source of personal rights, for government itself is limited by the

prior and superior rights of the people who form it. People form governments, governments don't form people, a theme that is developed crisply
in an economic context in James Buchanan and Gordon Tullock (1962).
One problem with this formulation is that no one truly knows how to
accomplish this as a pragmatic as distinct from intellectual matter. Scott
Gordon (1999) presents several historical episodes where different societies have taken different approaches to limiting government. Moreover, it
is doubtful if this end can truly be achieved, certainly not if the accuracy
of Carl Schmitt's (1932) claim on behalf of the autonomy of the political
is granted. That claim cannot be denied, moreover, without also denying
both that exceptions will always arise that will require some action not
previously accounted for, and that the friend–enemy distinction is an
enduring quality of the conflict-based character of societies (Collins 1988;
Hirshleifer 2001).

The history surrounding the Fifth Amendment to the American
Constitution illustrates the challenge. That history over the past century
or so has increasingly run in the direction of governments taking property
for what are private uses and paying only partial or token compensation.
Despite its clear wording about public use and just compensation, the Fifth
Amendment does not seem to be a strong bar against governments taking
private property for private use while failing to pay just compensation. The
Fifth Amendment, along with any constitutional document, is just a piece
of parchment. While parchment paper is stronger than ordinary writing
paper, it is not sufficiently strong to deter rapacious interest groups from
using government as an instrument of predation.

In Federalist No. 48, James Madison noted that legislatures in Virginia
and Pennsylvania had repeatedly violated their state constitutions, acting
thereby as an instrument of predation on behalf of some people at the
expense of others, in sharp contrast to acting as an instrument of protection and preservation. Madison concluded his examination by noting
"that a mere demarcation on parchment is not a sufficient guard against
those encroachments which lead to a tyrannical concentration of all the
powers of government in the same hands." The articulation on parchment
of a declaration of limited government to protect and preserve is not by
itself sufficient to generate protection and preservation as the core activity
of government. There is a tenuous balance between liberalism on the one
hand and democracy on the other, as the American Founders recognized
(Holcombe 2002). A system of economic organization based on private
property will as a pragmatic matter, as distinct from a matter of necessity, be accompanied by some measure of government activity. Liberalism
is grounded in individual freedom and private property, but there is no
reason grounded in necessity to think that governments will preserve and

protect those rights when doing so requires aiding enemies over friends or passing up profitable political deals.

Even though there may be general agreement about the proper principles of governmental activity, that agreement often dissolves in the specifics of particular practice. Primo, Secundo, and Terzo might all affirm the principle of limited government, and yet Secundo and Terzo will participate willingly and even eagerly in taking Primo's property when doing so allows them to build a bird sanctuary at lower cost to themselves. To be sure, Secundo and Terzo may have some moral qualms about their use of politics to circumvent the market when they could have bought Primo's land rather than taking it. To subdue such qualms, they might invoke such Paretian derivations as strategic holdouts and free riders as a kind of therapy to ease their minds. This would allow Secundo and Terzo to convince themselves with reasonable conviction that Primo really valued the bird sanctuary, only refused to say so because he was holding out to get a higher price.

As Vincent Ostrom (1984) explains with particular cogency, and which Aligica and Boettke (2009) amplify, government involves a Faustian bargain: instruments of evil—power over other people—are to be employed because of the good they might do, recognizing that evil will also result. This raises the issue of the terms of that bargain. There are two principal approaches to securing more favorable terms. One approach looks primarily to education and related processes for cultivating virtue and wisdom within a population (Walker 1990). The claim here is that the wiser people are about the dangers of the Faustian bargain, the less eagerly they will embrace it. Parchment will serve as a stronger barrier to predatory uses of government as people become wiser in their understanding about such predatory uses of government.

The other approach looks primarily to a kind of opposition of interests to limit government predation. Metaphorically speaking, this alternative approach looks to guns more than to parchment (Wagner 1993), or at least considers that guns are a necessary complement to parchment. The basic principle behind this approach is for governmental action to require some concurrence among different participants with opposed interests. Such concurrence, it should be noted, is exactly what market exchange promotes. Within the frameworks of property and contract, Primo, Secundo, and Terzo will all concur in the market-generated outcome concerning the use of Primo's marshland. If that land becomes a bird sanctuary, this will be because Primo concurs with Secundo's and Terzo's desire to exercise dominion over the marshland. The testimony about Primo's concurrence lies in his willingness to cede control over the land to Secundo and Terzo. If that land becomes a shopping center, this will be because Secundo and

Terzo concur with Primo's desire to build a shopping center. The testimony about Secundo's and Terzo's concurrence lies in their unwillingness to make an offer that would be sufficient to convince Primo to cede control over the land.

Both approaches reflect a presumption that self-interest is predominant in all human activity, in government as well as in commerce. The justification for government resides in the need to control the darker side of self-interest. With self-interest being ineradicable, the problem of constitutional control becomes one of how to control the operation of self-interest within government while allowing government the ability to perform those governing tasks that its justification requires. Ultimately, the task would seem to require both parchment and guns, that is, both knowledge pertinent to the task and rightly aligned desires and incentives to act consistently with that knowledge. Knowledge and incentive, moreover, do not act in separable fashion, for knowledge is generated through practice and practice is shaped by incentive (Wagner 2002). For instance, Charles Warren (1932) describes how the general welfare clause of the American Constitution underwent a transformation from a strong limit on the ability of Congress to appropriate money to a situation where Congress could appropriate for whatever it chooses, so long as it pronounces that it has some good civic reason for doing so. The process Warren describes is clearly one of a continuing spiral involving both belief and incentive. One of the central themes of the classical approach to moral education was that morality was simply good conduct that was reduced to habit through practice. The ability successfully to take property through politics instead of relying upon market transactions is to engage in a contrary form of practice. This alternative form of practice, where legislative takings replace market transactions, may, if repeated sufficiently, become sufficiently habitual to promote alternative beliefs as to what comprises just conduct. Knowledge and incentive, parchment and guns, would seem to be nonseparable ingredients of constitutional order in the final analysis.

NOTES

1. I don't deny that politicians make what might be perceived as commitments during campaigns. Those so-called commitments, however, are vague generalities without specific content. Whatever content there might be will come later, and will emerge through interaction among numerous interested parties.
2. Newberg et al. (2001) advance an explanation grounded in neurological observations of fMRIs to argue for a biological basis for belief in God in some fashion.
3. For what it's worth, George Mason, after whom George Mason University is named, opposed ratification of the Constitution, as he was one of the anti-federalists.
4. With respect to congruence between private law and public law, the Germanic tradition

of *ordnungstheorie*, set forth in Walter Eucken (1952), reflects the same spirit as the Fifth Amendment to the American Constitution. Leipold and Pies, eds. (2000) is a valuable collection of essays in this tradition. Kaspar and Streit (1998) is a valuable textbook written from within this tradition. Rath (1998) is a complementary monograph that connects Walter Eucken and Max Weber. Two highly valuable papers that convey the central ideas of *ordnungstheorie* are Vanberg (1988) and Streit (1992).

5. Carlo Cattaneo has been described as the Italian version of De Tocqueville in stressing the significance of the entities of civil society, in contrast to customary economic efforts to reduce society to states and markets, as Filippo Sabetti (2010) explains.

References

Acocella, N. (1998), *The Foundations of Economic Policy*, Cambridge: Cambridge University Press.

Alchian, A.A. (1950), 'Uncertainty, evolution, and economic theory', *Journal of Political Economy*, 58, 211–21.

Alexander, J.C. (2006), *The Civil Sphere*, Oxford: Oxford University Press.

Aligica, P.D. (2014), *Institutional Diversity and Political Economy: The Ostroms and Beyond*, Oxford: Oxford University Press.

Aligica, P.D. and P.J. Boettke (2009), *Challenging Institutional Analysis and Development: The Bloomington School*, London: Routledge.

Aligica, P.D. and V. Tarko (2012), 'Polycentricity: From Polanyi to Ostrom, and beyond', *Governance*, 25, 237–62.

Aligica, P.D. and V. Tarko (2014), 'Crony capitalism: Rent-seeking, institutions, and ideology', *Kyklos*, 67, 156–76.

Aron, R. (1967), *Main Currents in Sociological Thought*, vol. II, New York: Basic Books.

Aydinonat, N.E. (2008), *The Invisible Hand in Economics*, London: Routledge.

Backhaus, J.G. (1978), 'Pareto and public choice', *Public Choice*, 33, 5–17.

Baier, A. (1997), *The Commons of the Mind*, Chicago, IL: Open Court.

Barabási, A.-L. (2002), *Linked: The New Science of Networks*, Cambridge, MA: Perseus.

Bates, R.H. et al. (1998), *Analytic Narratives*, Princeton, NJ: Princeton University Press.

Bator, F.M. (1958), 'The anatomy of market failure', *Quarterly Journal of Economics*, 72, 351–79.

Baumol, W.J. (1965), *Welfare Economics and the Theory of the State*, 2nd ed., London: G. Bell and Sons.

Becchio, G. (2014), 'Carl Menger on states as orders, not organizations: Entangled political economy into a neo-Mengerian approach', *Advances in Austrian Economics*, 18, 55–66.

Becker, G.S. (1965), 'A theory of the allocation of time', *Economic Journal*, 7, 493–517.

Beito, D.T. (2000), *From Mutual Aid to the Welfare State*, Chapel Hill, NC: University of North Carolina Press.

Bergh, A. and R. Höijer (2008), *Institutional Competition*, Cheltenham, UK and Northampton, MA, USA: Edward Elgar.

Berlin, I. (1991), *The Crooked Timber of Humanity: Chapters in the History of Ideas*, New York: Knopf.

Berman, H.J. (1983), *Law and Revolution: The Formation of the Western Legal Tradition*, Cambridge, MA: Harvard University Press.

Bertalanffy, L. (1968), *General Systems Theory*, New York: George Braziller.

Besley, T. (2006), *Principled Agents? The Political Economy of Good Government*, Oxford: Oxford University Press.

Bilo, S. and R.E. Wagner (2015), 'Neutral money: Historical fact or analytical artifact?', *Review of Austrian Economics*, 28, 139–50.

Blankart, C.B. and G.G. Koester (2006), 'Political economics versus public choice', *Kyklos*, 59, 171–200.

Boettke, P.J. (1998), 'Economic calculation: The Austrian contribution to political economy', *Advances in Austrian Economics*, 5, 131–58.

Boettke, P.J. (2001), *Calculation and Coordination*, London: Routledge.

Boettke, P.J. (2007), 'Liberty vs. power in economic policy in the 20th and 21st centuries', *Journal of Private Enterprise*, 22, 7–36.

Boettke, P.J. and A. Marciano (2015), 'The past, present, and future of Virginia political economy', *Public Choice*, 163, 53–65.

Bolsinger, E. (2001), *The Autonomy of the Political: Carl Schmitt's and Lenin's Political Realism*, Westport, CT: Greenwood Press.

Bongiorno, A. (1930), 'A study of Pareto's treatise on general sociology', *American Journal of Sociology*, 36, 249–70.

Boudreaux, D.J. and R.G. Holcombe (1989), 'Government by contract', *Public Finance Quarterly*, 17, 264–80.

Boulding, K.E. (1956), *The Image: Knowledge in Life and Society*, Ann Arbor, MI: University of Michigan Press.

Boulding, K.E. (1970), *Economics as a Science*, New York: McGraw-Hill.

Boulding, K.E. (1971), 'After Samuelson, who needs Adam Smith?', *History of Political Economy*, 3, 225–37.

Boulding, K.E. (1985), *The World as a Total System*, Beverly Hills, CA: Sage.

Bourdieu, P. (1990), *The Logic of Practice*, Stanford, CA: Stanford University Press.

Bourdieu, P. (1998), *Practical Reason: On the Theory of Action*, Stanford, CA: Stanford University Press.

Bowles, S. and H. Gintis (1993), 'The revenge of homo economicus: Contested exchange and the revival of political economy', *Journal of Economic Perspectives*, 7, 83–102.

Brennan, G. and L. Lomasky (1993), *Democracy and Decision: The Pure*

Theory of Electoral Preference, Cambridge: Cambridge University Press.

Brennan, G. and P. Pettit (2004), *The Economy of Esteem*, Oxford: Oxford University Press.

Bruni, L. (2012), *Genesis and Ethos of the Market*, New York: Palgrave Macmillan.

Buber, M. (1923 [1958]), *I and Thou*, New York: Scribner's.

Buchanan, J.M. (1960), 'The Italian tradition in fiscal theory', in J.M. Buchanan, ed., *Fiscal Theory and Political Economy*, Chapel Hill, NC: University of North Carolina Press, pp. 24–74.

Buchanan, J.M. (1964), 'Fiscal institutions and efficiency in collective outlay', *American Economic Review*, Proceedings, 5, 227–35.

Buchanan, J.M. (1967), *Public Finance in Democratic Process*, Chapel Hill, NC: University of North Carolina Press.

Buchanan, J.M. (1968), *The Demand and Supply of Public Goods*, Chicago, IL: Rand McNally.

Buchanan, J.M. (1969), *Cost and Choice*, Chicago, IL: Markham.

Buchanan, J.M. (1975a), 'The Samaritan's dilemma', in E. Phelps, ed., *Altruism, Morality, and Economic Theory*, New York: Russell Sage, pp. 71–85.

Buchanan, J.M. (1975b), *The Limits of Liberty: Between Anarchy and Leviathan*, Chicago, IL: University of Chicago Press.

Buchanan, J.M. (2005), 'Afraid to be free', *Public Choice*, 124, 19–31.

Buchanan, J.M. and R.D. Congleton (1998), *Politics by Principle, Not Interest: Toward Nondiscriminatory Democracy*, Cambridge: Cambridge University Press.

Buchanan, J.M. and G.F. Thirlby, eds. (1973), *L.S.E. Essays on Cost*, London: Weidenfeld & Nicolson.

Buchanan, J.M. and G. Tullock (1962), *The Calculus of Consent: Logical Foundations of Constitutional Democracy*, Ann Arbor, MI: University of Michigan Press.

Buchanan, J.M. and Y.J. Yoon, eds. (1994), *The Return to Increasing Returns*, Ann Arbor, MI: University of Michigan Press.

Buchanan, J.M. and Y.J. Yoon (2000), 'Symmetric tragedies: Commons and anticommons', *Journal of Law and Economics*, 43, 1–13.

Budziszewski, J. (2003), *What We Can't Not Know*, Dallas, TX: Spence.

Bueno de Mesquita, B. et al. (2003), *The Logic of Political Survival*, Cambridge, MA: MIT Press.

Camerer, C.F. and R. Thaler (1995), 'Anomalies: Dictators, ultimatums, and manners', *Journal of Economic Perspectives*, 9, 209–19.

Campbell, S. (1986), 'The four Paretos of Raymond Aron', *Journal of the History of Ideas*, 47, 287–98.

Caplan, B. (2007), *The Myth of the Rational Voter*, Princeton, NJ: Princeton University Press.

Chaitin, G., N. da Costa, and F.A. Doria (2012), *Gödel's Way: Exploits into an Undecidable World*, London: Taylor & Francis.

Cheung, S.N.S. (1975), 'Roofs or stars: The stated intents and actual effects of a rents ordinance', *Economic Inquiry*, 13, 1–21.

Clinton, H.R. (1996), *It Takes a Village and Other Lessons Children Teach Us*, New York: Simon & Schuster.

Coase, R.H. (1974), 'The lighthouse in economics', *Journal of Law and Economics*, 17, 357–76.

Coleman, J.S. (1990), *Foundations of Social Theory*, Cambridge, MA: Harvard University Press.

Collins, R. (1988), *Theoretical Sociology*, San Diego, CA: Harcourt Brace Jovanovich.

Collins, R. (1998), *The Sociology of Philosophies: A Global Theory of Intellectual Change*, Cambridge, MA: Harvard University Press.

Commons, J.R. (1934), *Institutional Economics*, New York: Macmillan.

Congleton, R.D. (2011), *Perfecting Parliament: Constitutional Reform, Liberalism, and the Rise of Western Democracy*, Cambridge: Cambridge University Press.

Congleton, R.D., A.L. Hillman, and K.A. Konrad, eds. (2008), *Forty Years of Research on Rent Seeking*, Berlin: Springer.

Coyne, C.J. (2008), *After War: The Political Economy of Exporting Democracy*, Stanford, CA: Stanford University Press.

Coyne, C.J. (2013), *Doing Bad by Doing Good: Why Humanitarian Action Fails*, Stanford, CA: Stanford University Press.

Cristi, R. (1998), *Carl Schmitt and Authoritarian Liberalism: Strong State, Free Economy*, Cardiff: University of Wales Press.

Da Empoli, A. (1941), *Lineamenti teorici dell'economia corporativa finanziaria*, Milano: Giuffrè.

Damasio, A.R. (1994), *Decartes' Error: Emotion, Reasoning, and the Human Brain*, New York: Putnam.

Davis, O.A. and A.B. Whinston (1961), 'The economics of urban renewal', *Law and Contemporary Problems*, 26, 105–17.

De Angelo, H. (1981), 'Competition and unanimity', *American Economic Review*, 71, 18–27.

DeCanio, S. (2014), *Limits of Economic and Social Knowledge*, Houndmills, UK: Palgrave Macmillan.

De Jasay, A. (1985), *The State*, Oxford: Basil Blackwell.

De Jasay, A. (1997), *Against Politics: On Government, Anarchy, and Order*, London: Routledge.

De Jouvenel, B. (1948), *On Power: Its Nature and the History of its Growth*, London: Hutchinson.

De Jouvenel, B. (1961), 'The chairman's problem', *American Political Science Review*, 55, 368–72.

Demsetz, H. (1967), 'Toward a theory of property rights', *American Economic Review*, Proceedings, 57, 347–59.

Dennett, D.C. (1978), *Brainstorms: Philosophical Essays on Mind and Psychology*, Cambridge, MA: MIT Press.

De Tocqueville, A. (1835 [2002]), *Democracy in America*, Chicago, IL: University of Chicago Press.

De Viti de Marco, A. (1888), *Il carattere teorico dell'economia finanziaria*, Rome: Pasqualucci.

De Viti de Marco, A. (1936), *First Principles of Public Finance*, London: Jonathan Cape.

Dobb, M. (1969), *Welfare Economics and the Economics of Socialism*, Cambridge: Cambridge University Press.

Downs, A. (1957), *An Economic Theory of Democracy*, New York: Harper & Row.

Downs, A. (1967), *Inside Bureaucracy*, Boston: Little, Brown.

Durkheim, E. (1915 [1965]), *Elementary Forms of Religious Life*, New York: Free Press.

Eckert, R.D. and G.W. Hilton (1972), 'The jitneys', *Journal of Law and Economics*, 15, 293–325.

Eisenberg, T. and H. Farber (2003), 'The government as litigant: Further tests of the case selection model', *American Law and Economics Review*, 5, 94–133.

Elias, N. (1939 [1982]), *The Civilizing Process*, New York: Pantheon Books.

Elias, N. (1939 [1991]), *The Society of Individuals*, Oxford: Basil Blackwell.

Emmett, R.B. (2006), 'De gustibus est disputandum: Frank H. Knight's response to George Stigler and Gary Becker's "De gustibus non est disputandum"', *Journal of Economic Methodology*, 13, 97–111.

Emons, W. (1997), 'Credence goods and fraudulent experts', *RAND Journal of Economics*, 28, 107–19.

Enelow, J.M. and M.J. Hinich (1984), *The Spatial Theory of Voting*, Cambridge: Cambridge University Press.

Enelow, J.M. and M.J. Hinich (1990), *Advances in the Spatial Theory of Voting*, Cambridge: Cambridge University Press.

Epstein, J.M., ed. (2006), *Generative Social Science*, Princeton, NJ: Princeton University Press.

Epstein, R.A. (1985), *Takings: Private Property and the Power of Eminent Domain*, Cambridge, MA: Harvard University Press.

Epstein, R.A. (1993), *Bargaining with the State*, Princeton, NJ: Princeton University Press.

Epstein, R.A. (1995), *Simple Rules for a Complex World*, Cambridge, MA: Harvard University Press.

Epstein, R.A. (2014), *The Classical Liberal Constitution*, Cambridge, MA: Harvard University Press.

Eucken, W. (1952), *Grundsätze der Wirtschaftspolitik*, Tübingen: Mohr Siebeck.

Eusepi, G. and R.E. Wagner (2010), 'Polycentric polity: Genuine vs. spurious federalism', *Review of Law and Economics*, 6, 329–45.

Eusepi, G. and R.E. Wagner (2011), 'States as ecologies of political enterprises', *Review of Political Economy*, 23, 573–85.

Eusepi, G. and R.E. Wagner (2013), 'Tax prices in a democratic polity: The continuing relevance of Antonio De Viti de Marco', *History of Political Economy*, 45, 99–121.

Fasiani, M. (1949), 'Contributi di Pareto alla scienza delle finance', *Giornale degli Economisti*, 8, 129–73.

Fausto, D. (2003), 'An outline of the main Italian contributions to the theory of public finance', *Il Pensiero Economico Italiano*, 11, 11–41.

Fawcett, H. (1871), *Pauperism: Its Causes and Remedies*, London: Macmillan.

Fink, A. and R.E. Wagner (2013), 'Political entrepreneurship and the formation of special districts', *European Journal of Law and Economics*, 35, 427–39.

Foldvary, F. (1994), *Public Goods and Private Communities*, Aldershot, UK: Edward Elgar.

Frank, R.H. (1987), 'If homo economicus could choose his own utility function, would he want one with a conscience?', *American Economic Review*, 77, 593–604.

Franklin, J. (2009), *The Wolf in the Parlor: The Eternal Connection between Humans and Dogs*, New York: Henry Holt.

Friedman, M. (1953a), *Essays in Positive Economics*, Chicago, IL: University of Chicago Press.

Friedman, M. (1953b), 'Choice, chance, and the personal distribution of income', *Journal of Political Economy*, 61, 277–90.

Garnett, R.F. Jr., P. Lewis, and L. Ealy, eds. (2015), *Commerce and Community: Ecologies of Social Cooperation*, London: Routledge.

Georgescu-Roegen, N. (1971), *The Entropy Law and the Economic Process*, Cambridge, MA: Harvard University Press.

Gigerenzer, G. (2008), *Rationality for Mortals*, Oxford: Oxford University Press.

Gode, D.K. and S. Sunder (1993), 'Allocative efficiency of markets with zero-intelligence traders', *Journal of Political Economy*, 101, 119–32.

Goldberg, J. (2008), *Liberal Fascism*, New York: Random House.

Gordon, S. (1999), *Controlling the State: Constitutionalism from Ancient Athens to Today*, Cambridge, MA: Harvard University Press.

Gottfried, P.E. (1990), *Carl Schmitt: Politics and Theory*, New York: Greenwood Press.

Greve, M.S. (2012), *The Upside-Down Constitution*, Cambridge, MA: Harvard University Press.

Grice-Hutchison, Marjorie (1978), *Early Economic Thought in Spain, 1177–1749*, London: Allen & Unwin.

Grossman, S.J. and J.E. Stiglitz (1976), 'Information and competitive price systems', *American Economic Review*, 66, 246–53.

Grossman, S.J. and J.E. Stiglitz (1980), 'On the impossibility of informationally efficient markets', *American Economic Review*, 70, 393–408.

Hanke, S.H. and R.A. Walker (1974), 'Benefit-cost analysis reconsidered: An evaluation of the mid-state project', *Water Resources Research*, 10, 898–908.

Hayek, F.A. (1937), 'Economics and knowledge', *Economica*, 4, 33–54.

Hayek, F.A. (1945), 'The use of knowledge in society', *American Economic Review*, 35, 519–30.

Hayek, F.A. (1967), 'The theory of complex phenomena', in *Idem, Studies in Philosophy, Politics, and Economics*, Chicago, IL: University of Chicago Press, pp. 22–42.

Hayek, F.A. (1973), *Rules and Order*, Chicago, IL: University of Chicago Press.

Hayek, F.A. (1974 [1989]), 'The pretense of knowledge', *American Economic Review*, 79, 3–7.

Hebert, D. and R.E. Wagner (2013), 'Taxation as a quasi-market process: Explanation, exhortation, and the choice of analytical windows', *Journal of Public Finance and Public Choice*, 31, 163–77.

Heller, M. (1998), 'The tragedy of the anticommons: Property in the transition from Marx to markets', *Harvard Law Review*, 111, 621–88.

Himmelfarb, G. (1983), *The Idea of Poverty*, New York: Alfred A. Knopf.

Himmelfarb, G. (1992), *Poverty and Compassion: The Moral Imagination of the Late Victorians*, New York: Vintage.

Hirshleifer, J. (2001), *The Dark Side of the Force: Economic Foundations of Conflict Theory*, Cambridge: Cambridge University Press.

Holcombe, R.G. (2002), *From Liberty to Democracy: The Transformation of American Government*, Ann Arbor, MI: University of Michigan Press.

Holcombe, R.G. and A.M. Castillo (2013), *Liberalism and Cronyism: Two Rival Political and Economic Systems*, Arlington, VA: Mercatus Center.

Hoppe, H.H. (2001), *Democracy: The God that Failed*, New Brunswick, NJ: Transaction.

Hotelling, H. (1929), 'Stability in competition', *Economic Journal*, 39, 41–57.

Hughes, J.R.T. (1977), *The Governmental Habit: Economic Controls from Colonial Times to the Present*, New York: Basic Books.

Huizinga, J. (1950), *Homo Ludens: A Study of the Play Element in Culture*, Boston, MA: The Beacon Press.

Ikeda, S. (1997), *Dynamics of the Mixed Economy*, London: Routledge.

Jacobs, J. (1992), *Systems of Survival*, New York: Random House.

Jaffé, W. (1976), 'Menger, Jevons, and Walras de-homogenized', *Economic Inquiry*, 14, 511–24.

Johnson, M. (2014), 'James M. Buchanan, Chicago, and post war public finance', *Journal of the History of Economic Thought*, 36, 479–97.

Kant, I. (1784 [1991]), 'Idea for a universal history with a cosmopolitan purpose', in H.S. Reiss, ed., *Kant's Political Writings*, Cambridge: Cambridge University Press, pp. 41–53.

Kaspar, W. and M.E. Streit (1998), *Institutional Economics: Social Order and Public Policy*, Cheltenham, UK and Northampton, MA, USA: Edward Elgar.

Kauffman, S. (2014), 'On ethical and intellectual failures in contemporary economics', *Advances in Austrian Economics*, 18, 259–82.

Kenyon, D.A. and J. Kincaid, eds. (1991), *Competition among States and Local Governments*, Washington, DC: Urban Institute.

Key, V.O. (1966), *The Responsible Electorate: Rationality in Presidential Voting, 1936–1960*, Cambridge, MA: Harvard University Press.

Keynes, J.M. (1936), *The General Theory of Employment, Interest, and Money*, New York: Harcourt Brace.

Kirzner, I. (1973), *Competition and Entrepreneurship*, Chicago, IL: University of Chicago Press.

Kirzner, I. (1979), *Perception, Opportunity, and Profit*, Chicago, IL: University of Chicago Press.

Klein, D.B. (2011), *Knowledge and Coordination*, Oxford: Oxford University Press.

Klemperer, V. (2006), *The Language of the Third Reich*, New York: Continuum.

Knight, F.H. (1960), *Intelligence and Democratic Action*, Cambridge, MA: Harvard University Press.

Knight, J. and J. Johnson (2011), *The Priority of Democracy*, Princeton, NJ: Princeton University Press.

Koppl, R. (2002), *Big Players and the Economic Theory of Expectations*, New York: Palgrave Macmillan.

Krause, M. (2015), 'Buoys and beacons in economics', *Journal of Private Enterprise*, 30, 45–59.

Lachmann, L. (1956), *Capital and Its Structure*, London: Bell and Sons.
Lachmann, L. (1971), *The Legacy of Max Weber*, Berkeley, CA: Glendessary Press.
Lasswell, H.D. (1936), *Politics: Who Gets What, When, How*, New York: McGraw-Hill.
Latour, B. (2005), *Reassembling the Social: An Introduction to Actor-Network Theory*, Oxford: Oxford University Press.
Leeson, P.T. (2005), 'Endogenizing fractionalization', *Journal of Institutional Economics*, 1, 75–98.
Leeson, P.T. (2006), 'Cooperation and conflict: Evidence on self-enforcing arrangements and heterogeneous groups', *American Journal of Economics and Sociology*, 65, 891–907.
Leeson, P.T. (2008), 'Coordination without command: Stretching the scope of spontaneous order', *Public Choice*, 135, 67–98.
Leeson, P.T. (2012), 'Ordeals', *Journal of Law and Economics*, 55, 691–714.
Leibowitz, A. and R.D. Tollison (1980), 'A theory of legislative organization', *Quarterly Journal of Economics*, 94, 261–77.
Leipold, H. and I. Pies, eds. (2000), *Ordnungstheorie und Ordnungspolitik: Konzeptionen und Entwicklungsperspektiven*, Stuttgart: Lucius & Lucius.
Levy, D.M. and S.J. Peart, eds. (2008), *The Street Porter and the Philosopher: Conversations on Analytical Egalitarianism*, Ann Arbor, MI: University of Michigan Press.
Levy, D.M. and S.J. Peart (2013), 'How the Virginia School got its name', Richmond, VA: Jepson School of Leadership Studies.
Lewis, P.A. (2012), 'Emergent properties in the work of Friedrich Hayek', *Journal of Economic Behavior and Organization*, 82, 368–78.
Lovejoy, A.O. (1936), *The Great Chain of Being*, Cambridge, MA: Harvard University Press.
Lovejoy, A.O. (1961), *Reflections on Human Nature*, Baltimore, MD: Johns Hopkins University Press.
Luttmer, E.G.J. (2007), 'Selection, growth, and the size distribution of firms', *Quarterly Journal of Economics*, 122, 1103–44.
MacCallum, S. (1970), *The Art of Community*, Menlo Park, CA: Institute for Humane Studies.
Maine, H. (1864), *Ancient Law, 5th ed.*, New York: Henry Holt.
Makowski, L. (1983), 'Competition and unanimity', *American Economic Review*, 73, 329–39.
Makowsky, M.D. and R.E. Wagner (2009), 'From scholarly idea to budgetary institution: The emergence of cost-benefit analysis', *Constitutional Political Economy*, 20, 57–70.
Marberger, D. and R. Peterson (2013), *Economic Decision Making Using Cost Data*, New York: Business Expert Press.

Marshall, A. (1920), *Principles of Economics*, 8th ed., London: Macmillan.

Martin, A. and R.E. Wagner (2009), 'Heterogeneity, voting, and the political economy of public policy', *Public Finance and Management*, 9, 393–415.

McCaleb, T.S. and R.E. Wagner (1985), 'The experimental search for free riders', *Public Choice*, 47, 479–90.

McChesney, F. (1997), *Money for Nothing: Politicians, Rent Extraction, and Political Extortion*, Cambridge, MA: Harvard University Press.

McCloskey, D.N. (2006), *Bourgeois Virtues: Ethics for an Age of Commerce*, Chicago, IL: University of Chicago Press.

McCloskey, D.N. (2010), *Bourgeois Dignity: Why Economics Can't Explain the Modern World*, Chicago, IL: University of Chicago Press.

McCormick, R.E. and R.D. Tollison (1981), *Politicians, Legislation, and the Economy*, Boston, MA: Kluwer Academic Publishers.

McIlwain, C.H. (1947), *Constitutionalism: Ancient and Modern*, rev. ed., Ithaca, NY: Cornell University Press.

McKean, R.N. (1965), 'The unseen hand in government', *American Economic Review*, 55, 496–505.

McKean, R.N. (1968), *Public Spending*, New York: McGraw-Hill.

McLure, M. (2007), *The Paretian School and Italian Fiscal Sociology*, Houndmills, UK: Palgrave Macmillan.

McNulty, P. (1968), 'Economic theory and the meaning of competition', *Quarterly Journal of Economics*, 82, 639–56.

Meade, J.E. (1952), 'External economies and diseconomies in a competitive situation', *Economic Journal*, 62, 54–67.

Meade, L. (1986), *Beyond Entitlement: The Social Obligations of Citizenship*, New York: Free Press.

Meadows, D.H. (2008), *Thinking in Systems: A Primer*, White River Junction, VT: Chelsea Green.

Meier, H. (1995), *Carl Schmitt and Leo Strauss: The Hidden Dialogue*, Chicago, IL: University of Chicago Press.

Menger, C. (1883 [1985]), *Investigations into the Method of the Social Sciences*, New York: New York University Press.

Miceli, T.J. (2005), 'Dispute resolution', in J.G. Backhaus, ed., *The Elgar Companion to Law and Economics*, 2nd ed., Cheltenham, UK and Northampton, MA, USA: Edward Elgar, pp. 393–403.

Michels, R. (1962), *Political Parties: A Sociological Study of the Oligarchical Tendencies of Modern Democracy*, New York: Collier Books.

Mill, J.S. (1863), *On Liberty*, Boston, MA: Tichman and Fields.

Milonakis, D. and B. Fine (2009), *From Political Economy to Economics*, London: Routledge.

Minasian, J. (1964), 'Television pricing and the theory of public goods', *Journal of Law and Economics*, 7, 71–80.

Mitchell, W.G. and R.T. Simmons (1994), *Beyond Politics: Markets, Welfare, and the Failure of Bureaucracy*, Boulder, CO: Westview Press.

Moberg, L. and R.E. Wagner (2014), 'Default without capital account: The economics of municipal bankruptcy', *Public Finance and Management*, 14, 30–47.

Montemartini, G. (1900), 'Le basi fondamentali della scienza finanziaria pura', *Giornale degli Economisti*, 21, 555–76.

Montemartini, G. (1902), *Municipalizzazione dei Publici Servigi*, Milan: Società Editrice Libraria.

Mosca, G. (1947), *Elementi di scienza politica*, 4th ed., Bari: G. Laterza.

Mosca, M. (2011), *Antonio de Viti de Marco: Una Storia degna di Memoria*, Milan: Bruno Mondadori.

Mueller, D.C. (2003), *Public Choice III*, Cambridge: Cambridge University Press.

Munger, M.C. and K.M. Munger (2015), *Choosing in Groups: Analytical Politics Revisited*, Cambridge: Cambridge University Press.

Murphy, L. and T. Nagel (2002), *The Myth of Ownership*, Oxford: Oxford University Press.

Murray, C. (1985), *Losing Ground*, New York: Basic Books.

Nelson, P. (1970), 'Information and consumer behavior', *Journal of Political Economy*, 78, 311–29.

Newberg, A.B., E.G. D'Aquili, and V. Rause (2001), *Why God Won't Go Away: Brain Science and the Biology of Belief*, New York: Ballantine.

Neyman, J. (1950), *First Course in Probability and Statistics*, New York: Henry Holt.

Niskanen, W.A. (1971), *Bureaucracy and Representative Government*, Chicago, IL: Aldine.

Niskanen, W.A. (1978), 'The prospect for liberal democracy', in J.M. Buchanan and R.E. Wagner, eds., *Fiscal Responsibility in Constitutional Democracy*, Leiden: Martinus Nijhoff, pp. 157–74.

Noteboom, B. (2007), 'Methodological interactionism: Theory and application to the firm and to the building of trust', *Review of Austrian Economics*, 20, 137–53.

Oakeshott, M. (1975), *On Human Conduct*, Oxford: Clarendon Press.

O'Driscoll, G.P. and M.J. Rizzo (1985), *The Economics of Time and Ignorance*, Oxford: Basil Blackwell.

Ostrom, V. (1962), 'The water economy and its organization', *Natural Resources Journal*, 2, 55–73.

Ostrom, V. (1973), *The Intellectual Crisis in American Public Administration*, Tuscaloosa, AL: University of Alabama Press.

Ostrom, V. (1984), 'Why governments fail: An inquiry into the use of instruments of evil to do good', in J.M. Buchanan and R.D. Tollison, eds., *Theory of Public Choice II*, Ann Arbor, MI: University of Michigan Press, pp. 422–35.

Ostrom, V. (1987), *The Political Theory of a Compound Republic*, 2nd ed., Lincoln, NE: University of Nebraska Press.

Ostrom, V. (1996), 'Faustian bargains', *Constitutional Political Economy*, 7, 303–08.

Ostrom, V. (1997), *The Meaning of Democracy and the Vulnerability of Societies: A Response to Tocqueville's Challenge*, Ann Arbor, MI: University of Michigan Press.

Paganelli, M.P. (2014), 'Adam Smith and entangled political economy', *Advances in Austrian Economics*, 16, 37–54.

Pantaleoni, M. (1911), 'Considerazioni sulle proprieta di un sistema di prezzi politici', *Giornale degli Economisti*, 42, 9–29, 114–33.

Pareto, V. (1927 [1971]), *Manual of Political Economy*, New York: Augustus M. Kelley.

Pareto, V. (1935), *The Mind and Society*, New York: Harcourt Brace, originally published as *Trattato di Sociologia Generale* (1915, revised 1923).

Patrick, M. and R.E. Wagner (2015), 'From mixed economy to entangled political economy: A Paretian social-theoretic orientation', *Public Choice*, 164, 103–16.

Pauly, M.V. and M.R. Redish (1973), 'The not-for-profit hospital as a physicians' cooperative', *American Economic Review*, 63, 87–99.

Persson, T. and G. Tabellini (2000), *Political Economics: Explaining Economic Policy*, Cambridge, MA: MIT Press.

Pinker, S. (2002), *The Blank Slate: The Modern Denial of Human Nature*, New York: Viking.

Plott, C.R. and M.E. Levine (1978), 'A model of agenda influence on committee decisions', *American Economic Review*, 68, 146–60.

Podemska-Mikluch, M. (2014), 'Public policy: Object of choice or emergent phenomena? Learning from implementation of the Medical Reimbursement Act in Poland', *Advances in Austrian Economics*, 18, 93–110.

Podemska-Mikluch, M. and R.E. Wagner (2013), 'Dyads, triads, and the theory of exchange: Between liberty and coercion', *Review of Austrian Economics*, 26, 171–82.

Polanyi, M. (1958), *Personal Knowledge*, Chicago, IL: University of Chicago Press.

Polya, G. (1945), *How to Solve It*, Princeton, NJ: Princeton University Press.

Polya, G. (1954), *Mathematics and Plausible Reasoning*, 2 vols., Princeton, NJ: Princeton University Press.

Potts, J. (2000), *The New Evolutionary Microeconomics: Complexity,*

Competence, and Adaptive Behaviour, Cheltenham, UK and Northampton, MA, USA: Edward Elgar.

Prigogine, I. (1997), *The End of Certainty: Time, Chaos, and the New Laws of Nature*, New York: The Free Press.

Primo, D.M. (2007), *Rules and Restraint: Government Spending and the Design of Institutions*, Chicago, IL: University of Chicago Press.

Pruett, K.D. (2000), *Fatherneed: Why Father Care is as Essential as Mother Care for Your Child*, New York: Free Press.

Puviani, A. (1903), *Teoria della illusione finanziaria*, Palermo: Sandron. German translation: *Die Illusionen in der öffentlichen Finanzwirtschaft*, Berlin: Dunker & Humblot, 1960.

Rajagopalan, S. and R.E. Wagner (2013), 'Constitutional craftsmanship and the rule of law', *Constitutional Political Economy*, 24, 295–309.

Rath, C. (1998), *Staat, Gesellschaft, und Wirtschaft bei Max Weber und bei Walter Eucken*, Egelsbach: Hänsel-Hohenhausen.

Raudla, R. (2010), 'Governing the budgetary commons: What can we learn from Elinor Ostrom?', *European Journal of Law and Economics*, 30, 201–21.

Rawls, J. (1971), *A Theory of Justice*, Cambridge, MA: Harvard University Press.

Read, L. (1958), *I, Pencil*, Irvington-on-Hudson, NY: Foundation for Economic Education.

Reder, M.W. (1982), 'Chicago economics: Permanence and change', *Journal of Economic Literature*, 20, 1–38.

Reder, M.W. (1999), *Economics: The Culture of a Controversial Science*, Chicago, IL: University of Chicago Press.

Reiff, P. (1966), *The Triumph of the Therapeutic*, New York: Harper and Row.

Reiss, H.S., ed. (1991), *Kant: Political Writings*, Cambridge: Cambridge University Press.

Resnick, M. (1994), *Turtles, Termites, and Traffic Jams: Explorations in Massively Parallel Microworlds*, Cambridge, MA: MIT Press.

Richardson, S.O. (2011), *The Political Economy of Bureaucracy*, London: Routledge.

Riker, W. (1962), *The Theory of Political Coalitions*, New Haven, CT: Yale University Press.

Rizzo, M.J. (2015), 'The problem of rationality: Austrian economics between classical behaviorism and behavioral economics', P.J. Boettke and C. Coyne, eds., *Oxford Handbook of Austrian Economics*, Oxford: Oxford University Press, pp. 364–92.

Robbins, L. (1952), *The Theory of Economic Policy in English Classical Political Economy*, London: Macmillan.

Roberts, P.C. (1971), *Alienation and the Soviet Economy*, Albuquerque, NM: University of New Mexico Press.

Rogowski, R. (1974), *Rational Legitimacy*, Princeton, NJ: Princeton University Press.

Romer, P.M. (1986), 'Increasing returns and long-run growth', *Journal of Political Economy*, 94, 1002–37.

Rosenberg, N. (1960), 'Some institutional aspects of the *Wealth of Nations*', *Journal of Political Economy*, 68, 557–70.

Rowley, C.K., R.D. Tollison, and G. Tullock, eds. (1988), *The Political Economy of Rent Seeking*, Dordrecht: Kluwer Academic Publishers.

Rubin, P.H. (2002), *Darwinian Politics*, New Brunswick, NJ: Rutgers University Press.

Runst, P. and R.E. Wagner (2011), 'Choice, emergence, and constitutional process: A framework for positive analysis', *Journal of Institutional Economics*, 7, 131–45.

Sabetti, F. (2010), *Civilization and Self-Government: The Political Thought of Carlo Cattaneo*, Lanham, MD: Rowman & Littlefield.

Samuels, W.J. (1966), *The Classical Theory of Economic Policy*, Cleveland, OH: World Press.

Samuelson, P.A. (1954), 'The pure theory of public expenditure', *Review of Economics and Statistics*, 36, 387–89.

Samuelson, P.A. (1955), 'Diagrammatic exposition of a theory of public expenditure', *Review of Economics and Statistics*, 37, 350–56.

Schelling, T.C. (1978), *Micromotives and Macrobehavior*, New York: Norton.

Schlicht, E. (1998), *On Custom and the Economy*, Oxford: Clarendon Press.

Schmitt, C. (1923), *Die Geistesgeschichtliche Lage des Heutigen Parlamentarismus*, Munich: Dunker and Humblot.

Schmitt, C. (1932 [1996]), *The Concept of the Political*, Chicago, IL: University of Chicago Press.

Schoeck, H. (1969), *Envy: A Theory of Social Behavior*, New York: Harcourt Brace.

Schumpeter, J.A. (1918 [1954]), 'The crisis of the tax state', *International Economic Papers*, 4, 5–38.

Schumpeter, J.A. (1934), *The Theory of Economic Development*, 2nd ed., Cambridge, MA: Harvard University Press.

Schumpeter, J.A. (1954), *A History of Economic Analysis*, New York: Oxford University Press.

Selgin, G. (1988), *The Theory of Free Banking*, Totowa, NJ: Rowman & Littlefield.

Selgin, G. and L.H. White (1999), 'A fiscal theory of government's role in money', *Economic Inquiry*, 37, 154–65.

Shackle, G.L.S. (1961), *Decision, Order, and Time in Human Affairs*, Cambridge: Cambridge University Press.

Shackle, G.L.S. (1968), *Uncertainty in Economics and Other Reflections*, Cambridge: Cambridge University Press.

Shackle, G.L.S. (1972), *Epistemics and Economics*, Cambridge: Cambridge University Press.

Shapiro, D. (2007), *Is the Welfare State Justified?*, Cambridge: Cambridge University Press.

Shughart, W.E. II and L. Razzolini, eds. (2001), *The Elgar Companion to Public Choice*, Cheltenham, UK and Northampton, MA, USA: Edward Elgar.

Simmons, R.T. (2011), *Beyond Politics: The Roots of Government Failure*, Oakland, CA: Independent Institute.

Simon, H.A. and C.P. Bonini (1958), 'The size distribution of business firms', *American Economic Review*, 48, 607–17.

Simons, H.C. (1938), *Personal Income Taxation*, Chicago, IL: University of Chicago Press.

Skarbeck, D. (2014), *The Social Order of the Underworld: How Prison Gangs Govern the American Penal System*, Oxford: Oxford University Press.

Smith, A., B. Yandle, and R.E. Wagner (2011), 'A theory of entangled political economy, with application to TARP and NRA', *Public Choice*, 148, 45–66.

Smith, D. (2014), 'Heterogeneity and exchange: Safe-conducts in Medieval Spain', *Review of Austrian Economics*, 27, 183–97.

Smith, V.L. (2008), *Rationality in Economics*, Cambridge: Cambridge University Press.

Somin, I. (2013), *Democracy and Political Ignorance: Why Smaller Government is Smarter*, Stanford, CA: Stanford University Press.

Sonstelie, J.C. and P.R. Portney (1978), 'Profit maximizing communities and the theory of local public expenditure', *Journal of Urban Economics*, 5, 263–77.

Soros, G. (2013), 'Fallibility, reflexivity, and the human uncertainty principle', *Journal of Economic Methodology*, 20, 309–29.

Spruynt, H. (1994), *The Sovereign State and Its Competitors*, Princeton, NJ: Princeton University Press.

Staniland, M. (1985), *What is Political Economy?*, New Haven, CT: Yale University Press.

Stigler, G.J. and G.S. Becker (1977), 'De gustibus non est disputandum', *American Economic Review*, 67, 76–90.

Storing, H.J. (1981), *What the Anti-Federalists Were For*, Chicago, IL: University of Chicago Press.

Storr, V. (2008), 'The market as a social space', *Review of Austrian Economics*, 21, 135–50.

Storr, V. (2013), *Understanding the Culture of Markets*, London: Routledge.

Streit, M.E. (1992), 'Economic order, private law, and public policy: The Freiburg school of law and economics in perspective', *Journal of Institutional and Theoretical Economics*, 148, 675–704.

Suits, B. (1967), 'Is life a game we are playing?', *Ethics*, 77, 209–13.

Susskind, L. and A. Friedman (2014), *Quantum Mechanics: The Theoretical Minimum*, New York: Basic Books.

Szasz, T. (1961), *The Myth of Mental Illness: Foundations for a Theory of Personal Conduct*, New York: Harper & Row.

Tanzi, V. (2011), *Government versus Markets: The Changing Economic Role of the State*, Cambridge: Cambridge University Press.

Thaler, R.H. and C.R. Sunstein (2008), *Nudge: Improving Decisions about Health, Wealth, and Happiness*, New Haven, CT: Yale University Press.

Tinbergen, J. (1952), *On The Theory of Economic Policy*, Amsterdam: North-Holland.

Tollison, R.D. and R.E. Wagner (1991), 'Romance, realism, and economic reform', *Kyklos*, 44, 57–70.

Tononi, G., O. Sporns, and G.M. Edelman (1999), 'Measures of degeneracy and redundancy in biological networks', *Proceedings of the National Academy of Sciences*, 96, 3257–62.

Trump, D.J. (1987), *The Art of the Deal*, New York: Random House.

Tsebelis, G. (1991), *Nested Games: Rational Choice in Comparative Politics*, Berkeley, CA: University of California Press.

Tullock, G. (1965), *The Politics of Bureaucracy*, Washington, DC: Public Affairs Press.

Tullock, G. (1967), 'The welfare costs of tariffs, monopolies, and theft', *Economic Inquiry*, 5, 224–32.

Tullock, G. (1971), 'The charity of the uncharitable', *Economic Inquiry*, 9, 379–92.

Tullock, G. (1989), *The Economics of Special Privilege and Rent Seeking*, Boston, MA: Kluwer.

Vanberg, V. (1988), '*Ordnungstheorie* as constitutional economics', *ORDO*, 39, 17–31.

Vriend, N.J. (2002), 'Was Hayek an ace?', *Southern Economic Journal*, 68, 811–40.

Wagner, A. (2014), *Arrival of the Fittest: Solving Evolution's Greatest Puzzle*, New York: Current.

Wagner, R.E. (1988), '*The Calculus of Consent*: A Wicksellian retrospective', *Public Choice*, 56, 153–66.

Wagner, R.E. (1992), 'Crafting social rules: Common law vs. statute law, once again', *Constitutional Political Economy*, 3, 381–97.

Wagner, R.E. (1993), *Parchment, Guns, and Constitutional Order*, Aldershot, UK: Edward Elgar.

Wagner, R.E. (1997), 'Parasitical political pricing, economic calculation, and the size of government', *Journal of Public Finance and Public Choice*, 15, 135–46.

Wagner, R.E. (2002), 'Complexity, governance, and constitutional craftsmanship', *American Journal of Economics and Sociology*, 61, 105–22.

Wagner, R.E. (2004), 'Public choice as an academic enterprise: Charlottesville, Blacksburg, and Fairfax retrospectively viewed', *American Journal of Economics and Sociology*, 63, 55–74.

Wagner, R.E. (2006a), 'Retrogressive regime drift within a theory of emergent order', *Review of Austrian Economics*, 19, 113–23.

Wagner, R.E. (2006b), 'States and the crafting of souls: Mind, society, and fiscal sociology', *Journal of Economic Behavior and Organization*, 59, 516–24.

Wagner, R.E. (2007), *Fiscal Sociology and the Theory of Public Finance*, Cheltenham, UK and Northampton, MA, USA: Edward Elgar.

Wagner, R.E. (2010a), *Mind, Society, and Human Action: Time and Knowledge in a Theory of Social Economy*, London: Routledge.

Wagner, R.E. (2010b), 'Change within permanence: Time and the bivalent logic of economic analysis', *Advances in Austrian Economics*, 14, 181–203.

Wagner, R.E. (2010c), 'Raising vs. leveling in the social organization of welfare', *Review of Law and Economics*, 6, 421–39.

Wagner, R.E. (2011a), 'Municipal corporations, economic calculation, and political pricing: Exploring a theoretical antinomy', *Public Choice*, 149, 151–65.

Wagner, R.E. (2011b), 'Promoting the general welfare: Political economy for a free republic', in J. Postell and B.C.S. Watson, eds., *Rediscovering Political Economy*, Lanham, MD: Lexington Books, pp. 135–57.

Wagner, R.E. (2012a), 'A macro economy as an ecology of plans', *Journal of Economic Behavior and Organization*, 82, 433–44.

Wagner, R.E. (2012b), 'The institutional framework for shared consumption: Deemphasizing taxation in the theory of public finance', *Public Finance and Management*, 12, 5–20.

Wagner, R.E. (2012c), *Deficits, Debt, and Democracy*, Cheltenham, UK and Northampton, MA, USA: Edward Elgar.

Wagner, R.E. (2012d), 'Viennese kaleidics: Why it's liberty more than policy that calms turbulence', *Review of Austrian Economics*, 25, 283–97.

Wagner, R.E. (2013), 'Choice versus interaction in public choice: Discerning the legacy of the *Calculus of Consent*', in D.R. Lee, ed., *Public Choice, Past and Present*, New York: Springer, pp. 65–79.

Wagner, R.E. (2014a), 'Entangled political economy: A keynote address', *Advances in Austrian Economics*, 16, 15–36.

Wagner, R.E. (2014b), 'Richard Epstein's *Classical Liberal Constitution*: A public choice refraction', *New York University Journal of Law & Liberty*, 8, 360–88.

Wagner, R.E. (2014c), *American Federalism: How Well Does It Support Liberty?*, Arlington, VA: Mercatus Center.

Wagner, R.E. (2015a), 'Virginia political economy: A rational reconstruction', *Public Choice*, 163, 15–36.

Wagner, R.E. (2015b), 'Welfare economics and second-best theory: Filling imaginary economic boxes', *Cato Journal*, 35, 133–46.

Wagner, R.E. and D. Yazigi (2014), 'Form vs. substance in selection through competition: Elections, markets, and political economy', *Public Choice*, 159, 503–14.

Walker, G. (1990), *Moral Foundations of Constitutional Thought: Current Problems, Augustinian Prospects*, Princeton, NJ: Princeton University Press.

Walters, S.J.K. (2014), *Boom Towns: Restoring the Urban American Dream*, Stanford, CA: Stanford University Press.

Warren, C.O. (1932), *Congress as Santa Claus*, Charlottesville, VA: Michie.

Webber, C. and A. Wildavsky (1986), *A History of Taxation and Public Expenditure in the Western World*, New York: Simon and Schuster.

White, L.H. (1999), *The Theory of Monetary Institutions*, Oxford: Blackwell.

White, L.H. (2012), *The Clash of Economic Ideas*, Cambridge: Cambridge University Press.

Wicksell, K. (1896), *Finanztheoretische Untersuchungen*, Jena: Gustav Fischer.

Wicksell, K. (1958), 'A new principle of just taxation', in R.A. Musgrave and A.T. Peacock, eds., *Classics in the Theory of Public Finance*, London: Macmillan, pp. 72–118.

Wicksteed, P. (1910), *The Commonsense of Political Economy*, 2 vols., London: Macmillan.

Wieser, F. (1926), *Das Gesetz der Macht*, Vienna: Julius Springer.

Wildavsky, A. (1975), *Budgeting: A Comparative Theory of Budgetary Processes*, Boston, MA: Little, Brown.

Willett, T.D., ed. (1988), *Political Business Cycles*, Durham, NC: Duke University Press.

Wilson, J.Q. (1995), *On Character*, Washington, DC: American Enterprise Institute.

Wilson, W. (1885), *Congressional Government*, Boston, MA: Houghton Mifflin.

Wittman, D. (1989), 'Why democracies produce efficient results', *Journal of Political Economy*, 97, 1395–424.

Wittman, D. (1995), *The Myth of Democratic Failure*, Chicago, IL: University of Chicago Press.

Young, R.A. (1991), 'Tectonic policies and political competition', in A. Breton et al., eds., *The Competitive State*, Dordrecht: Kluwer Academic Publishers, pp. 129–45.

Index

Acocella, N. 35
action in society, logical vs. non-logical
    94, 97–100, 126–7, 184
    behavioral economics as deceptive
        105–9
    environmental influences and
        97–102, 105, 114–16
    reciprocal relation between cost and
        choice 100–104, 138–9
agenda control 78
agent-based computational modeling
    7, 18
agreement distinguished from
    acquiescence 190–93
Alchian, A.A. 146
Alexander, J.C. 47
Aligica, P.D. 128, 133, 207
analytical narratives 86
anti-commons 70
approbation as cousin of envy 91,
    94–5
Aron, R. 184
autonomy of the political 93–7
Aydinonat, N.E. 40, 164

Backhaus, J. 30, 127
Baier, A. 1
Barabási, A.L. 28, 76, 161
Bates, R.H. 86, 176
Bator, F. 13
Baumol, W.J. 3
Becchio, G. 83, 94
Becker, G.S. 102, 187
Beito, D.T. 130, 195
Bergh, A. 135
Berlin, I. 25, 85, 94, 96
Bertalanffy, L. 60
Besley, T. 113, 125, 155, 164
Big Players 62–3, 90
Bilo, S. 8
Blankart, C.B. 18

blind men of Hindustan *see* knowledge
    as invariably incomplete
Boettke, P.J. 3, 5, 136, 207
Bolsinger, E. 94, 142, 180
Bongiorno, A. 98
Bonini, C.P. 177
Boudreaux, D.J. 46, 180
Boulding, K.E. 7, 30, 47, 99
Bourdieu, P. 88
Bowles, S. 164
Brennan, G. 48, 128
Bruni, L. 47
Buber, M. 94
Buchanan, J.M. 2–3, 5, 7, 10, 17–18,
    21–2, 29, 36, 47, 68–70, 74, 92,
    100, 104, 120, 133, 138–9, 149,
    168, 195–6, 206
Budziszewski, J. 199
Bueno de Mesquita, B. 19, 115

Camerer, C. 106
Cantillon, R. 8
capital accounts and political entities
    125, 146–9, 151–4
    cities and hotels 44–6,
        154–60
    municipal bankruptcy 45–6
Caplan, B. 127–8
Castillo, A.M. 128
centralized mindset 42, 144
civic association and civil society
    47–9
Coase, R.H. 2, 15–16, 17
collective property as analytically
    incoherent 21–2
Chaitin, G. 6, 60, 178
Cheung, S.N.S. 122, 148
Clinton, H. 48
Coleman, J.S. 92
Collins, R. 5, 59, 80, 186, 206
Commons, J.R. 75, 153, 164

competition and selection through
election 111–16
form vs. substance in selection for
qualities 116–27
Congleton, R.D. 68–9, 149
Cristi, R. 94
crooked timber of humanity 85, 94–7,
195

Da Empoli, A. 68, 70, 149
Damasio, A.R. 89
Davis, O.A. 107
De Angelo, H. 155
DeCanio, S. 7, 56
De Jasay, A. 94
De Jouvenel, B. 52, 70, 76, 116, 161
democracy, generic form vs. particular
instances 51–4
democratic oligarchy 76–8, 116, 162,
170
Demsetz, H. 86–7
Dennett, D. 85, 188
De Tocqueville, A. 203
De Viti de Marco, A. 4, 68
diamond–water paradox 8–9, 14
Dobb, M. 3
Downs, A. 103, 111
Durkheim, E. 187
dyadic relationships *see* triadic
relationships in political economy

Eckert, R. 17
economic calculation
and collective action 138–43
and enterprise valuation 28–9, 103
impossibility of for political
enterprises 29–30, 143
parasitical political calculation 136–8
property rights and 142–3
economic theory, distinguishing text
and subtext 38–9
Eisenberg, T. 104
Elias, N. 47–8, 87, 197
eminent domain and American
constitution 38
Emmett, R.B. 186–7
Emons, W. 30
Enelow, J.M. 36, 140
Epstein, R.A. 38, 72, 79, 124, 164, 170,
181, 187, 194

Eucken, W. 73, 120, 201
Eusepi, G. 4, 44, 68, 84, 162
extended present and history of
economics 5–8

Farber, H. 104
Fasiani, M. 109
Faustian bargains 49–51, 187, 194, 207
Fausto, D. 3
Fawcett, H. 131
federalism as cartelized system of
governments 78–82
federalism as competition among
governments 78–80
Fine, B. 1
Fink, A. 141
Foldvary, F. 45, 157
form vs. substance in economic theory
83–5, 89–93, 115–16
Frank, R.H. 196
Franklin, B. 72, 162, 187
Franklin, J. 25, 95
Friedman, A. 34
Friedman, M. 3, 131
Friend–enemy distinction 96, 142

Garnett, R.F. 47
Georgescu-Roegen, N. 74
Gigerenzer, G. 97, 100
Gintis, H. 164
Gödel, K. 6
Goldberg, J. 181
Goode, D.K. 128
Gordon, S. 206
Greve, M. 79, 162, 195
Greyhound and Amtrak as alternative
business ventures 84, 158–9
Grice-Hutchison, M. 8
Grossman, S. 7, 18

Hamilton, A. 193
Hanke, S.H. 204–5
Hayek, F.A. 7, 18, 39–40, 63, 96, 135,
186, 203
Hebert, D. 51, 142
Heller, M. 70
Hilton, G. 175
Himmelfarb, G. 131
Hinich, M.J. 36, 140
Hirshleifer, J. 35, 206

history of economics, alternative
    orientations toward
    classical vs. neoclassical 8–10
    institutions vs. allocations as focal
        points 9–10, 16–17
Höijer, R. 135
Holcombe, R.G. 46, 128, 206
Hoover, H. 99
Hoppe, H.H. 52
Hotelling, H. 140
Hughes, J. 28, 72, 120
Huizinga, J. 92
human nature and political economy
    25, 34, 94

intelligence and democratic action
    127–9
invisible hands and spontaneous
    ordering 12–13, 40–41, 44, 91–2,
    144–5, 147, 164–5
Italian tradition of public finance 3–4

Jacobs, J. 13, 44
Jaffé, W. 9
Jevons, W.S. 9
Johnson, J. 39
Johnson, M. 10

Kant, I. 25, 94
Kenyon, D.A. 80
Key, V.O. 127
Kincaid, J. 80
Kirzner, I. 17, 176
Klein, D. 136
Klemperer, V. 124, 188, 191
Knight, F.H. 10, 127–8, 187
Knight, J. 39
knowledge
    as invariably incomplete 7–8, 12, 18,
        39–40, 63, 96, 133, 136, 186
    as assembled through transactions
        16–17, 50–51, 67–8
Koester, G.G. 18
Koppl, R. 62–3, 90
Krause, M. 16

Lachmann, L. 152
Lange, O. 3
Leeson, P.T. 71, 90
Leibowitz, A. 150

Lerner, A.P. 3
Levine, M. 78
Levy, D.M. 2, 95
Lewis, P. 86
liberalism and democracy 49–50, 76–9,
    201–2
Liepold, H. 201
Lincoln, A. 99
Lomasky, L. 128
Lovejoy, A. 1, 6, 48, 91, 95, 189
Luttmer, E.G.J. 177

MacCallum, S. 45, 157
Madison, J. 206
Maine, H. 21
majority voting and minority faction
    53–4
majority voting, qualified vs. simple
    20–21
Makowski, L. 155
Makowsky, M.D. 204
Marberger, D. 168
Marciano, A. 3
Marshall, A. 31
Martin, A. 37
McCaleb, T.S. 50
McChesney, F.S. 201
McCloskey, D. 132, 197
McCormick, R. 26, 150
McIlwain, C. 205
McKean, R. 44
McLure, M. 3, 126, 184
McNulty, P. 14
Meade, J. 13
Meade, L. 133
Meadows, D. 59
median voter 18–19, 41, 67
Menger, C. 9–10, 83, 94, 203
method and substance, reciprocal
    relationship between 166–9,
    188–90
Miceli, T.J. 103
Michels, R. 76, 161
micro–macro relationship as ecological
    and not aggregative 42–3, 85–6
Mill, J.S. 8–9, 94
Milonakis, D. 1
Minasian, J. 15
Mitchell, W.C. 36
Moberg, L. 45, 125

Montemartini, G. 121
moral imagination 73–4, 195–202
  global vs. local forms of 198–202
moral syndromes, commercial and
    guardian 44
Mosca, G. 76, 161
Mosca, M. 4
Munger, M. 20
Murphy, L. 21
Murray, C. 132

Nagel, T. 21
Nelson, P. 29
Neyman, J. 170
Niskanen, W.A. 80, 103
Noteboom, B. 89
Nutter, G.W. 2

O'Driscoll, G.P. 71
Ostrom V. 12, 18–19, 44, 49, 78, 145,
    162, 187, 194, 203
other worldly vs. this worldly schemes
    of thought 189–90

Paganelli, M.P. 83
Pantaleoni, M. 138, 144, 147, 149, 151,
    163, 167, 175
parades vs. pedestrian crowds, as
    templates for political economy
    40–42, 55–6, 165
parasitical political pricing 147–51, 167
Pareto efficiency 14, 67
Pareto, V. 29, 32, 35, 56, 70, 85, 94,
    97–9, 106, 109, 126–8, 131, 169,
    184, 188, 205
Patrick, M. 28, 35
Pauly, M.V. 154
Peart, S. 2, 95
Persson, T. 37, 52, 113, 164
Peterson, R. 168
Pettit, P. 48
Pies, I. 201
Pinker, S. 132
Plott, C.R. 78
Podemska-Mikluch, M. 64, 75, 116,
    123–4, 137, 164
Polanyi, M. 38–9
political economy
  additive 32–3, 35–40, 60, 68, 198
  entangled 1, 28, 33–5, 40–44, 54–6,

    61, 64–5, 83, 85, 90, 114, 127–9,
    164–6
  liberal 3–4, 8, 11, 22
  polycentrism and 52–3, 78, 202
  progressivism and 5, 12–13, 15, 21,
    39, 118, 181, 190
  Virginia tradition of 1–5, 10–11, 13,
    18–19, 26
  see also human nature and political
    economy; systems theory
political property rights 25, 69
politics as peculiar business practice
    26–30, 84, 113, 150–51, 153–4
Polya, G. 11, 111
Portney, P. 46
Potts, J. 58, 61, 167
power, etiology of 70–71, 93–4, 96
praxeology–catallaxy dichotomy
    superior to micro–macro
    dichotomy 87–8
Prigogine, I. 60
Primo, D. 69, 145
property rights and self-ordered
    systems 66–71
property rights as social relationships
    26, 69–70, 83
Pruett, D.K. 132
public choice *see* political economy,
    Virginia tradition of
public goods theory
  in relation to plausible and
    demonstrative reasoning 16,
    66
  lighthouses and 16–17
public policy as shell game 56, 59,
    62–5, 202–5
purposive action 84, 88
  practical rather than theoretical
    88–9, 104–5
  see also sentiment in relation to
    reason
Puviani, A. 4

raising vs. leveling as welfare principles
    130–35
Rajagopalan, S. 56, 94
rationality *see* action in society
Raudla, R. 104
Rawls, J. 199
Read, L. 137

reasoning in economics, types of
  demonstrative 11–15, 22, 25, 106
  plausible 11–15, 22, 24, 25, 106–8
Reder, M. 1–2, 55
Redish, M.R. 154
Reiff, P. 48
Reinert, E. 189
Resnick, M. 42, 144
Ricardo, D. 9, 10
Richardson, S.O. 103
Riker, W. 23, 173
Rizzo, M.J. 71, 108
Robbins, L. 13
Rogowski, R. 54
Romer, P. 7
Rowley, C.K. 201
Rosenberg, N. 9
Rubin, P. 113
Runst, P. 153

Samaritan's dilemma 92, 133–4
Samuels, W. 13
Samuelson, P.A. 15, 47, 66, 68, 167
scale-free polities 28, 75–8, 160–62
Schelling, T.C. 203
Schlicht, E. 200
Schmitt, C. 38, 50, 69, 78, 94, 96, 120,
  142, 183, 193, 206
Schmölders, G. 4
Schumpeter, J.A. 18, 92, 149, 182
self-governing systems *see* invisible
  hands and spontaneous ordering
Selgin, G. 180
sentiment in relation to reason 85,
  188
Shackle, G.L.S. 61, 139
Shapiro, D. 133
Shoeck, H. 48, 91
Simmons, R.T. 36
Simon, H.A. 177
Simons, H.C. 69, 130
Skarbeck, D. 70
Smith, A. 3, 8–10, 34
Smith, D. 71
Smith, V. 108
social contract *see* agreement
  distinguished from acquiescence
Somin, I. 116
Sonstelie, J. 46
Soros, G. 59

Spruynt, H. 45
status vs. contract in governance of
  social interaction 21, 28
Staniland, M. 2
Stigler, G.J. 187
Stiglitz, J. 7, 18
Storing, H.J. 191
Storr, V. 34
Suits, B. 91–3
Sunder, S. 128
Sunstein, C. 84, 105
Susskind, L. 34
systems theory 2, 55–6
  action level vs. system level 62–3,
    65, 92
  controlling vs. influencing 59,
    61–2
  creative systems 58, 59–61, 71–5
  robotic systems 56–61
Szasz, T. 89, 97

Tabellini, G. 37, 52, 113, 164
Tanzi, V. 63
Tarko, V. 128, 133
Thaler, R. 84, 105–6
Thirlby, G.F. 168
Tinbergen, J. 35
Tollison, R.D. 26, 59, 150, 204
Tononi, G. 125
triadic relationships in political
  economy 64, 74–5, 164–6, 168–9,
    172–3
  and political money laundering
    169–71
Trump, D. 163, 170
Tsepelis, G. 91
Tullock, G. 2, 5, 17–18, 21–2, 36, 98,
    103, 173, 201, 206
turbulence
  as intensified through political
    action and public ordering
    172–3
  as natural feature of healthy social
    economy 171

ultimatum games 106–9
unfunded liabilities as systemic lying
  126–7

Vriend, N. 7, 18

Wagner, A. 60
Wagner, R.E. 3–5, 8, 16–18, 20–21,
     25, 28, 35, 37, 42, 44–6, 48,
     50–51, 56, 59, 62, 64, 68, 71–2,
     75, 79–80, 84, 86, 94, 111, 116,
     123–5, 130, 137–8, 141–2, 145,
     151, 153, 157, 162, 164, 167, 171,
     175, 187, 191, 195, 198, 204,
     207–8
Walker, G. 197, 207
Walker, R.A. 204–5
Walras, L. 9–10
Warren, C.O. 208
Webber, C. 48

Whinson, A.B. 107
White, L.H. 180
Wicksell, K. 21–2, 24, 150
Wicksteed, P. 100
Wieser, F. 70, 94
Wildavsky, A. 48, 145
Willett, T.D. 180
Wilson, J.Q. 133
Wilson, W. 12, 19
Wittman, D. 113

Yazigi, D. 111, 125
Yeager, L.B. 2
Yoon, Y. 7, 70